Advance Praise f
BEING HUMAN AND A BU

T0010424

"Thorough, informative, and written like a narrative from a lifelong friend—Klein weaves theory and storytelling together in a graceful and exciting way. A wonderful collection of ancient voices from India to Tibet, gathered here in the pages to further dissipate the devious myth of separateness."—Sharon Salzberg, author of *Lovingkindness* and *Real Happiness*

"*Being Human and Buddha Too* contains a lifetime of meditation on our deeply human capacity for contemplation, reflections on our brokenness and wholeness, and insights into the vastness and intimacy of our lives. Anne Klein weaves together a rich tapestry of memories of her decade of living with Tibetan teachers, texts, ideas, practices, and inspirations; her own deeply poetic reflections on wholeness and separation; and Tibetan voices from the Great Perfection tradition from Longchenpa to Jigme Lingpa and Adzom Paylo Rinpoche, talking about the pathways that wind through karma and impermanence to wisdom and awakening. In the language of the tradition, this is a book written in the jeweled letters of hard-fought realization and the easy grace that precedes and follows it."—David Germano, professor of Tibetan Buddhist studies and executive director of the Contemplative Sciences Center at the University of Virginia

"Anyone who has even thought about a practice or whose mind has alighted even once on the paths of buddhas and bodhisattvas will benefit from this book. Read Longchenpa's fourteenth-century *Sevenfold Mind Training* in its simplicity, and ordinary experience will become a door to wholeness. Then read the oral commentaries by Adzom Rinpoche and Anne Klein to find elegant insights on Dzogchen. The best of Indian, Tibetan, and Western traditions are strung together in this book—a garland of clear jewels that cannot help but reflect the open sky."—Laurie Patton, professor of religion and president, Middlebury College, author of *Bringing the Gods to Mind* and *House Crossing: Poems*, and translator of *The Bhagavad Gita*

All the Teacher's bountiful teachings without exception, it is well known,
   free the ongoing flow of beings' body, speech, and mind and
      are here gathered in these crucial mind-training points. *I am sure.*
         So, people with a heart for teachings, train your minds.

When you mind-train to discern mind and its nature,
   all untoward thoughts hanging onto self
      are finally free in their own ground. *I have no doubt.*
         Naturally seeing reality is astounding. *I'm amazed.*

Practicing just this way, dissolve your ideas
   into their ground, the frill-free Sheer Form (dharmakāya).
      Let the uncontrived, incalculable way things are,
         wholly free of contrivance, be a rich, serene stillness

Wherein you are effortlessly secure
   in seeing the real state, just as it is,
      of a mind grasping at everything. All now goes empty.
         You've met your true nature, a blissful buddha essence. *Marvelous!*

With this, Gyurme Thupten Gyatso, also known as Pema Wangyal, a speaker on behalf of the glorious Dharma, voiced this poem in praise of this book that brings together the crucial mind-trainings, translated and composed by the richly learned Khewang Rigzin Drolma. May it be victorious. May it be auspicious.

སྟོན་པའི་ཚོས་ཕྱུང་མ་ལུས་ཇི་སྙེད་ཀུན། །
ཐམས་ཅད་གང་ཟག་རྒྱུད་དེ་གྲོལ་བ་ལགས། །
ཀུན་འདུས་བླ་སྤྱོད་གནད་འདི་རིས་པར་ཤེམས། །
དེ་ཕྱིར་ཚོས་ལྷན་སྐྱེ་པོས་བློ་སྦྱངས་མཛོད། །

ཤེམས་དང་ཤེམས་ཉིད་བློ་སྤྱོད་མཛོད་ཤེས་ན། །
ཐ་མར་བདག་ཏུ་འཛིན་པའི་ཚོག་ངན་ཀུན། །
རང་སར་ཉིད་དུ་གྲོལ་བ་ཞེ་མི་ཚོག །
རང་བཞིན་ཚོས་ཉིད་མཐོང་བ་ཨེ་མ་མཚར། །

དེ་ལྟའི་རྣལ་འབྱོར་ཇེ་བཞིན་བྱེད་པ་ལ། །
ཚོས་སྐུའི་སྟོས་པ་བྲལ་བའི་རང་སར་གཞིགས། །
མ་བཅོས་ཆེས་གདབ་བྲལ་བའི་གནས་ལུགས་ཉིད། །
ཐམས་ཅད་བཅོས་པ་མེད་པར་ལྷུག་མེར་ཞོག །

དེ་ཀའི་དང་ནས་ཚོས་ཀུན་བདག་འཛིན་བློ། །
ཇི་ལྟར་ཇི་བཞིན་མཐོང་བའི་གནས་ལུགས་ལ། །
བརྟན་པའི་སྟོལ་མེད་དང་གི་སྟོང་པར་གྱུར། །
རང་བཞིན་བདེ་གཤེགས་སྙིང་པོ་མཐལ་བར་རྣད། །

ཅེས་པ་འདི་ནི་དཔལ་ༀ་ཚོས་སྐྱ་བ་འགྱུར་མེད་ཐུབ་བསྟན་རྒྱ་མཚོའམ་པདྨ་དབང་གི་
རྒྱལ་པོས་མཁས་དབང་རིག་འཛིན་སྐྱོལ་མ་མཚོག་གིས་བསྐུར་ཚོས་མཛོད་པའི་བློ་སྐྱོང་
གི་གནད་འདུས་པའི་ཚོས་ལ་བསྟོད་པ་དང་བཅས་སྐུལ་པ་ཕི་ཏུ་ཡར་ཕྱུབས་མ་ནརྒོ། །

Adzom Paylo Rinpoche

House of Adzom is a special multifaceted series featuring new resources on the historical context, people, and practices connected with Adzom Drukpa (1842–1924), a vital figure who influenced Tibet's initial encounter with modernity. Adzom Drukpa was a visionary, scholar, and treasure revealer (*gter ston*), as well as an influential political force central to reshaping Dzogchen education and nonsectarianism in his era. He was a key lineage holder of Jigme Lingpa's *Longchen Nyingthig* and Khyentse Wangpo's *Chetsun Nyingthig*. He founded the great printing press at Adzom Gar, the third largest in Tibet. He was student to some of the most significant nineteenth-century Nyingma teachers, including Patrul Rinpoche and Jamyang Khyentse Wangpo. He was teacher to supremely illustrious Dzogchen practitioners of the next generation, including Terton Lerab Lingpa, Khyentse Chokyi Lodro, and Dilgo Khyentse Rinpoche. Each volume illuminates in unprecedented richness unique features of Adzom Drukpa's life and work, or that of significant lineal forerunners and successors.

Being Human and a Buddha Too
Longchenpa's Sevenfold Mind Training for a Sunlit Sky

This first volume in the *House of Adzom* series centers on Longchenpa's seven trainings in bodhicitta. Anne C. Klein's (Lama Rigzin Drolma) original composition engages Adzom Paylo Rinpoche's quintessential reflections and explores Jigme Lingpa's five pith practices along with his detailed commentary on the trainings. Weaving into these Longchenpa's creative integration of sutra, tantra, and Dzogchen, she orients the discussion toward resolving our most challenging questions about what awakening involves and how it relates to the truth of our human situation right now. The seven trainings are revered as foundational for Dzogchen practitioners and include contemplations on impermanence, the adventitiousness and short duration of happiness, the multiple causes of death, the meaninglessness of our worldly activities, the value of recognizing Buddha's good qualities, the import of a teacher's pith instructions, and nonconceptual meditations on bliss and emptiness, clarity and emptiness, and, ultimately, on reality itself.

BEING HUMAN
AND A
BUDDHA TOO

· · · · ·

Longchenpa's Sevenfold Mind Training
for a Sunlit Sky

Longchenpa's *Sevenfold Mind Training:*
Practical Instructions on the Foundational Practices

སྦྱོན་འགྲོ་སེམས་སྦྱོང་བདུན་གྱི་དོན་ཁྲིད།

Prologue by Adzom Paylo Rinpoche,
oral commentary on the *Sevenfold Mind Training*

Anne Carolyn Klein,
Lama Rigzin Drolma
Dawn Mountain Research Institute

Wisdom

Wisdom Publications
132 Perry Street
New York, NY 10014 USA
wisdomexperience.org

Library of Congress Cataloging-in-Publication Data
Names: Klein, Anne C., 1947– author. | A-dzoms-dpa'-lo Rin-po-che, 1972 or 1973–,
    author. | Klong-chen-pa Dri-med-'od-zer, 1308–1363. Sngon 'gro sems sbyong bdun
    gyi don khrid.
Title: Being human and a Buddha too: Longchenpa's sevenfold mind training for a sunlit
    sky: Longchenpa's Sevenfold Mind Training: Practical Instructions on the Founda-
    tional Practices / original composition by Anne Carolyn Klein; prologue by Adzom
    Paylo Rinpoche, oral commentary on the Sevenfold Mind Training, translated and
    edited by Anne Carolyn Klein in discussion with Adzom Paylo Rinpoche.
Other titles: Sngon 'gro sems sbyong bdun gyi don khrid. English
Description: First edition. | Somerville : Wisdom Publications, 2023. |
    Series: House of Adzom; volume 1 | Translation of: Sngon 'gro sems sbyong bdun gyi
    don khrid. | Includes bibliographical references and index.
Identifiers: LCCN 2022059438 (print) | LCCN 2022059439 (ebook) |
    ISBN 9781614297581 (paperback) | ISBN 9781614297772 (ebook)
Subjects: LCSH: Rnying-ma-pa (Sect)—Doctrines. | Rdzogs-chen. | Blo-sbyong. |
    Spiritual life—Rnying-ma-pa (Sect)
Classification: LCC BQ7662.4 .K48813 2023 (print) | LCC BQ7662.4 (ebook) |
    DDC 294.3/444—dc23/eng/20230206
LC record available at https://lccn.loc.gov/2022059438
LC ebook record available at https://lccn.loc.gov/2022059439

ISBN 978-1-61429-758-1   ebook ISBN 978-1-61429-777-2

27 26 25 24 23   5 4 3 2 1

Cover and interior design by Gopa & Ted2, Inc.

Printed on acid-free paper that meets the guidelines for permanence
and durability of the Production Guidelines for Book Longevity of the
Council on Library Resources.

Printed in the United States of America.

Please visit fscus.org.

Dedicated to real awakening in the most wholesome sense
by everyone,
whoever, wherever, and whenever they may be.

CONTENTS

Preface

BUDDHISM ARRANGES ITSELF into paths and processes. Dzogchen, the Great Completeness, understands all these to move toward a natural state of wholeness. In the process, the path's inexpressible secret is revealed. This process is also the story of rivers seeking their ocean, of pained and promising humans like ourselves contending with something at once utterly foreign and also inseparability intimate with our human being. The river's journey looks long and winding. And yet the ocean is not only the river's destination but its source. The secret, if we can believe it, is that the river already is the ocean, and that we, all our anguishing to the contrary, may already be whole.

To feel whole is a state of intimacy with everything we know, sense, and are. Intimate with our sorrow, intimate with our joy, free in our fullness, easy and open to others. Like the sun that lights the sky, our loving knowing shows up everywhere.

Such is the premise of Tibet's most profound and secret teachings. Even when we are understandably skeptical about this, we want to look for ourselves. We sense something more is possible. That we need not be trapped inside our silhouettes, a solo sojourner on the road of life. This is not what we want. But then what? What does awakening involve and how does it relate to the truth of our situation right now? Do we lose or amplify our humanness in the process? Our exploration of Longchenpa's sevenfold trainings, seven steps toward the wholeness Dzogchen celebrates, is in response to these questions, long a source of intense speculation for practitioners and philosophers alike.

All Dzogchen practices facilitate appreciation of the radical inclusiveness of our nature. These practices dissipate the separateness that ordinarily structures our experience. Other people, cultures, colors, tastes, and everything else our senses take in, seem outside of us. Do they not? For Dzogchen, for its own unique reasons, all this apparent separateness is simply a byproduct of confused imagination. Its resolution is in plain sight.

With this in mind, we encounter the open secret through the brilliant mind of Longchen Rabjam (1308–64) and the writings of his spiritual heir, Jigme Lingpa (1730–98). We reflect on their teachings on the seven trainings and their other philosophical or poetic Dzogchen writings that help amplify what those trainings make possible. We also follow the pivots by which Longchenpa, as Longchen Rabjam is also known, in other writings moves the reader-practitioner from sūtra teachings on impermanence and emptiness to Dzogchen recognition of an unceasing dynamism that permeates all experience. To clarify this further we include an oral commentary on Longchenpa's *Sevenfold Mind Training* text by Adzom Paylo Rinpoche, one of the great Dzogchen masters in Tibet today, and widely considered an incarnation of Jigme Lingpa.

In this way we ride the great current of ancient voices from India and Tibet, reaching back to the earliest days of Buddhist writing and practice, borne forward to our time, when the possibility for wholeness in the world has never seemed more vital.

INTRODUCTION

THE BIG PICTURE: AT HOME IN WHOLENESS

SCIENCE AND MYSTICS say everyone is connected. We are all children of the Big Bang. We come from space. Everything we see and touch comes from space. Our blood carries iron, sourced in the explosive energy of supernovas. We are not a smallness separate from this grandeur. We are nourished by it and contribute to it. My breath, my iron, was once in someone else's body, and will be again. Yours likewise. With this vast perspective in mind, who among us is a stranger?

Wholeness and connection are central to our existence. But we rarely live as if they are. Our unwieldy sense of separateness is at the core of our suffering. How to repair this is the main lesson we humans need to learn. We feel separate from others, from society, yet we don't want to be alone. We feel separate from our own greatest potential, yet we want to succeed. We feel separate from our feelings and yearn to feel more alive. We don't want to feel fragmented, yet wholeness eludes us. Separateness is suffering. The separateness we address here is not the same as difference and disagreement. Wholeness is not one color. It is definitely not a call for everyone to be the same. It's about not getting so lost in the drama in front of us that we forget a deeper ground that holds everything. The earth we stand on holds us all. The passion for wholeness blazingly recognizes the multiplicities it contains.

Our sense of what is possible is always in dialogue with obstructionist proclivities provided by our psyches and social surround, which hide in plain sight what is actually available to us. This is not a small thing!

> Nothing hinders waking more
> than remaining unaware
> of what is already there,
> right there without fuss or strain.[1]

Buddhist views on our human potential offer an optimism-cum-realism that seems unparalleled in contemporary schemata of human possibility. To explore such discourse, we cannot do better than consult a tradition whose very name suggests the truth and necessity of our actual and potential state of completeness.

This great completeness is known in Tibet as Dzogchen. "Dzog" means complete, perfect, whole, and all inclusive, and "chen" means great—underscoring that everything, just everything, is part of this picture. This inclusive reality teems with a variety that never breeches its wholeness. In an ancient poem from the Bon Dzogchen tradition, the voice of reality puts it like this:

> Nothing, not even one thing,
> does not arise from me.
> Nothing, not even one thing,
> dwells not within me.
> Everything, just everything,
> emanates from me.
> Thus I am only one!
> Knowing me is knowing all.
> Great bliss.[2]

Such poetic exultation helps make the familiar strange, thinning out our addiction to the ordinary. The opaqueness in our self-sight fades a bit. Awakening, not to mention buddhahood, may sound esoteric or distant, yet Dzogchen's vision is exactly the opposite. Our sensibilities reveal themselves as naturally primed for the open expanse of inclusivity.

At their best, spiritual, political, social, religious, and psychological systems provide beacons toward wholeness; they are healers of separation. Villains and victims, politicians and those who serve them, as well as the horrific behavior of despots and of nations, peoples, races, and religious standard-bearers who use their power to hate and harm—these are all mired in structures that for the time being preclude wholeness.

On a personal level, there are simple ways to feel more complete: Walking in the woods. Looking at the sky. Sitting quietly with dear ones. In every case, feeling oneself safe in such a larger space is healing and holy. When I am relaxed, feeling safe and among friends, I have no wish to harm anyone. Writ large, this is transformative. In the middle of the Vietnam War, Thich Nhat Hanh famously advocated compassion for the villains and the victims, the hungry and the hunted. He also said, "If I could not be peaceful in the midst of danger, then the kind of peace I might have in simpler times is meaningless."[3] This is not easy. Yet it is possible. In the midst of a cruel racist history, and as a direct target of its menace while spearheading the civil rights movements of the twentieth century, Martin Luther King said, "I believe that unarmed truth and unconditional love will have the final word in reality."[4] Gandhi famously noted that an eye for an eye would make the whole world blind. We must counter injustice with everything we have. But we must not, and in fact ultimately cannot, utterly separate from one another.

Our ordinary human mind might rebel against what might sound like too much acceptance in these calamitous times—so much of the precious Amazon sold to oil interests, the unbearable US school-to-prison pipeline, all products of economic and racial injustices that threaten our world's priceless reroutes . Loss of connection to oneself and to a larger social contract fuels the multi-sourced turmoil we now experience. Recognizing our connectivity begins with seeing clearly into our own human experience. The closer we look, the less we may be able to separate it from what Buddhists call awakening.

The ideas and practices discussed here invite wholeness into our lived experience. Cultural, personal, sexual, racial, and all other distinguishing characteristics contribute to a grand horizon that has no limit. Variety does not create separateness because, again, wholeness is not sameness. Our lived experience is infinitely variable. And appreciation of variety is part of the path to wholeness. Wholeness is blissfully unboring. Or, as Borges put it, "Ecstasy does not repeat its symbols."[5]

Recognizing the connections among things is a game changer. Awareness of intricate interdependencies behind climate change, human migration, economic disparities, and more is crucial. Recognizing interdependence can catalyze whole-hearted dedication to bring about maximum opportunities for everyone. Kindness and a sense of connection, a recognition that we are all in this together, changes priorities. It is a natural extension of the golden rule, central to spiritual traditions around the world. The seven trainings are for embracing unbounded benevolence toward all life.

The ocean is home to infinite waves and ripples, the nature of all of them is water. Our personal wholeness is home to infinite waves of experiences we do or do not want. Yet all of this occurs within the scope of experience. And all experience has the nature of knowing—some kind of awareness underlies every part of experience.

At its most subtle, this knowing is what Dzogchen calls our "incorruptible mind nature." Recognizing this is at the heart of Great Completeness practice. Such recognition conduces to kindness and joy, natural human qualities that can surface any time and enhance our experience right in that moment.

There is no barrier between ordinary and awakened conditions. From the perspective of Dzogchen, humans and buddhas are simply different ways of arising from the general ground of being. In the course of the seven trainings we flow back and forth between human and more awakened states, just as we do in everyday life. Right from the start, the state of being human holds intimations of awakening, even as it obstructs that very thing.

We glimpse these possibilities all the time. A college semester abroad brought me a glorious taste of freedom. I hitchhiked with friends over the San Bernadino pass, walking for miles on the lip of road, praying for a ride, then climbing high onto a transport truck. We spent hours roaring through the mountains, their silhouettes massive against the bright or starlit sky. After sunset, the driver stopped at a small village near Tolve where a kind family put us up for the night. A few days later, headed toward Italy's boot, our hearts full, our stomachs often empty, a rough-looking driver gave us each a slice of warm Sicilian pizza. The world felt like a very friendly place, a seamless whole of adventure and possibility.

In Brindisi we caught a night-boat to Patras and disembarked in high spirits around dawn, the newly lit sky shining up the sea. I was relaxed and excited. Nothing was required and everything seemed possible. I walked slowly along the quay with my friend, not talking, letting my senses melt into blue vistas as far as the eye could see, the golden sun lying low, sky and water shining everywhere, feeling an intimate part of this expansive display and filled with a simple love for all of it. Something in me said, *This is how it really is. Never forget how this feels.* It was a kind of vow. I didn't speak of it to anyone, and I didn't forget, but I also had no idea what I might do in connection with this unprecedented exaltation of completeness. Awe and curiosity about this glorious feeling became a palpable force.

Many religious traditions have narratives of a wholeness that existed before variety was born, before separateness emerged, before there was light. Or, more personally, before any thought arose, or before our interfused infant senses condensed into a localized "me."

The boundary between uninterrupted vastness and the onset of variety is, after all, the moment of creation. The impulse to inquire into this process is at the heart of science and the pulsing center of spiritual, psychological, and phenomenological inquiry. Consider the familiar words of Genesis:

> In the beginning God created the heavens and the earth. The earth was without form and void, and darkness was upon the face of the deep. And the Spirit of God moved over the face of the waters.
>
> And God said, "Let there be light," and there was light.

And God saw that the light was good, and God separated the light from the darkness. God called the light Day, and the darkness he called Night.[6]

The oldest religious document in human history, India's *Ṛgveda* also touches the mystery of a time before time:

Then even nothingness was not, nor existence.
There was no air then, nor the heavens beyond it ...
The One breathed windlessly and self-sustaining.
There was that One then, and there was no other.
At first there was only darkness wrapped in darkness,
All this was only unillumined water ... [7]

Later Indian traditions speak variously of atman, brahman, emptiness, and buddha nature or reality as being eternally present in everyone. And in the Gospel of Thomas, the cosmic vision of Genesis becomes a very personal relationship with originary light:

Jesus said, "If they say to you, '*Where do you come from?*' Say, 'We come from the light; the place where the light [first] came into being ...' If they say to you, '*Who are you?*' Say, 'We are the children [of the light] ...'"[8]

For Genesis, the *Ṛgveda*, and the Gospel of Thomas, creation's opening salvo is light itself. Creation generates boundaries between light and dark, creator and created, and the scriptures then immediately breech that boundary by suggesting the reader's connection with both sides of it, light and dark.

In the *Ṛgveda,* we are children of the One. For Saint Thomas, creation means we are children of light. The Tibetan master Padmasambhava, widely known as Guru Rinpoche and forefather of Tibet's Great Completeness traditions, also fused the cosmic and the personal. The fabled Indian king Indrabhūti discovered him, looking like an eight-year-old child, sitting alone inside a giant lotus flower. Naturally curious, the king asks, Who are you and where are your parents? The child responds:

My father is the wisdom of spontaneous awareness
My mother is the all-good space of all things
My caste is indivisible space and awareness
I have taken the unborn reality realm as my homeland.[9]

The wholeness of a sunlit sky, the radically cosmic and intimate unities of the Great Completeness, resonate with all the above. From the earliest days of Dzogchen, its practitioners played with and explored the expansive, intimate horizon they saw as their real homeland.

Over the centuries, these yogis, poets, and spectacular thinkers created a magnificent legacy of practices, poetry, and philosophy evoking an innate completeness. The Dzogchen Heart Essence literature describes a fundamental ground that exists existentially prior to the division into buddha and ordinary being. This is known as the general ground (*spyi'i gzhi*) that has not yet been divided into saṃsāra or nirvāṇa. Longchenpa invokes it this way:

Previously, before me
there were neither buddhas nor ordinary beings...
Previously, before me
there was not even the name "buddha"...
Buddhas are born from me.
I am the ultimate meaning of unborn sheer knowing.[10]

There are many such statements in Dzogchen writings. Stories by definition have beginnings and endings. Instructions on practice and practice itself, however, reveal that this ground is actually a state that exists simultaneously, if secretly, with all the limitations that create the human-buddha dichotomy in the first place.

Only a wisp, which is not exactly anything, separates buddhas and humans. This sensed separation from our birthright of wholeness yields pain, restlessness, and dissatisfaction; it is not an abstract metaphysical idea. The tragedies of human history turn on an unwarranted sense of separation from those whom we identify as "not us." The not us, human or animal, seem fair game for colonization, slaughter, enslavement, and general exclusion from rights of any kind. These lines between friend and enemy, superior and lackey, grow vivid to the extent that we forget the larger creativity from which all emerged. And this creativity, for Dzogchen at least, is not a past event; it is an ongoing presence in the sky-space of our being.

I knew none of this when I first learned, through random reading in my teens, that the line between buddhas and humans wasn't so very real, a claim that struck me as absurd but interesting.

AN OPEN SECRET

When I was in high school, the few books on Zen then available intrigued me. But when I read that everyone, including me, was already awakened or already a buddha, I put the book down. How could anyone say such a thing? It just seemed impossible. I looked in the mirror, no Buddha there. Still, my curiosity was piqued. But information was hard to come by.

In college the only Asia-related course I could find was a semester of Old Vedic. After college, and after a master's in Buddhist studies from the University of Wisconsin, Madison, I studied Tibetan texts and practices with teachers raised and educated in traditional Tibet, sometimes in India or Nepal, and sometimes as part of graduate studies at the University of Virginia. I learned there were foundational principles to support this wild idea that we are all already buddhas, or the almost equally wild notion that with time we could become one—principles like impermanence, especially the changeability of my own mind and how, when you look really closely, things are different than they first appear. Slowly it sank in that none of us are as stuck as we think. The game of life is a game of change. And change means . . . change! It means possibility. The steely feel of my indignation softened a tad. Studies and practices in impermanence, causality, emptiness, and compassion—all essentialized in the seven trainings—slowly softened into curiosity my earlier incredulity about the "buddha within" idea. Being introduced to Dzogchen the following decade softened it further.

In 1996 I was inspired to create a pilgrimage to Tibet with a few friends in order to visit places connected with Jigme Lingpa's Vast Expanse Heart Essence (*Longchen Nyingthig*) Dzogchen lineage. The greatest serendipity of my life was meeting the now-legendary Tibetan lama in the lineage of Longchenpa who was early in life identified as an incarnation of Jigme Lingpa. This was Adzom Paylo Rinpoche. It was only the second time he had come to Central Tibet from his native Kham.

Almost immediately, in the small nunnery where he was staying, and in between giving teaching to monks and nuns who descended single file in long lines from the high retreat caves all around us, singing songs of devotion, he raised the question that I'd been cooking on for so long, and upped the ante considerably: "Do you believe you can awaken in this lifetime?"

What would it be like, I had to wonder anew, to believe in this possibility? I certainly found it attractive and didn't really argue with it anymore, but . . . did I really believe it? I believed it doctrinally by then, but seeing *this* as part of me *now,* and not in some distant time but *soon*, was a wholly different matter.

Perhaps you can appreciate this from your own experience. Would you, right now, like to consider what qualities would you most like to embody? Qualities such as ease, confidence, clarity, or kindness, for example? Take a moment to stop and imagine actually having them in full measure. What would it feel like to walk through your house, to meet friends or strangers with those qualities in play? Can you imagine others having those same qualities in full? Does it impact you in some way to imagine these qualities? Are they not then already in fact present in your experience, already part of you, even if not robustly developed?

Slowly, finally, I began to get, in a more embodied way, that this matter was not a theory about an abstract possibility, nor was it anything I could just decide. I would have to connect what I "knew" about Buddhism with my own real-time felt sense of things. I still didn't know what awakening was, of course, but I was learning that there were ways of training that involved something quite different than gathering information.

Learning to distinguish conceptual abstraction from lived experience was a key step in the process. Getting that understanding from my head into my bones continues to be a compelling part of learning and practice, and was the subject of my earliest books. Being willing to leave the safe haven of ideas for the messier arena of experience was part of the challenge. I learned that I liked the creative space in which knowing and wondering flow forward together.

When we look into our actual experience, there are endless clues about where this might lead. A pioneering researcher into finely seen human experience, Claire Petitmengin, recently wrote: "Most of the time, we are cut off from ourselves, from what vibrates and lives within us, and this disconnection has catastrophic consequences in all areas of existence. Retrieving contact with our experience is the precondition that would allow the regaining of our lucidity, our dignity, and the courage to change our model of society."[11]

The entire Buddhist tradition, starting with the practice of mindfulness so well known today, encourages a new familiarity with experience. At the same time, both Buddhism and science encourage us to cognitively understand the framework in which we live. Lived experience and cognitive understanding are distinctive and mutually enriching ways of knowing.

Longchenpa says that wisdom is present in every mind and body. This wisdom is not a knowing *about* something else; it is sheer knowing, seeing itself. It doesn't gaze outward or inward. It wakes up to its own unstoppable, incorruptible nature, like fresh water moistening or recognizing itself in its spontaneous, elemental rush down a mountain. Everything we experience is in the field of our knowing. There is no "out there" beyond that.

This is not something to take anyone else's word for. Can you separate your knowing from what it knows? Your senses from what they sense—sounds, sights, and all the rest? You don't have to decide now, it's part of our ongoing exploration here.

For Longchenpa, sheer knowing is the support and essence of every experience. We just haven't noticed this before. In retrospect, my glory moment by Patras harbor showed me something like that.

In a flash, something indescribably new was suddenly as obvious as the noonday sun. There was no separation here between knowing and what I knew. Knowing and known were equally part of the blue air and water, the whole horizon felt as intimate as it was vast. The real secret, hard to believe but in the end impossible to ignore, is that this shining is the way of all knowing.

But how does this happen? How is it, really?

Backlit by Completeness

Do you remember learning to read? Did you learn individual letters first, or did you start with one-syllable words? Do you remember the shock of learning that a final "e" is not pronounced? The magic of not just looking at letters but reading!

When I saw a family friend, not much older than this five-year-old me, open a book and read it out loud, I was filled with admiration and ambition. How did he do that? How could *I* do that? Soon enough, I practiced at home with a book about a girl taking her first train ride. My first day, I could not get past the opening sentence. Then each day after, without understanding why, without any further instruction, I could read a little further. So I felt, deep in my bones, that learning can naturally unfold, step by step. Learning the alphabet of course was necessary, but that didn't explain why I could now read today what I couldn't read yesterday. I didn't try in any special way or ask anyone's help. I just showed up and my ability increased. The same thing happened when I learned to count. Each morning, I stood by our third-floor living-room window, looking down on the street below. Each day I could count a little higher than before. I didn't consult anyone or practice in between. The knowing was in there. Apparently it just needed incubation.

What I really think happened is that I learned to relax. After reading that first sentence, I was just too excited to go on. It wasn't the ability to read that threw me off, it was my habitual tight holding to a life-long conception of myself as someone who could not read. Breaking into a new identity, even a highly desired one, is a challenge. That challenge made me just tense enough that I couldn't continue reading. But by the next day I was used to seeing myself as someone who could read one sentence, so I could read a second. But a whole page? Not yet. So each morning I read until I reached that day's barrier, the moment when my self-sense as someone who could not read would rise up and I would freeze. I oscillated continually between these recently crystallized identities of reader and nonreader. Before I started to read, there was no such division. And now it wasn't because of mysterious letters that I couldn't go further. I just wasn't ready to be a certain idealized version of myself—a reader. Once I relaxed into the truth of that reader identity, it was easy to go on. This pattern is still true for me today. In writing this book, in practicing the paths it describes, I am repeatedly showing up, getting stuck, then relaxing enough to make the next step possible. Relaxing makes us more whole, more available to our knowing. Moving into a new identity as a reader comes more easily. The same is true as we move back and forth from our ordinary human experience to more awakened states.

In large and small ways, I discover over and again how stress holds me back from joy and creativity. It is also hard on the body. But stress, no matter how ubiquitous, is not our natural state. It causes us to withdraw, lash out, lose our expansiveness. It divides us from deeper reserves of knowing, and especially from intimacy with ourselves and others. In practice, shedding *identification* with stress allows the currents of wakefulness to flow through us, just as taking a deep breath makes for relaxation.

The trainings discussed here reckon with our hopes, fears, and negative ideation as well as with the potential we have to be increasingly free from these. Confidence, trust, and commitment are essential. Modern culture seems to value skepticism, yet often rewards certainties of dubious merit: the glamorously confident movie stars, the ideologically fired-up politician, the profit-monger CEO. The confidence needed in these trainings is not of this type. It does not thrive on fanfare. It is a genuine certainty in our capacity to access something authentic in ourselves, something as basic as the capacity to read, and to recognize this capability in others.

It took me only a few decades to recognize that my skepticism about awakening was based, first of all, on having no idea what Buddhist traditions actually meant by this, and, second, on not knowing that there was actually a process for approaching it. Finally, and most important of all, it was based on my assumption that awakening lay entirely outside the bounds of natural human experience. In fact, exactly the opposite is true. Dzogchen in particular emphasizes that wakening is basic and intrinsic. Learning to get out of our own way is the challenge.

Dzogchen is for the ancient Nyingma Buddhist and Bon traditions the most sacred, swift, and hidden of the great traditions of Tibet. Longchenpa's seven trainings for the Great Completeness seek to loosen what binds us from wholeness and thereby allow us to experience what Dzogchen describes as our real nature, our vast expanse.[12] The trainings engage your entire body, energy system, and mind. They reflect Longchenpa's key observation that wisdom suffuses the entire human body and mind and distils the elements that transform ordinary flesh and blood into a body of living wisdom.

JIGME LINGPA'S REFLECTIONS ON LONGCHENPA'S SEVENFOLD MIND TRAINING

Jigme Lingpa's expansive reflections on Longchenpa's seven trainings, his unique story-meditations, his pith practices, and the additional meditative instructions he brings forward show how these trainings engage every step of Nyingma's nine pathways.[13] In the first three chapters of Part 3 we introduce Jigme Lingpa's text expanding on Longchenpa's seven trainings and note especially his teaching stories and pith instructions, along with the important role of imagination and the centrality of a compassionate heart, culminating in Longchenpa's distillation of the channel-wind practices' subtle integration of mind and body.

This puts us in a good position to appreciate the pivots by which Longchenpa moves practitioners toward Dzogchen's wisdom narrative that runs like a river through all the trainings. The wisdom narrative we refer to here has been transmitted from teacher to student, going back at least to the time of Longchenpa. Throughout Buddhist traditions from the time of the Buddha, human relationship is always part of the equation.

Longchenpa's own pivots toward Dzogchen, drawn from select philosophical and poetic writings, form the organizing principles of the closing two chapters of Part 3. Along the way, and in between chapters, we touch sequentially into Jigme Lingpa's five pith practices, found in his own discussion of the seven trainings. These distill the wisdom trail into single-sentence meditations that can inform our own wisdom turn for a lifetime.

Over time, these practices elicit new understanding and fresh feelings, gently undoing habitual distancing and feelings of separateness in relation to the world and to ourselves. As a vital foundation for all of this, we now start with Part 1, Longchenpa's own very succinct text on these seven trainings,[14] to which I've appended a section on the background of the seven trainings. Part 2 is Adzom Paylo Rinpoche's oral commentary on the trainings. His distilled discussion of all seven trainings is the prologue and context for my reflections on them in seven chapters in Part 3.

PART 1

Sevenfold Mind Training
by Longchenpa

SEVENFOLD MIND TRAINING

With body, speech, and mind I offer deepest homage
to lama, yidam, and ḍākinī hosts.
I clarify here how to enter in stages
the manifest heart-meaning by way of
these seven practical instructions for training and purifying
    your mind.[15]

T HE "PRECIOUS COPPER LETTERS"[16] describes seven mind trainings that make it possible for fortunate beginners gradually to
enter the direct import of their own sheer awareness.[17] The first of the
seven methods practiced is contemplation on impermanence. [324.1]

First Mind Training:
Reflection On Impermanence
Outer impermanence includes the changeability of the four seasons,
as well as seconds and minutes of the day and night. Inner impermanence includes the changeability of your own aggregates associated with the four elements.[18] These are as impermanent as a mass
of water bubbles, disintegrating immediately and having no actual
essence. The most intimate or secret impermanence is the death of
your mother, father, and relatives, and in time this will be your own
situation as well, will it not?! Nothing guarantees that you will not die
today or tomorrow.

From the depths of your heart reflect: "I could die tonight, or I
could die tomorrow." Focus on this without being distracted even for
a moment. No other living beings you see have transcended death
either. Meditate on the uncertainty of just when anyone's death will
occur. In this way, you will see that all conditioned phenomena have
the nature of impermanence and that they themselves are instances
of impermanence. Your ability to sustain attention on this is the

measure of attaining this training. With this meditation you fulfill the requirement of turning your mind away from cyclic existence.

Second Mind Training: Temporary and Lasting Happiness

The full spectrum of suffering and unfortunate rebirths comes about due to our unwholesome actions. All high rebirths and pleasures come about due to our wholesome actions. [325.1] What a shame! The highs and lows of cyclic existence are by nature like a water wheel, shifting and incapable of enduring. Liberation, which is awakening, is the ideal way to avoid ending up in cyclic existence. Lacking this, your mind remains unstable and is greatly deceived.

If you remain on the path to liberation, the temporary happiness and excellent good qualities associated with a good rebirth will be present in your mindstream. Just like buddhas' heirs, the heroic-minded bodhisattvas, you will gain long-lasting happiness of unsurpassed awakening, as have the buddhas.

Unless you enter the path to liberation, you will end up in unfortunate destinations due to unwholesome actions, and even though wholesome actions bring high status, you cycle again into unfortunate destinations.

Your recognizing that all activities are causes of pain is thus the measure of attaining this training. This makes it imperative that weariness with cyclic existence arises in your mindstream.

Third Mind Training: Reflecting on the Multiple Conditions for Death

Once born into cyclic existence, there is nothing reliable or trustworthy. Even when you mean to be helpful, harm results. Just eating or drinking can be a cause of illness or death. Even once you acquire some basic necessities, they turn out to be just what our enemy or some thief is coveting. Hoping to get some help, you call a friend or relative, upon which occasion they become an enemy who harms you. Even if they don't harm you, they speak negatively about you or malign you for no reason! No matter what you do, people are displeased, and this situation continues without end. What a pity!

Once you reflect wholeheartedly on the attitude of living beings, you see that, as mentioned already, even though you try to help, some are satisfied and some are not. No matter how you look at it, nothing is categorically beneficial.

Whatever you do is by its very nature unsatisfying. Those many things that bring about illness or death definitely do not bring manifest help or benefit. Except for the lama and the Three Jewels, nothing is undeceiving. Your heartfelt yearning for and offerings to them are sources of happiness. This being so, reflect: "A range of wholesome attitudes is all I need." Reflect on the good and bad conditions you have already experienced, on what you are doing now, and on your activities in the future. Then feel world-weariness and modulate your attitude.

The measure of attaining this training is your giving rise to compassion for beings in the six realms and reflecting how appropriate it is to see all your activities as offerings to the Three Jewels and your teacher.

Fourth Mind Training: The Pointlessness of All Activities [327.2]

Our activities in this life involve protecting our dear ones, thwarting our enemies, multifarious business details, wanting profit and fame, having desire and hatred, receiving friendly advice from others, arrogance, seeking pleasant conversation and the like, taking enjoyment with friends, and putting together a grand home and so forth. But no matter what you have done, after you die none of these will benefit or accompany you.

Whatever you might have done yesterday, or before that, is nothing but a memory, like last night's dream, never to return. What you see before you today is like tonight's dream. Beyond that, all activities in all your tomorrows are like tomorrow night's dream.

Our assorted past pursuits—pointless desire, hatred, quarrels, likes, dislikes, chasing after happiness, fending off suffering—are a waste of time. What a pity! Worldly appearances are illusions—deceptive and beguiling. The measure of gaining this training is to feel very powerfully the need, starting today, to completely give up attitudes associated with nonrealization. It is therefore vital to enter into a teacher's practical instructions.

Fifth Mind Training: Relying on the Buddhas' Good Qualities [328.3]

Now, reflect in this way. "Buddha is beyond all defects of cyclic existence: buddha's form blazes with the indications and marks of Buddhahood, a buddha's speech turned the wheel of the dharma, and a buddha's great heart-mind does not stir from the state of primordial knowing. Buddha is the sole excellent leader of the entire world and its gods, our refuge and ultimate recourse. Therefore I must attain buddhahood! Unless I become a buddha, there is no benefit."

"It is impossible to attain buddhahood without cultivating the path. No matter what, then, I must meditate. I must one-pointedly strive to emulate the astonishing accomplishments of the amazing realized beings in the past who attained liberation after undertaking many difficulties and practicing alone in isolation. Like them, I also must put aside this life's activities and practice in a remote area alone." And so it is. The measure of gaining this training is to give rise in your mindstream to the thought: "Without meditation, there is no finding buddhahood. Therefore I must meditate." Therefore, when it comes to meditation, fortitude[19] is essential.

Sixth Mind Training: Reflecting on the Lama's Practical Instructions [329.3]

Reflect that the lama is your guide to becoming free from the endless depths of the samsaric ocean; the method that liberates is a great boat consisting of your lama's instructions. It is therefore important to practice precisely as you are taught. Lacking practice, you will constantly be tormented by the illness that is suffering. Your exceedingly loving teacher is a king of physicians.

Reflect: "It is vital for me to take up with fortitude the practical instructions, medicinal nectar." Then consider the many reasons for this.[20] The measure of gaining this training is when, through this cultivation, you ask yourself, "What is the use of this life's activities?"

and conclude that you will focus entirely on practicing your lama's practical instructions. Therefore it is important to set your mind one-pointedly on the practical instructions without setting your mind on other activities.

Seventh Mind Training: Threefold Nonconceptual Contemplation [330.1]

These three trainings in nonconceptual meditation each have their own instructions:

1. *Training in the nonconceptual state of bliss and emptiness.* At the top of your central channel is an upside down letter *haṃ* from which nectar descends when you attend to the fire blazing forth from the letter *ah* at your navel. This nectar completely suffuses all four channel-wheels, as well as the lesser channels. In this way, contemplate the arising of bliss and emptiness.

Pull your energy up from below while pressing down from above, and fix your mind on a white *ah* at your heart.[21] Bliss is the skillful means that gives rise to the wisdom of emptiness.

2. *Training in the nonconceptual state of clarity and emptiness* [330.4]. After expelling three stale breaths, feel that all appearances have dissolved into light and merged with the blue sky. As you inhale, this shimmering enters and fills your body. Through holding your joined energies (*rlung kha sbyar*), clarity and emptiness arise. Through this practice realization will come. Also, when it is cold, meditate that your energy is hot, and when it is hot, consider that it is cool to the touch. This is a key point.

There are additional explanations of many styles of meditation regarding wind—the fire-wind in summer, the wind-wind in the fall, the water-wind in winter, and the earth-wind in spring—using color and the sense of touch as antidotes. These are simply elaborations [of the key point already given].[22]

3. *Nonconceptual Training with Respect to Reality.* Relaxing your body and your mind from deep within while your eyes remain still, meditate without either expanding your concepts or reeling them in. This meditation will enable you to focus your mind anywhere and,

following that, to remain longer and longer with your mind in a sky-like state free of concepts.

Thus the measure of your gaining this training is that your bodhicitta inevitably increases more and more more through this practice.

Epilogue

Thus through the key meaning of the profound foundational
    practices[23]
contained in this array of teaching points on the seven mind
    trainings,
its wholesomeness rising white like the snowy mountains,
may beings without exception find their site of exquisite peace.
Through what continues from training in my previous births,
in this life I am wise in the Supreme Vehicle's heart-meaning.
And so with benevolent intelligence
I clearly revealed its profound meaning.

Fortunate beings, take this fine portal to the profound heart
    meaning
as your crown ornament. This excellent path
is a chariot for seeking the liberation,
swiftly accomplished through my writings here.

Teaching points on the seven foundational mind trainings were completed on the slopes of the White Skull Snow Mountain by a yogi in the Supreme Vehicle, Longchen Rabjam. I have entrusted it to the glorious sovereign lady of mantra [Ekazati], Rāhula and the oath bound [Vajrasadhu]. Keep it secret from those who are not vessels for it. Bestow it on the fortunate ones.

Sealed to Silence.
Commitment.
Wholesome. Wholesome. Wholesome.

BACKGROUND ON THE SEVEN TRAININGS

Tibetan chronicles place one of Longchenpa's own previous incarnations at the center of the origin stories of imperial Tibet. This was Princess Pematsal, daughter of Tibet's second great Buddhist king, Trisong Detsen, who ruled from 755 to 797 CE. She died while still a child, and at her grieving father's request was briefly returned to life by none other than Padmasambhava, who blessed her to take rebirth in the future and introduce a new cycle of Heart Essence Dzogchen teachings to Tibet. Six hundred years later, we are told, she was born as Longchen Rabjam.[24]

During those six hundred years, the Heart Essence teachings of the great Indian master Vimalamitra, who traveled to Tibet in the ninth century, prevailed. His main teachers included Jñānasūtra and Śrī Singha. All three went to China, with Vimalamitra and Śrī Singha spending time at China's famous Wutai Shan, the five-peaked sacred mountain northeast of Beijing. Vimalamitra is said to be there to this day. Adzom Paylo Rinpoche has written of encountering him there in vision.[25]

The broad Dzogchen tradition in Tibet traces itself to eighth-and-ninth-century Tibet, the very period during which Chan was emerging in Tang-dynasty China. Contemporary scholarship sees consolidation of Tibetan Dzogchen during the tenth or even twelfth centuries. However, there is evidence of conversations between early forms of Dzogchen and Chan from a quite early period, especially about the respective merits of the classical, gradual path of India versus the swift, even instantaneous, path made famous by early Chan writings, especially the *Platform Sūtra*.[26] Even before that, some of the early Mahāyāna sūtras, as we will see, contain threads that later become central to Dzogchen.

During the six centuries between the death of the princess and her prophesied rebirth as Longchen Rabjam, Tibetan culture became thoroughly infused with the Buddhism flowing in from India. Huge collections of Indian Buddhist literature were translated into Tibetan during a four-hundred-year collaboration between Indian pandits and Tibetan lotsawas, culminating in Atiśa's eleventh-century visit to Tibet. In addition to this prodigious translation enterprise, Tibetans soon began writing their own commentaries and composing countless practice texts that offered experiential entry to the Buddha's teaching. There has not been such a sustained and extensive cultural transference of Buddhist literature until Tibetan works began to be translated into English in the late twentieth century, and still going strong.[27]

In the fourteenth century, Longchenpa undertook a vast collation of the major Dzogchen traditions that had been set in motion since the eighth century. In this collection, known as the *Fourfold Heart Essence* (*Snying thig ya bzhi*), he lays out and comments on Vimalamitra's *Heart Essence*, as well as on Guru Rinpoche's *Dākinī Heart Essence*. The seven trainings is included in one of its most famous subsections known as the "Precious Copper Letters."

The earliest flows of Buddhist literature from India to Tibet included sūtras, tantras, and the early Dzogchen tantras. Tibet's first Buddhists, the Nyingma ("Old Ones"), were quick to synthesize this growing body of practices and philosophical reckoning, which they organized into nine pathways or vehicles. Paths based on sūtras, outer tantras, and inner tantras address increasingly subtle obstructions to the practitioner's recognition of an incorruptible wholeness and are therefore typically presented as a hierarchy crowned by Dzogchen. However, close readings, and experience itself, suggests they are more hologram than ladder.

From its own perspective, Dzogchen is present in every part of it and is not simply the top rung of a vertical ascent, just as all rungs are part of a ladder, and the ladder is expressed in every rung. All nine pathways participate in some degree in the seven trainings. As Adzom Rinpoche says below, "Everything from the foundational practices through to the actual basis is itself a great completeness, a real perfection." The Great Completeness makes clear that it includes all nine paths, even as it teaches the distinguishing characteristics of each. All of them to some degree amplify the seven trainings. Thus the ninth vehicle of Dzogchen, the Great Completeness, not only culminates the other eight paths but also holds, and in that sense backlights, all of them.[28]

Sūtra practices emphasize reflection on key principles such as impermanence, the four truths, dependent arising, and emptiness. These themes are related to the first three vehicles, the initial triad of the nine paths. In both inner and outer tantras, the second and third sets of three, a subtle embodied sensitivity is conjoined with a flowering imagination as one learns to see oneself as a fully awakened being. In Dzogchen, all thought and imagination resolves into the groundless ground of reality. Only when we reach that peak, the ninth pathway, can we see clearly how all other paths, the whole mountainside, is there to support us.

That Great Completeness, again, is all-inclusive reality. Since nothing is excluded, it is an unbounded wholeness. This means reality is not somewhere else. It is at any and every moment inseparable from our ordinary body, speech, and mind. Much of the core literature from which Longchenpa draws include passages in which reality describes itself. We find, for example, these evocative lines in the *All-Creating Majesty*:

> I, creator of everything, encompass the three awakened
>   Buddha dimensions.
> All things, however they manifest,
> are uncontrived in nature, essence, and loving responsiveness.
> I reveal these dimensions as my suchness.[29]

Variation and Simplicity

Practitioners sometimes feel it should be enough simply to sit and be. Why should we chant, why imagine such a variety of worlds and beings? And why do Tibetans have so many different practices? The intuition behind this question is valid: reality is indeed very simple. Yet its unceasing dynamism yields infinitely diverse expressions. To know one person well, we need to see the range of different ways they express themselves—to children, to colleagues, at the movies, over dinner. How much more is this true of an endlessly creative reality?

And we ourselves are variable. Sometimes we are agitated, sometimes annoyed, sometimes incredulous—the varieties of our reactivity are infinite. Our different proclivities are best addressed through different styles of practices. Tibetan traditions offer many such. Feeling jittery? Learn to settle body, breath, and mind. Feeling hateful? Cultivate love or a relationship with Avalokiteśvara. Feeling fearful? Cultivate an unstoppable strength through a relationship with the tiger-riding Dorje Drolo. And, finally, recognize that the real nature of all these, and yourself, is the same. One nature, infinite variety. Unborn, unceasing. Seeing this is the heart of Dzogchen.

To recognize all practice and experience as backlit by its own great completeness is to find a horizon that never narrows. This can't make sense to our ordinary human mind, but it is not nonsensical. And it can be experienced.

Longchenpa makes clear that his seven trainings, while replete with insights common to other Buddhist paths, are pathways to Dzogchen. He draws the main headings for this practice from an ancient tantra, the *Sole Child Scripture* (*Bu gcig*), attributed to Garab Dorje. The seven topics he names become the blueprint for Longchenpa's layout of the seven trainings, outlined below. In parenthesis next to each training is the topic that Jigme Lingpa chooses to emphasize in his own exposition of these same seven:

1. impermanence (existential aloneness)
2. the adventitiousness of happiness and its short duration (karmic cause and effect)
3. the multiple causes of death (suffering of the six realms)
4. the meaningless of our worldly activities (importance of the relationship with your teacher)
5. reliance on the buddha's good qualities (necessity of meditation)
6. the teacher's practical guidance (discarding the ten unwholesome acts)
7. three meditative experiences leading to reality: nonconceptual meditation on bliss and emptiness, clarity and emptiness, and reality itself (wisdom and breath)

In closing his commentary on his *Precious Dharmadhātu Treasury*, Longchenpa writes, "In the past, I signed treatises I authored by several names," and notes that these different names are clues to the subject matter of the text. He caps this by saying, "In works that reveal the way of abiding as an inconceivable spacious expanse I have signed the name Longchen Rabjam."[30] To reveal such a way of abiding is to find the Dzogchen view. This is how he signs the seven trainings.

Also, in the colophon to the trainings, he writes, "I have entrusted this [text] to the glorious sovereign lady of mantra [Ekazati], to Rāhula and the oath bound [vajra sadhu Dorje Lekpa]. Keep it secret from those who are not vessels for it! Bestow it on the fortunate ones! Sealed to Silence. *Kha tham*." Ekazati is the protectress of Dzogchen, and Rāhula, of the Nyingma Treasure tradition, is also part of Dzogchen. By asking them to protect this text, Longchenpa is further indicating that we are to understand its Dzogchen pedigree. And elsewhere he says straight out: "These key instructions on the foundational practices of the seven mind trainings serve as steps that lead to the primordial nature," which is another key topic in Dzogchen.

Further, Longchenpa himself, in listing the categories of his extensive writings, names five, which he says "summarize the heart essence of profound meaning." At the head of this list is his *Sevenfold Mind Training*, and he notes that the five together make up the cycle of "sacred practical instructions" connected with the *Profound Heart Essence* of Vimalamitra.[31]

I mention these points because, on the face of it, Longchenpa's text seems to focus on many topics covered in the early phases of the path: impermanence, the fleeting nature of worldly happiness, a wish to focus on more enduring happiness, to develop compassion, and to practice sincerely. Longchenpa wants us to know from the outset the full horizon of these practices. He leaves it up to us to uncover how these trainings in fact function as portals to Dzogchen. Moreover, especially through Jigme Lingpa's discussion, to understand that in engaging these practice, we are not only training for Dzogchen but already participating in it.

To identify the status of this work as a Dzogchen text is helpful and also provocative. Dzogchen is famous for its direct unmasking of ordinary mind. Are we humans practicing to be buddhas? Are we buddhas masquerading as humans? Given that the ground of all human experience is reality, is there even such a thing as "merely human"? In fact, the more I look into it, the more the question "Can I awaken" starts to stand on its head. For one potent moment I wonder, "How can I not!" In a similar vein, Rumi notes that "God loves you" is the only possible sentence, because once this is known, you are dissolved into God and no other pronoun remains.[32]

Nonetheless, my everyday mind, ingeniously protective of the "me" that is its main devotional object, balks at undoing the descriptions by which I carve out my separateness. I easily forget that being different and being separate are not at all the same thing. Wholeness is compelling precisely because it embraces all difference. I long for wholeness to the extent that I feel burdened by the existential loneliness of separation and also to the extent that I feel threatened by the violence, born of alienation, that results. At this most fundamental human level, there are many things wholeness can heal.[33]

Experience confirms that curiosity and conviviality are truer than our apparent divides. Since the dawn of human life on Earth we have learned from one another, traded in goods and ideas. Our recognizing that this co-arisen, fluid nature is truer and more beneficial than black-and-white, us-versus-them assumptions has been key to much of our social awakening. We're different, and difference is entertaining as well as enriching. To confuse difference with inequality is a huge error! Overcoming our sense of difference, or separateness, requires persistence and patience. Yet every step forward is evidence that the divide between ourselves and our ultimate best selves, even buddhahood, is greatly exaggerated. The first six of Longchenpa's trainings reshape the ordinary mind through cultivating clarity about impermanence, cause and effect, compassion, and commitment. The purpose is to reverse misleading assumptions that lie at the edge of our awareness. All are associated with some type of othering. Twoness goes hand in hand with our ordinary human mind.

For Longchenpa "ordinary mind" refers to any consciousness that reifies sense objects. Still, Longchenpa emphasizes that "the root of ordinary mind is found in primordial wisdom . . ."[34] This is a tremendous statement and a centerpiece of Dzogchen. It means that humans and buddhas—our ordinary mistakenness and our awakened potential—are not separated by a chasm in the way that I had imagined when I first heard about buddha nature and recoiled at the absurdity of suggesting that I already participated in any kind of buddha-ness. To the contrary, Longchenpa is saying that the heart of awakening is the root of even the most rambunctious parts of us. In this he echoes the earliest Indian Buddhist emphasis on the mind's intrinsic luminosity and the great potential in every living being.[35]

The more my mind trends toward separation and distance, the more idealization and defamation run rampant. The space of my experience shrinks, its potential for emotional or psychic-physical expansiveness cramped. Peace and justice require a social sense of wholeness, and a wisdom consonant with wholeness trends to connection and care.

Ordinary mind is a powerful habit. We've relied on our ordinary mind for everything our whole lives. Conceding its limitations, and getting ready to try an alternative, is a crucial fork in the road. Confronting this can be quite a drama for practitioners.

In addressing the habits of mind that impede vast vistas, the seven trainings integrate all registers of practice. Every part of our being is engaged—intellect, imagination, vocalization, body, and our senses. Stillness and imagining, sound and silence, enhance each other. Finally, all dissolve into their source, the heart of all knowing, whose dynamism continuously yields new formations.

Jigme Lingpa in *Stairway,* his commentary on the seven trainings, writes that "the infinite number of approaches that comprise the traditions of sūtra and tantra can be shown [in a single sitting]."[36] This path-river flows through many landscapes, and Jigme Lingpa here points out that the stages of the path, the different parts of our spiritual landscape, are profoundly connected. There is a natural flow through them, as the seven trainings and associated pith practices will reveal. The more we experience this flow, the more we also grow clear about how we impede it. This clarity opens toward wholeness. By connecting the other eight vehicles to Dzogchen's unique vision, Jigme Lingpa shows practitioners how Longchenpa's seven trainings combine sūtra, tantra, and Dzogchen. The very different skills that are hallmarks of these three perspectives are integrated. All elements are meaningfully connected and their variety enriches the wholeness in which they, like us, participate.

When you start to touch into the nature you're seeking, you may balk, just as I balked years ago at reading a few lines I was perfectly capable of reading. My ordinary mind, my conception of myself as unable to read, was still the only identity familiar to me. When it felt threatened, I felt threatened. Ordinary mind does not want to disappear or be one-upped. Ordinary mind wants to run the show and protect its own deceptions. Ordinary mind, desperate to understand reality, just can't. And it certainly does not want to dissolve into it. So we are stuck. We are seized by doubt. We may turn away and decide it's too hard. Or we are intrigued and wonder how we might put our toe in the wisdom water.

Ordinary Mind and Wisdom Mind

Practice is not only about righting our errors, nor is it only about unveiling our natural wisdom qualities. We need both gestures. Buddhism's karmic narrative mirrors our ordinary face and helps us brighten it. Buddhism's wisdom narrative resonates with our true face, what Zen calls our face before our mother was born. Jigme Lingpa reminds us:

> Mahāyāna has two aspects:
> the perfection (paramita) approach
> and the unsurpassable Vajrayana.[37]

Karma is the story of our brokenness; wisdom speaks to our wholeness. In karmic narratives, awakened mind is something we strive for, the culmination of much effort on a lengthy path. In Dzogchen's wisdom narratives, awakened mind is the goal as well as the ground. It is path as well as path's fruition. The karmic narrative teaches us how to move toward wisdom; the wisdom narrative teaches us how to see that wisdom is already here. Both are essential.

Longchenpa's gnostic turns—his pivots toward already present wisdom—are signposts for moving from brokenness to wholeness, for discovering that wisdom is always right here. This is not an objective fact, yet it is something we can validly sense and celebrate. Wisdom is something alive. Just like us.

In the coming chapters, we trace Longchenpa's arc from karmic to wisdom narratives and amplify his pivots as they relate to the seven trainings, drawing especially from two of his famous seven treasures, *Precious Dharmadhātu Treasury* and *Precious Treasury of Philosophical Systems*. He suggests we do well in approaching wisdom with awe and wonder. "How amazing," he often says, modeling those very states.

We highlight the moves by which he brings ordinary karmic perspectives into alignment with wisdom so that, finally, love and compassion cease to become goals of the path and are recognized as the very nature of everything already.[38] Awakened mind is revealed as the actual ground of everything, our own incorruptible nature.[39]

Everything is either wisdom or a distortion of it. The wisdom Dzogchen describes is intrinsically infused with kindly responsiveness. We start to see that, just as we are effortlessly already part of the vast universe, we are also part of wisdom, part of responsive kindness. The path itself is a kindly wholeness.

Adzom Rinpoche: A Pilgrim's Progress through the Sevenfold Mind Training

In the next section Adzom Paylo Rinpoche, widely regarded as the greatest Dzogchen master in Tibet today, discusses the seven trainings. His elucidation of these anchors my subsequent discussion of them in Part 3, where I look at the trainings through the lens of Jigme Lingpa's commentary on them and draw as well from other works by Longchenpa. In the process, we continue to appreciate the pivots by which Longchenpa, as well as practitioners, can shift from karmic to wisdom perspectives.

In the holy Buddhist month of Sagadawa, 1996, I was standing in the back of a truck that was taking our pilgrimage group from Samye, Tibet's first monastery, to the main meadow of Samye Chimphu, one of the central sacred places of Tibet. A young Tibetan nun grabbing on to the truck's side next to me wore a pin with a monk's face on it. I asked her who he was. She said he was a great lama who was right now visiting Chimphu and that we could meet him He was staying at a small Ani Gompa (now extensively rebuilt).

The truck delivered us to a meadow below the Gompa where our group set up camp for the night. Next morning we set out to find him. I scouted the way, climbing a rocky path in the bright air until we reached a small nunnery nestled in a flat clearing on the mountain-side. We were admitted to Rinpoche's room, where he sat, powerful as a mountain, on the wooden platform that served as a bed at night and conversation seat during the day.

When, on behalf of the group, I asked whether he would teach us, his immediate response was, "Do you mean teach you all at once or one by one?" I was taken aback for a moment, hesitant in the face of this astounding generosity. But I collected myself enough to gratefully accept on behalf of the group and then participated with my friend Michele Martin in translating these very personal exchanges for each of us.

By the time the personal instructions concluded, including pauses in the conversation when he transmitted entirely new bandwidths of experience with his eyes, my orientation had gently shifted and has been shifting ever since. Some wider horizon is absolutely possible. And it is most definitely not what I had thought.

PART 2

Prologue by Adzom Paylo Rinpoche,
a Commentary on Longchenpa's
Sevenfold Mind Training

IN THE WINTER of 2007–8, Adzom Paylo Rinpoche taught the seven trainings on Whidbey Island, Washington, and in Germany. In 2010 he encouraged me to ponder, teach, and write about them. "There can be no better foundation for practice!" he called out in his hearty way. "I'll sign my name to it," he said, his right hand vigorously writing in the cool air. Now he introduces them to you. His careful and caring oral teaching directs our gaze to the sunlit sky within, and to appreciating how Longchenpa and then Jigme Lingpa bring these seven trainings home.[40]

Adzom Paylo Rinpoche was early in his life recognized as an incarnation of several figures key to Tibet's cultural identity, including King Trisong Detsen, Vimalamitra, Ngari Panchen, Jigme Lingpa, and, in his most recent past life, Pema Wangyal, a son of Adzom Drukpa (d. 1924), who was instrumental in bringing Jigme Lingpa's *Heart Essence* cycles into twentieth-century eastern Tibet and infusing them with reflections from his own experience. When Adzom Drukpa was thirty-two years old, he had a luminously clear vision of Jigme Lingpa, whom he described as exceptionally kind. Many years later he observed that Jigme Lingpa had been most impactful of all his teachers.[41] One doesn't need to believe in visions or even reincarnation to recognize the visceral connections Buddhist practitioners find among the figures now embodied in Adzom Rinpoche.[42]

In these straight-to-the-heart reflections, we hear Rinpoche's own hearty voice on the import and structure of the seven trainings, which touch on every part of the path, from instructions on hearing, to the trainings on impermanence and compassion, up to the esoteric seventh training that engages the channels and winds in service of nonconceptual bliss, clarity, and insight into reality. Key elements of the Dzogchen path are implicit in his crystallization of these seven trainings, which he regards as an outstanding foundation for moving through the entire path.[43]

• • ● • •

THE INTENTION TO TRAIN THE MIND

Right from the start, joy is important because it cleanses the mind. So take joy in the opportunity we have right now to light up our foggy minds with the wisdom teachings of Longchen Rabjam, the profound master from Tibet. Longchenpa was deeply learned and deeply accomplished in practice. He lived, taught, and wrote in fourteenth-century Tibet and we have not seen the likes of him since. Take joy and greet these teachings with real courage and strength of mind. Let enthusiasm rise up and fortify your readiness to further your bodhicitta, your powerful aspiration to benefit all beings. This intention yields many good qualities of tremendous benefit. At best, we will have wholly unfabricated bodhicitta.

Why is bodhicitta so important? It brings our minds vastness as well as courage. With such a mind we can overcome our powerful habit of sustaining a pervasive sense of me-ness, of holding onto self. This erroneous holding is the taproot for all our afflictions and pain. Bodhicitta banishes them. Bodhicitta is necessary at all times, regardless of our activity. Bodhicitta destabilizes the very ground of our grasping at "me." When that grasping dissolves, our heart easily embraces all living beings. Let our every action be motivated by the intention to benefit everyone. Indeed, the aim of all our practice, of all our training—including especially these seven trainings from Longchenpa—is the flourishing of our bodhicitta, our awakened mind.

We awaken through our pure intention to benefit others. Our first focus is on the needs of living beings. For their sake, we have a second focus, our own awakening into the complete omniscience of buddhahood. This makes it possible for us to address their suffering. We are not separate from other living beings! As Maitreya said, developing bodhicitta is the ultimate purpose of all our practice and training.

Bodhicitta, awakened mind, yields the ultimate fruit. Filled with courage and determination to bring about this fruition, we are ready to overcome all sloth and impediments. Every single one of us wants the same thing. We want to avoid suffering and we want to enjoy happiness. Yet suffering comes our way through the ripening of our five main afflictions. This happens because we don't directly know our own nature. So we train to bring forth the clarity, wisdom, and compassion that lead to complete awakening. This dispels all mental fogginess.

Crucial for these endeavors is our own heartfelt confidence, what Buddhists call faith. This heartfelt confidence, a state of great receptivity, is of four types: the heartfelt confidence that is clarifying, that seeks to awaken, that has confident conviction in cause and effect, and that remains irreversibly on the path.

First, we have heartfelt clarifying confidence (*dvang pa'i dad pa*). Clarifying confidence makes you feel very alive. Meeting your teacher, studying or practicing the dharma, you find that your mind is vivid, clear, and enthusiastic. You feel inspired. You are animated, you are clear. This bright confidence brings clarity and dispatches mental sluggishness. It clarifies the all-base (*kun gzhi, ālaya*). This has significance. The all-base is dull. It obscures. It is the ground of failing to recognize your own nature. Such unawareness is discordant with awareness. Heartfelt confidence dispels some of that ignorance and at the same time reveals what is genuinely meaningful.

In short, the basis of not knowing or not recognizing your nature (*ma rig pa, avidyā*) is the all-base. The path, by contrast, is knowing what behaviors to adopt and what to discard. Its fruition is buddhahood. In all these ways, this first type of heartfelt confidence is a cause of banishing what obstructs and a cause of further development. Understanding this well is important.

The second type of faith, the heartfelt confidence that wants to awaken (*'dod pa'i dad pa*), is a wish that comes about through the clarifying confidence that is its cause. It is vital that your goal be clear. This kind of confidence propels us on the path. Your goal has become clear, like fog lifting on the road before you. You see where you are headed.

Does wanting to achieve the path seem like desire? And that such wanting is wrong? But all desires are not the same! You need not quash *all* wanting. Aśvaghoṣa calls the young Gautama's wish to picnic in a pleasure garden "the desire that would end all desire" because it is en route to this pleasuring that he encounters an old man, a sick man, a corpse, and, finally, the joyful mendicant who inspires him to leave home intent on liberation.

Desires can help or obstruct. We are talking here about the desire to practice, a wish born of pure intention and wanting to benefit others. This kind of wanting is not at all like the wanting of your own desires. Wanting something in order to benefit others is wholly unlike worldly desires, which do not bring you to awakening. The cause is different, and its effect also different. It's important and necessary to have desire and a goal. Otherwise you won't get there. Without a cause there can be no effect, no fruition.

Your desire to practice is a cause of your ability to benefit others. Worldly desires are about your own happiness. Seeking to help others releases the limitations of purpose you place around your actions. Focusing on self only yields more suffering. It cannot lead to awakening. Your desire for practice, on the other hand, can bring happiness to everyone, including yourself. This is a big difference. So direct your mind to this purpose and accomplish it. Such intentionality is necessary for accomplishing anything. You don't build a house without some intention to channel your energy.

The third type of openhearted devotion is heartfelt conviction in cause and effect (rgyu 'bras yid ches gyi dad pa). Spiritually as well as materially, we live in an ongoing process of cause and effect. The power and validity of cause and effect means that the path can fulfill our wishes. A cause that is authentic and right gives rise to an effect that is also authentic and right. We need confident understanding of this principle. Intention and desire alone are not enough.

We must train in the actual methods that bring about awakening. This brings us confidence in the process of the path and in Buddha's foundational teachings on cause and effect. It's important to investigate this, to probe the matter with questions, to look at it scientifically. This is how we develop complete certainty (nges shes) regarding causality. This interdependence is what we bring to the path and what allows the path to function.

Everything living, as well as everything without life, arises from causes. This is how ordinary phenomena all around us come to be. These things are conventional truths and they come about through one thing: relying on one another. These are what we have to work with. Knowing this well supports our development. In this way too, you start to see that your life is really the effect of its own prior causes. This reveals the existence of past lives. We recognize that we are now in the present, walking toward our future.

The fourth, irreversible heartfelt confidence (*phyir mi ldog pa'i dad pa*) is an openhearted confidence that will never revert. Until you gain authentic knowing (*tshad ma, pramāṇa*), you rely on inference based on the authority of scripture. Once you have authentic, direct experience of cause and effect, you no longer need to rely on scripture or inference. Your knowing is irreversible. As Vasubandhu said:

> Hearing dispels ignorance like a lamp banishes darkness.
> Meeting rightness is the supreme increaser [of goodness].[44]

All good qualities come from superb knowing (*shes rab, prañjā*). Wisdom is inexhaustible and complete (*shes rab mthar phyin pa*). We need to rely on an excellent teacher who can explain this well. If we can't follow the meaning we hear, if we don't understand its logic, we can consult scriptural authority. When Buddha said, "I will speak to you well," he meant that he would speak well in order to provide temporary and final antidotes to our ignorance and our afflictions. In this way, blessings are given and teachings are offered. Buddha himself was accomplished in all these ways and these accomplishments also affected his listeners.

We also train in meditation. The wisdom arising from meditation brings forth boundless expressions of the teachings: words without limit can emerge. New dimensions of meaning can come forth from a single word. The most sublime and marvelous (*phun sum tshogs pa, sampanna*) wisdom knows everything; it encompasses the entire spectrum of knowing. When such abundance of cognitive understanding is married to action, it reveals all skillful methods and it enables us to cut through all the misunderstandings that limit us. This wisdom has insight, volition, and power. It is inexhaustible. This is what can arise through listening—or study—and personal reflection.

Compassion is a supreme method for realizing emptiness. The most excellent practitioners, on meeting other living beings, see their pain and therefore have compassion for them. This compassion gives rise to wisdom. We need to unite our understanding of emptiness with compassion.

Buddha advised, "Listen well, really well, without any distraction to sensory objects." Listening that is authentic (*tshad dang ldan pa*) means that you are attending without a lot of extraneous thoughts arising. This is good.

When he urged us to listen well, Buddha made three points. First, we are to give up coarse conceptualizing when we listen. Second, we keep our mind, our eyes, and our ears focused on the teaching. Third, in doing so we become like an upright vessel, able to hold its contents without spilling. Simply sitting still will not accomplish good listening! Patrul Rinpoche describes this situation in *Words of My Perfect Teacher*: "The body is straight and still, but mind has run off to the marketplace."

Understand that, in listening well, you will not be falling asleep, nor will you be overly stressed. Neither too tight nor too loose! Keep to the middle way. As Majik Labdron said, "Tighten by tightening, loosen by loosening. The view's very essence is there." This is the view on which we reflect and meditate. Don't attempt the impossible by trying to touch your fingertip with that same finger. Your finger will get twisted; you cannot succeed.

It is good so many people feel an affinity for the Great Completeness, Dzogchen. But you need to understand well the exact ways in which it is excellent. The Tibetan word *dzog* means that which is complete, that which is perfect. Everything from the foundational practices (*sngon 'gro*) through to the actual basis of practice is itself a great completeness, a real perfection.

Before an airplane can take to the skies, it has to be assembled on the ground. Likewise, the foundational practices allow us to develop the airplane that is Dzogchen. Skillful means and wisdom are the two wings of this plane. When it is fully operational we can guide our actual support—the fully operative plane—to buddhahood. Without this foundation, it is not complete, not perfect. It is not *dzog* (complete).

The Great Completeness includes all the good qualities of all nine pathways. All the beneficial qualities coalesce in it and can be elaborated from it. Dzogchen, swiftest of all paths, can like one swift arrow slice through all pathways to reach the state of complete awakening. This complete perfection is called "great," or *chen*, because there is nothing greater than it, no greater purpose, no higher or vaster reality. On the basis of Dzogchen's unique practical instructions (*man ngag*) we can attain buddhahood very quickly, so long as we have a suitable karmic connection with it. Few in words, profound in meaning, Dzogchen easily brings swift fruition to those connected to it. The ordinary path of the perfections takes many lifetimes.

Dzogchen is the awakened state, the grace-mind (*dgongs, saṃdhāya*) of all buddhas, past, present, and future. It is the heart-blood, the essential vital bright orb of the lama, the special deity or yidam, and the ḍākinīs, the sky-streaming wisdom women.

Foundational practices help make us capable of genuinely accessing Great Completeness teachings. How do they do this? Access requires that we ourselves be persons of great completeness. So some preparation is needed. When a person of great completeness caliber meets the Great Completeness teachings, they are in sync. The practices work.

This training or purification of mind is necessary because right now our minds are under the power of their own grasping. "Mind" here refers to the functioning of our senses and our mental perception. Our minds grasp onto objects and take them to be true. As a result, we experience wanting, aversion, or ignorance. In other words, the way we perceive things gives rise to afflictions. And our afflictions inevitably yield suffering.

In order to train successfully, we need to understand our mind's errors and reverse them. Since suffering most essentially comes from our own minds, we train our minds to shift our way of perceiving so that we do not create suffering. We reorient ourselves to a more appropriate direction that is new for us. We break the spell of nonrecognition and reverse the processes leading to suffering. Buddha explained that the purpose of dharma is to lead us to awakening, to full realization. We need to be led to the ultimate awakened state through realizing the final emptiness, the actual nature of things. These teachings make us real candidates for the Great Completeness.

By engaging these mind trainings laid out by Longchenpa, we grow capable of great completeness. Through these trainings, we move from coarse to more and more subtle. We start to see everything as impermanent. This is quite obvious, so in that sense it is a more easily accessible part of the path. After this we are guided to the meaning that leads to the ultimate, the essential awakened grace mind of all buddhas.

TAKING REFUGE IN THE LAMA, DEITIES, AND ḌĀKINĪS

Longchenpa begins with an homage: "I bow to the lamas, special deities, and ḍākinīs." We pay homage to these three because we understand and are inspired by their great qualities. Blessings for our body, speech, and mind arise from the lama. We offer our lamas devotion through our body, speech, and mind in order to connect with their own. Their blessings help us overcome our ordinary sense of our body, speech, and mind. Our three portals awaken. These blessings, which are the grace-waves of awakened beings, flow through us. Even Buddha's kindness is surpassed by the kindness of our lama, our spiritual friend.

Secret mantra says that the lama embodies both the ordinary and extraordinary Three Jewels. The lama is the embodiment of awakened body, speech, and mind. And the lama's good qualities are equal to Buddha's own. Moreover, the lama is right here with us, able to offer personal guidance. We need this. Even buddhas rely on spiritual friends. And buddhas themselves are our spiritual friends. "In the future, I reveal myself as a spiritual friend to help beings."

The excellent lama is knowledgeable about dharma (*mkhas*), clear about how to be a guide, able to communicate clearly (*btsun*), and filled with compassion (*thugs rje*) and kindliness (*bzang*). They must in addition be skilled in hearing, reflecting, and meditation.

Listening, or study, brings understanding of the teaching. With reflection, one absorbs the words' meaning. Meditation yields realization of how things really are, the view. As a result, one becomes capable of teaching, debating, and composition and is inspired to benefit the minds of their students. When it comes to Dzogchen, we have intellectual understanding, meditative experience, and realization.

In addition to relying on the lama, we rely also on our personal deity, or *yidam*, who helps bring genuine flexibility to our minds. By relying on the yidam, our habits of mind (*phag chags*) begin to shift. One very strong habitual conditioning is clinging to our own body as self. In our practice, we replace our ordinary body with the divine form of the yidam, an awakened being with whom we feel a special relationship. We experience our own body as the yidam's divine form. In this way we remove a major reference point for grasping onto self. We also replace the sense of our ordinary speech and mind as the expression and awakened mind of this yidam. This is how we purify perceptions associated with self and our ordinary sense of body.

The ultimate *siddhi*, or power (*'grub pa*), is awakening itself. The three levels of saṃsāra—the desire, form, and formless realms—arise from our habitual tendencies. These tendencies lead to afflictions. Through our practice, we experience our body as the deity, our speech as mantra, and our mind as meditative stabilization. This is how we attain an indivisible wholeness of body, speech, and mind (*lus ngag sems gsum ngo bo dbyer med*). Such meditation connects us to the three buddha dimensions, or *kāya*. This is how we attain the accomplishments or feats (*siddhis*) that are inseparable from a buddha's own body, speech, and mind. And alongside these ultimate accomplishments, we get minor ones as well.

We also take refuge in the ḍākinī, our supportive friend. Everyone needs this kind of friend; no one succeeds alone. We need also to understand that the ḍākinīs engage in four kinds of helpful activities:

1. They *pacify* obstructions, illness, and obscurations.
2. They *increase* and *enrich*; they call forth adventitious circumstances not yet present, such as lifespan, merit, or prosperity.
3. They *magnetize*. If beings are not focusing well, for example, ḍākinīs strengthen their intention. In brief, they bring living beings' minds and energies (*rlung*) under control, including spirits who may be at loose ends. This is a function of gathering together and unifying loose ends of various kinds.
4. *Wrathful activities* are used when the other methods don't succeed, when we need to cut down or cut through something right in its own place in order to awaken.

A buddha's awakened body is the emanation dimension or formed form, the nirmāṇakāya. Awakened speech is the richly resplendent dimension or bright form, the saṃbhogakāya. And awakened mind is the sheer essence dimension or sheer form, the dharmakāya. These sheer, bright, and fully formed buddha dimensions are all connected with the awakened form of the lama. In this way, we ultimately find that our own body, speech, and mind are inseparable from the enlightened body, speech, and mind of the lama.

In fruition, our awakened body is the lama, our awakened speech is the yidam, and our awakened mind is the ḍākinī. Our identification with the three sources—Guru, Deva, and Ḍākinī—is our ultimate homage. We practice to recognize our indivisibility with them.

ON LONGCHENPA'S *SEVENFOLD MIND TRAINING*

Longchenpa's first full verse, as we have seen, offers homage by way of body, speech, and mind to the lama, yidam, and ḍākinī.

> Most respectfully, I offer homage through the three gates of
> my being.
> To the hosts of lama, yidam, and ḍākinī,
> I clarify the method of direct entry to the heart-meaning
> through seven teaching points for training your mind.

Readers of exceptional capacity will fathom the inner meaning of this text just by reading its title and opening words of homage. Those with good fortune and karmic connection will come to realization on the basis of the text.

Longchenpa composed this text to give a clear explanation of the seven trainings leading to such realization. These seven trainings are a method, a stage-by-stage path for entering our natural great completeness. We can't move forward without them. We need a method for realizing the ultimate. Our purpose in practicing this method, and Longchenpa's in writing about it, is to reverse all mistaken appearances so that we see correctly, so that they dawn for us as they really are. Our actual nature will appear. And when it does, we feel we gain a completely new kind of life. In his great generosity, Longchenpa lifts the veil here and clarifies the meaning.

After the homage, Longchenpa expresses his openhearted intention to benefit all, setting aside any lesser agenda. This aspiration is the ground of everything. Pride, for example, renders one unable to help others. Similarly, scholars interested in showing their erudition lack pure motivation. They are interested in fame and respect, consumed with competitiveness or a wish to advance their careers and dismantle someone else's. Without the proper causes, Longchenpa notes, we will be unable to help others. Pure and positive motivation makes his writing powerful. And listening with great joy to such teachings disperses our agitation and sleepiness. Our minds are clear. Thereby we can bring full attention to listening, integrating what we learn with our own intention to benefit beings. We do not just listen to these teachings, we practice them to completion.

When Longchenpa says that he will "bring forward this training for fortunate beginners with positive karma," he means that this teaching is for everyone who, by the power of their own previous listening, are able to respond fully to these teachings. The strength of their prior training means they can connect more easily with the path and more easily become familiar with sheer knowing, an open awareness, or *rig pa*, that they have already directly encountered.

All the teachings here accord with the "Precious Copper Letters" section of the *Fourfold Heart Essence* and are more fully elaborated in the extensive commentarial teachings in that collection.[45]

First Mind Training: Impermanence

The training on impermanence relates to Buddha's first teaching on unsatisfactoriness, the first ennobling truth, often called "the truth of suffering." The four characteristics associated with this first ennobling truth are impermanence, pain, emptiness, and selflessness.[46] Saṃsāra has the nature of suffering, the nature of impermanence.

Impermanence is something we can see directly. When we meditate on it we overcome our erroneous holding to permanence. Such meditation is vital, for impermanence reveals to us that existence is unsatisfactory. There are three elements here: first, how we train to understand impermanence; second, the measure of our success; and third, the result.

Meditation on impermanence moves from the more obvious outer, or coarse, types of impermanence to the most subtle, the most easily overlooked. We can see coarser forms directly, whereas we approach the more hidden or secret forms of impermanence through inference.

This is an important training. In the end we seek to realize outer, inner, and secret impermanence. In doing so, we find that everything our senses contact is impermanent. This recognition blossoms until the shifting nature of everything becomes more compelling than the illusory solidity that usually attracts our attention. We are being weaned away from conflating how things seem with how they really are.

The external or most obvious and coarse type of impermanence is the vessel in which we live, our world system. This world system comes together over a period of twenty countless eons. It abides and then disintegrates over another two countless eons, and after its destruction there are twenty eons in which it is altogether absent and there is only empty space.

Another example of external impermanence to which Longchenpa calls attention is the turning of the seasons. Every day is an example of impermanence. First comes morning, then noon, then evening.

Day follows night. Then it's gone. In the same way, every moment also has a head and a tail, enduring for only a speck of time. The wheel is always turning. Everything is always in flux. Nothing remains, ever.

Our bodies too are always in transition. First there is conception, then we are a fetus, then we take birth, live our life, experience our death. We are like bubbles that can burst at any moment. We are composed of the four elements, or of the five aggregates. These come together and then part. They have no essence. With every breath, there is the possibility for breath to stop, and then we die. This is the inner level of impermanence.

The next phase of this meditation is to observe that others are also impermanent. Like ourselves, they are conditioned, meaning that support for their lives comes together and then falls apart. Yet they look upon the things of this life as permanent! Seeing this, we cultivate compassion for them. Our compassion helps us do away with laziness and procrastination in our practice. It also orients us toward that which is enduring, the state of full awakening.

The secret level of impermanence encompasses all the changes that separate us from those we love, or leave us stuck with those we do not. And we can never declare with certainty that we will not die today. Recognizing the secret level of impermanence also means we see how our thoughts, moods, and mind are always changing. And so we accept things as they are.

When Buddha encountered the four great rivers of suffering—birth, old age, sickness, and death—he saw that dominion over his kingdom was pointless. In the end he would lose it anyway. He gave up his kingdom right then. He found it more meaningful to focus on something that could endure, the state of buddhahood.

It's fine to have enjoyment, but we can be careful about pursuing pleasure as if it's permanent, as if it will really last. We practice never to be distracted from this recognition. In our hearts, we maintain continuous awareness of impermanence. Don't feel that your meditation on impermanence leads to more suffering! Quite the contrary. With such practice, we head toward definitive understanding (nges shes) of our actual situation.

The measure of our success in this practice is that we diminish pre-occupation with meaningless worldly activity. We focus on actions whose fruits will endure, and we reverse the trend of investing ourselves in samsara. As a result, we reverse the causes that increase suffering and reverse our addiction to afflictions such as anger.

We all have deeply entrenched afflictions that cause us difficulty. We set about reversing the causal processes that ripen our suffering in saṃsāra. We reduce our involvement in desire and hatred. We reverse the negative trend of the cause and effect associated with cyclic existence ('khor ba'i blo ldog).

Second Mind Training: Fleeting Happiness

Once we have pacified our coarse mind by understanding imperma-nence, we move on to reflect on the temporary nature of happiness and learn to distinguish it from enduring happiness. In this way, skilled practitioners decrease the detrimental effects of their afflic-tions. Karma may ripen, and we may experience temporary or even somewhat stable happiness, but either way we don't fixate on these. We learn to distinguish the wholesome from the unwholesome, rec-ognizing that unwholesomeness arises due to our own erroneous mind, not causelessly.

The lower realms are obviously places of suffering. Yet the higher realms also bring suffering. Both are impacted by the suffering of per-vasive conditioning, which is present everywhere in saṃsāra. The measure of our success in this second training is that we see every-thing we are involved with as a cause of suffering, and so forever give up yearning for higher forms of samsaric existence. This is in accord with realizing the cause of suffering, the second noble truth.

Now we understand what gives rise to the cycles of our existence. Our decision to decamp from this situation deals a significant blow to our afflictions and opens the way for overcoming them completely. First we move away from them through the splendor of our determi-nation to be free from the afflictive patterns of cyclic existence. In the end, we overwhelm these afflictions with the splendor of our wisdom realizing selflessness. This means we are really determined to depart cyclic existence. Such determination on our part is essential. In this way, we realize the truth of cessation, the third ennobling truth. In addition, we need openhearted confidence and compassion.

These three, the determination to depart, confidence, and compassion, are essential to liberation. Our determination to depart cyclic existence helps us overcome afflictions, a process essential for liberation. This same determination also stabilizes our path, which in turn leads us to the realization of selflessness, timeless wisdom.

Third Mind Training: Compassion for All Saṃsāra

Our saṃsāra comes about through endless causes and conditions. Our minds are impacted by a multitude of circumstances. When we incorporate these conditions into mind training, we harness that very process of conditioning for a positive outcome. We orient ourselves toward what is reliable. We haven't yet fully decided that nothing in cyclic existence is stable or reliable. We now seek to become the kind of good practitioner who is not mastered by any samsaric circumstance.

Our unwholesome actions are motivated by afflictive tendencies. The three negative physical actions that afflictions bring about are killing, stealing, and sexual misconduct. The four negative actions associated with speech are lying, harsh speech, divisive talk, and nonsensical, gossipy conversation. The three negative mental actions are covetousness, intention to harm, and wrong view.

Wholesome actions associated with the body are generosity, protecting life, and pure ethics. Wholesome actions associated with speech are speaking truth, harmonious discourse, and kind words or recitation of teachings and mantra. Training in these undermines and reverses negative habits.

The three wholesome mental actions are, first, cultivating a helpful mind (phan sems) to counter malice—that is, instead of ill will you have a mind intending to benefit others. Second, since contentment itself is true wealth, our cultivation of contentment counters jealousy and upends covetousness. And cultivation of devotion will reverse wrong views. We don't seek just to avoid negative actions but to cultivate positive ones. These three cultivations are a great support for liberation.

We ourselves create all three realms of cyclic existence: the desire, form, and formless realms. These realms come about through our actions, not because of an external deity. Through mind training we recalibrate the causes and conditions of our lives. We train to reverse the processes that ripen our suffering and further our saṃsāra, learning to use these circumstances in a way that works positively for us. We train not to be carried away by afflictions, the source of our future suffering. We train to reverse cyclic existence, not to extend it.

As Longchenpa observes, thinking that cyclic existence will somehow pay off is just wishful thinking. Skilled practitioners are not overwhelmed or mastered by any circumstance. They easily decrease the detrimental effects of their own negativity.

Buddha said, "Cyclic existence is really very strange. We place our hope in what cannot fulfill us, while we fail to hope for what can actually come to pass." Cyclic existence is unpredictable. You may want to help someone for no reason. Or someone criticizes you for something you did not do, and even though the matter in question is minor, it gets blown out of proportion. Worldly activities are endless.

Since wants and afflictive desires can never be sated, they will drive us on without end. That's the cycle. Our own afflictions assist our plunge into suffering. Negative actions, motivated by our afflictive reaction patterns, give birth to the three lower realms. The teachings speak of uniting skillful means with wisdom. Wisdom means real insight into how things are, and we link this understanding with the skillful means of compassion.

Longchenpa tells us, "Don't indulge in saṃsāra! Direct your mind to liberation." In order to release ourselves from the whirlpool of habit patterns—our own saṃsāra—we must disarm our afflictions. When we realize selflessness, we deal a heavy blow to our [mistaken] sense of self. Lasting happiness comes from realizing exactly this selflessness. Until then, afflictions distort our perception.

Our orientation is based on bringing benefit to living beings. Mind training helps us turn toward enduring happiness, a happiness not subject to impermanence. Whenever we have the fire of ultimate happiness, we naturally have the smoke of temporary benefits. These benefits include finding situations where obstructions are decreased, where we have good health, and so on. Such temporary benefits come on the way, but our focus remains on accessing the stable happiness that is ultimate.

At the same time, we continue to view saṃsāra as something we can turn away from by reducing negative actions and their causes. We cultivate openhearted confidence, compassion for all beings, and the clear intention to depart saṃsāra. These three, as we have said, are vital to our path of awakening.

Success means realizing that our worldly karmic perceptions are entirely without essence. All the same, they prevent us from finding a path, and so prevent us from tasting the fruits of the path. Thus it is vital to have the second type of heartfelt confidence, strongly seeking enlightenment. This kind of heartfelt resonance is fundamental for us. Otherwise we do not move along the path.

The purpose of the excellent dharma is to vanquish negativity, bring forth all good qualities, and thus find happiness. Take joy in reading or listening to these special teachings. Engage in learning with the intention to benefit everyone.

All beings are just like you in wanting happiness and doing their best to avoid suffering. Practice with the intention of stabilizing the enduring happiness of buddhahood for yourself and all of them. These are all key points for your developing the correct view and correct meditation.

For your intention to blossom, you need to be a vessel for the teachings. The teaching itself consists of vowels and consonants, the condition for words coming forth. Being a vessel for the teaching means developing a relationship with the teaching such that your mind grows fertile and receptive. To see your teacher as Samantabhadra, the All-Good, and to consider yourself as Mañjuśrī, for example.

Everything that appears to our senses is erroneous! Things appear based on our own habit patterns and seeded predispositions. They arise due to unawareness. This ignorance, the unknowing (*ma rig pa*) that holds them to be true, is called an "obscuration" (*gti mug*) for how it grasps at what falsely seems so true.

The appearance of things as true is completely mistaken. It is dictated by our distorted habits. Our powerful habit of ignorance leads us to see and believe that everything we experience is solid and permanent. It is not. Buddhas see phenomena in an entirely different, awakened manner. Lesser bodhisattvas still have some clinging and fixation, but we ordinary beings have a tremendous amount of it. Our addiction to seeing things as true, solid, and lasting creates our desire, hatred, and ignorance, as well as pride and jealousy. These are the causes of our suffering.

The main point of our training, as we have seen, is to reverse these densely habitual ways of seeing and being. We encounter many circumstances in our lives—good, bad, and indifferent. Our afflictive engagement is never satisfied. We think we can get some benefit here, and instead become a slave to the objects we imagine are so solidly present around us. This is inevitable: once we understand that the objects, the things we see and touch, are erroneous, we ourselves, the subject of those perceptions, are certainly in error. Hence we must reverse these habitual tendencies, powerful as they are.

There are three important things to understand here: Everything we see or conceive is impermanent, mistaken, and without essence. What is essenceless has no meaning or purpose. Such things cannot possibly give rise to real or lasting happiness. Therefore we must turn our minds to what is reliable and true; they are sources of genuine happiness.

Fourth Mind Training: Our Pointless Activities

Our worldly activities are, in the end, without meaning or purpose. Meaning resides in what is true. To focus on the interests of this life is a function of being centered wholly in our particular sense of self. We are ego-fixated! Bodhisattvas are not like this. Their concern is for all living beings.

As Longchenpa observes, our worldly activities are driven by narrow interests—protecting our family, keeping friends close, competing with and overcoming our foes, being involved in business or agriculture. We do need to live and take care of things. The issue is how our self-fixation governs all these endeavors, making us a slave to saṃsāra, always serving and serving again the demands of our addiction to cyclic existence. But in the end there is no payoff. It is as if we've eagerly sought full-time employment in the Office of Conflict.

We want fame, we want to be acknowledged and honored by everyone. As a result, we are hollow at the core, precariously poised on a razor's edge.

In fact most of us are willy-nilly increasing our attachments, getting more enmeshed in family and working for good connections with friendly others. We also ripen our aversions, cultivate enmity, and stay away from those we regard as hostile. Which of these activities will help us when we come to die?

Let us turn our attention to what is really useful. Let us recognize that these things we now tend to so carefully and with all our life's energy are not useful. Soon they will pass away and become memories. They are like dreams. Nighttime brings us shorter dreams, our life is a longer dream. That is the only difference! You are a guest in your body.

All these things we now call ours—our houses, even the aggregates of our bodies—won't help us when we face our death. In that sense they are pointless, without meaning. We are training our minds to focus on what is genuinely meaningful and beneficial. What's the point of serving saṃsāra our entire lives when we can take nothing from it with us? We need to reflect very carefully on where benefit actually lies. Is it not ironic that Buddha successfully cultivated happiness in a cave, while wealthy people can be miserable in a palace?

Ordinarily speaking, we are badly deceived. We need to give up this life's deceptive goods like Buddha gave up his kingdom. Longchenpa says he feels as if a magician had lured him into this wholly false "reality." When he awoke from this, he sang a song of realization. Such songs are meant to bring joy and to allow beauty to blossom. Here is my own spontaneous song:[47]

Vast Expanse is Sheer Form found,
Great Array of all that's known,
Errorless Peak Path's Master,
Homage to you, Stainless Light.[48]

Bright rainbow form, Vast Expanse,
Resides, its essence changeless.
Just-there ground is all complete.
Beings throughout space, be well.

May I ever remain with
You, my exalted Teacher,
Tasting Dharma ambrosia.
May we all find Buddhahood.

It really is as if a magician conjured up the scenes of our lives and
we responded by getting completely absorbed in that. We suffer
greatly because of this. The appearances of this life won't follow you
for all time. Why should we be servants of fallible saṃsāra? Why not
serve what is flawless, and attend to the teachings' essential instructions? The measure of our success in this training is realizing we have
to let go of all these empty pursuits.

Fifth Mind Training: Buddha's Good Qualities

We suffer a great deal because of afflictions that arise due to our self-
concern and the way we invest our sense of self with solidity. Awakened beings, Buddhas, transcend this. As you remove afflictions, your
tight bondage to your falsely reified self decreases. This is an inter-
dependent process and it works the other way as well: as you loosen
the bonds of erroneous self-identification, your afflictions diminish,
no longer holding you in their grip. This is how Buddha accumulated
a vast store of merit which ripened into the Buddha body of thirty-two
marks and eighty-four signs.

The good qualities of awakened body, speech and mind are an inexhaustible wheel of ornamentation (*rgyan gyi 'khor lo*), the result of

an ocean of virtuous goodness. Such a person's mind is forever filled with a wish to benefit beings, all beings. Such a mind never veers from the immutable sheer essence dimension (*chos sku, dharmakāya*); wisdom continually flows forth from it. The splendor of Buddha's body, speech, and mind overwhelms the limitations of all ordinary beings. This awakened state is the purpose of these trainings. Like someone churning milk into butter, we engage our effort to manifest the incredible qualities of buddhahood.

Longchenpa counsels us to think deeply about accomplishing buddhahood, and therefore to focus single-pointedly on gaining the beneficial qualities that help us do so. For this we need to develop in meditation. Guru Rinpoche said, "I never said there is buddhahood without any meditation, or that accomplishments come without making any effort at all."

Great yogis engage in strict austerities and rigorous practice. This is how they purify the five poisons, thereby manifesting the qualities of awakening. Our own manifestation of these depends entirely on practice. Practice pacifies agitation and inspires us to more practice. Meditation is the cause. Awakening, called buddhahood, is the fruit. We are intent on practicing until we gain the result. The measure of our success in this training is that we wholeheartedly want to pursue practice.

Sixth Mind Training: Importance of The Teacher's Instructions

The ocean of our suffering is vast and deep. Our lama is the boatman. The boat itself consists of instructions. We use these instructions as a boat to take us to the other shore. We want to meditate on the preciousness and significance of the teacher's instructions. Our teacher is the boatman who helps us across the ocean. The teacher is a supreme monarch who removes the veils of saṃsāra. As students, we need the fortitude to carry out the instructions we receive in these mind trainings make our mind workable, capable of overcoming our afflictions. Each mind training supports the others. This is why we rely wholeheartedly on the lama.

The measure of our success is realizing that a narrow pursuit of this life's purposes alone is pointless. And we have nothing to rely on other than our lama's instructions. We need to review and reflect on this until we have become a perfect vessel for the teachings. Because what is needed is for us to accomplish the great qualities and benefits of buddhahood in this very life. In one single lifetime. So we relinquish our pointless pursuits and focus on the instructions we have received.

Seventh Mind Training: Three States beyond Thought

This is a subtle level of training. It yields an ability to fully rely on the good cause, our teacher, that leads to the good fruition of awakening. Suchness, or the nature of reality (*chos nyid, dharmatā*), is the essence of everything and nonconceptuality is the path to realizing this nature for ourselves.

Nonconceptuality is a method that can lead us to recognize the real nature of things, their reality. So rely on Longchenpa and realize the truth of bliss-emptiness in a state of nonconceptuality. Nonconceptuality is the source from which our good qualities arise. The lama is that source, in that the lama embodies the Three Jewels. Fleeting meditative experiences *(nyams)* of bliss, clarity, and nonconceptuality are methods by which we gradually can encounter reality.[49]

MEDITATIONS

First Nonconceptual Meditation: Indivisible Bliss and Emptiness

This meditation begins with bringing attention deep into the body and clearly seeing your central channel. It is deep blue, signifying the sheer essence dimension, and forms a hollow passageway, like a piece of bamboo. This hollow channel rises from your deep navel area, what Tibetans call the *mdo* (pronounced "doe"), where the body's three major channels converge.[50]

The top of this channel opens at your crown, where you imagine an upside-down white syllable *haṃ*, the size of a pea. This is said to have the nature of method. At the channels' bottom, four finger-widths below your navel, is a blazing red *ah*.[51] Its flame rises through your central channel as a luminous stream of warm light that purifies all your channels and chakras. It reaches your great-bliss crown chakra, associated with the formed form or emanation dimension (*nirmāṇakāya*), where its warmth dissolves the upside-down white syllable *haṃ*, from which white liquid light now descends, passing through your throat cakra, which is associated with the bright form or richly resplendent dimension (*saṃbhogakāya*), to the dharma wheel at your heart, which is associated with sheer form or sheer buddha dimension (*dharma-kāya*). It then reaches the manifestation wheel (*sprul 'khor, nirmāṇa-cakra*) at your navel center, which is associated with the naturally awakened dimension or full form (*svabhāvikakāya*).

Once your channels are completely suffused with nectar, you can engage the four applications (*sbyor ba gzhi*) of pulling in, settling, churning, and shooting out. First, pull energy in with your inhalation. Second, settle it down beneath your navel, then pull up from below as you push on it a bit from above, trapping a ball of breath-energy in the diaphragm area. Third, churn your lower belly to the right and then left, and again forward.[52] You hold your breath as you are able— but don't force it. Then, fourth, when you need to breathe, release the breath, sending it straight out from you like an arrow.[53]

To put this another way, we gently pull up the lower wind and press down the upper one. When we need to exhale, we relax and then resume. While doing this, focus on a white *ah* in your heart. Through this skillful means for developing bliss you achieve a stable realization of emptiness.[54]

While the instructions are simple, there are nuances that can only be communicated in person, so none of this should be attempted without guidance from an experienced teacher. It is easy to take it too far and bring harm to yourself.[55]

Second Nonconceptual Meditation: Indivisibility of Clarity Emptiness

Begin with the threefold or ninefold breath cleansing, breathing through your nose. Expel hatred through your right nostril as a smoky blue-blackness, and send desire through your left nostril as dark-red color. Expel ignorance through both nostrils as a smoky color. In this way you engage your breath to purify obscurations.

Immediately everything that exists, everything that you can see or sense, dissolves into light and then into blue-sky spaciousness. Inhale this while holding the vase as before, without, however, rotating the breath in your belly.[56] You need not hold very long, a little will do, until just before it feels awkward. Otherwise the energy may rise up to your heart, and this is dangerous. Use the medium vase breath, don't hold it too long, but go to your edge. Be easy, let your body and mind relax, and be with the nonconceptual state of clarity and emptiness.

If you are hot, feel that your breath energy is cold. If you are cold, feel that the breath energy is warm. This is a simple and very appropriate way of working with the energies and elements. More elaborately, we can say that in summer, when the fire element is dominant, we meditate water. In fall, when wind is dominant, we meditate earth. In winter, when water dominates, we meditate fire, and in spring, when earth is dominant, we meditate on wind. And if one wishes one can also work with the color associated with the antidote to the current season. Winter is white, spring is yellow, summer is red, fall is green. You can also meditate on the feel or touch of, for example, heat, cold, liquid, and so forth.[57]

However, the energy of space is always present, and all the elements are included in it. Therefore, simply working with hot and cold is sufficient. Longchenpa marvels at this practice and advises us to practice only this.

Third Nonconceptual Meditation: Realization of Reality

This meditation is for entering into our true condition without any conceptualizing. Your mind gains power from the one-pointed state and realizes vast spaciousness as it enters the unfabricated samādhi—meditative stabilization—of reality itself. In this way the primordial wisdom of buddhahood blossoms for you.

Rejoice! You have received an incredibly profound introduction to Dzogchen. Longchenpa said, "I have arranged these seven, which carry the key points so that practitioners can enter the exceedingly profound practice of the great completeness." Longchenpa's mind training spans from the foundational practices all the way to Dzogchen. He composed it so that the true meaning of how things are can become clear to us all. This method provides steps for entering the natural great completeness. It is a gradual process for developing understanding (*kho rim*).

Be relaxed, easy in your mind and body. Don't let your eyes flit here and there; let them rest without movement. Let your mind just be, not entertaining memories of the past or plans for the future. In this way, your mind is not following after anything. It simply rests. It stays put. And you gain the capacity to be your own master.

This is freedom. Through this you will recognize your mind-nature. Your mind-nature is like the sky and is equal to space. You are present in space, with utterly bare and wide-open, sheer awareness. This is the method for recognizing the true meaning of what is. Receiving this practice is like finding an excellent vehicle in which you can ride away from suffering. Its more subtle and profound dimensions emerge as you become familiar with the practice.

Longchenpa's name means vast (*chen*) expanse (*klong*). He achieved the rainbow body of clear light and abides there. May we accomplish the supreme view and spontaneous presence. May all our lives keep this connection to the guru. May all beings wake up in this maṇḍala.

Longchenpa wrote this at White Skull Mountain above Shugseb nunnery. "White" indicates the intention to benefit others. And, like a mountain, this practice is a source of many good qualities. Doing these practices prepares you to receive *semtri*, or mind guidance (*sems khrid*), in addition to further teachings. Mind guidance is the superhighway to awakening. Mind training is an outer level, something like dietary guidelines that are helpful to everyone. Mind guidance is specific to each individual. Like advice from your own doctor, it is personal, a one-on-one process. Our connection to these practices creates conditions in which this seed can bring about your awakening. May all benefit. This is my deepest and most sincere aspiration.

PART 3

Mind Trainings' Breadth and Depth:
Wisdom, Pith Practices,
and Dzogchen Perspective
in Jigme Lingpa and Longchen Rabjam

1. Horizons of Wholeness
and the First Mind Training

In opening his text with an homage to Guru, Deva, and Ḍākinī, Longchenpa, like Jigme Lingpa and Adzom Rinpoche after him, indicates that the seven trainings' perspective includes tantra as well as Dzogchen. Garab Dorje, on whose outline these seven are based, calls them "seven trainings in bodhicitta," and Adzom Rinpoche's teaching on these likewise makes bodhicitta central.

Jigme Lingpa calls his *Stairway to Liberation* an "instruction on the essential meaning" or "teaching points" (*don khrid*) of Longchenpa's seven trainings. In it, he offers detailed advice for practice. His take on the seven trainings has four crucial features. First, he anchors the seven in widely shared Buddhist principles as well as in uniquely tantric perspectives. He interweaves karmic and wisdom narratives, and he includes a touch of Dzogchen as well. Second, he amplifies the trainings through story-practices, something rarely if ever found in mind training manuals, yet a method that harkens back to Buddha's own way of teaching, as described in many sūtras. Third, he joins these story-practices to key elements of guru yoga and tantric elements of the path. Fourth, he includes pith practices that in the simplest possible ways guide the mind to its own nature. As he says, "Through relying on the flower of words, one comes to the fruit, the wordless and nonconceptual meaning."[58]

Jigme Lingpa is famous for his revelation of the Heart Essence Vast Expanse cycle of Dzogchen teachings, which became perhaps the most widespread of Heart Essence cycles in Tibet and is now widely practiced in Dzogchen communities around the world. Like Adzom Paylo Rinpoche, who is recognized as his incarnation, Jigme Lingpa was regarded as an incarnation of Trisong Detsen and Vimalamitra, and was prophesied by Guru Rinpoche in a treasure discovered in the fourteenth century.[59]

Jigme Lingpa had powerful visions of Longchen Rabjam during his second three-year retreat in the Flower Cave at Samye Chimphu in Central Tibet.[60] Some narratives name him a reincarnation of Longchen Rabjam.[61] In any case, Jigme Lingpa is most definitely a spiritual son of Longchenpa, having received full blessings, transmission, and permission to teach during course of the three visions he describes in his *Secret Autobiography*.[62]

Jigme Lingpa opens *Stairway to Liberation* with an homage to Samantabhadra, the all (*kun, samanta*) good (*bzang, bhadra*) reality, who is unobstructed and primordially awake. The practices Jigme Lingpa provides here can reveal the practitioner's own nature as likewise all good, unobstructed, and awake. Since this nature has always existed, it does not newly come into being and is thus "unborn," a simple epithet that in Dzogchen is shorthand for many aspects of experience that language cannot express.

Jigme Lingpa offers homage also to the first human master of Dzogchen, Garab Dorje, whose commentary on the *Sole Child Scripture* (*Bu gcig*)[63] reminds us to "reflect that all conditioned things are impermanent."[64]

To slow down and notice hitherto overlooked evidence of impermanence in everything dissolves our addiction to imagining that we and our surroundings are permanent. Following Longchenpa's instructions on the first training, we gradually digest the import of seasonal change, recognize our own and dear ones' mortality, and finally, as Adzom Rinpoche suggested, note the fleeting nature of our own turbulent emotions. In the second training we note the fleeing nature of happiness, and in the third we develop compassion by sensing into the profound sufferings of this world.

THE FIRST STORY-MEDITATION

The first three of the seven trainings might as well be called "welcome to the world of saṃsāra." Our realm is known in India as the *saha* world—a place where there is much to endure. What could symbolize our fragile state better than a rickety rowboat in a raging storm, roiled by giant sea swells carrying multiheaded monsters?[65] We'll be on it soon, because in the first training Jigme Lingpa invites us to imagine ourselves riding such a sea as our fearful regret intensifies. This is the first of his story-meditations, a method unique in the broad compass of mind-training practices.[66] And he tells us why he introduces this kind of practice. Longtime practitioners, he observes, may come to understand impermanence by reflecting on scripture, but beginners often do better with stories.[67] Who among us is not a beginner? My venerable teacher of forty years, the revered Dzogchen master Khetsun Sangpo Rinpoche, in talking with us students would often matter-of-factly include himself as part of the circle of "us beginners."

At the beginning of this first story-meditation, we find ourselves in a frightening place about which we know nothing, except that we are alone. Existential aloneness is a bleak state indeed. We sit there in miserable not knowing—what will we do? Approached by a white male and black female, we quickly agree to join them in search of a precious jewel in the City of Illusory Six Senses. (The name itself should be a warning, but it isn't. Such is our befuddlement.)

Setting out in a small boat with these new companions, we encounter one peril after another. This journey is a nightmare of sky-vaulting waves, multiheaded sea monsters, and whipping winds, until finally your boat is ready to break apart in the middle of the ocean. Gradually, you get it. You understand that this ocean of saṃsāra will never bring the happy security we seek. As you immerse ourselves in this drama, impermanence and mortality are no longer theoretical. Suddenly you know exactly how they feel. You perform your terror. Appalled, you find yourself facing the brute inevitability of your death for the very first time. You will never see family, friends, or country again.

You cry out. Your lamentations fill the air. And then your own teacher in the form of Guru Rinpoche, tantric and Dzogchen master par excellence, is right there, swaying in a gentle dance in the space before you. He brings home the point by spelling out the symbolism of your story. "You've been seeing saṃsāra as a precious jewel," he tells you, "when it's nothing but painful." This is what happens when you never consider your mortality. The man and woman who enticed you across the ocean—they are your own innate and entrained ignorance. "What will you do?" he asks. And then:

> Your panic intensifies, you pray with one-pointed concentration. When you are completely bewildered, without any idea of what to do next, straight from the guru's heart a web of white light comes forth to pierce your heart. Your boat capsizes, your mind leaves your body. You merge inseparably with the Guru and attain Buddhahood.[68]

This last phrase is a distilled guru yoga, a synopsized tantric practice. The vignette as a whole calls on the surging human instinct for survival while also pivoting toward a state of being that need never struggle to survive.

Once you have imagined all this, Jigme Lingpa gives his first of five pith instructions, a direct pivot toward that deeper, unassailable, state:

> Leave your thoughts of the three times to themselves, without support. Be wholly open and at ease. Then, whether your mind is active or at rest, simply maintain a state of mindful awareness.[69]

This pith instruction unfolds in three parts. The first step is to let go of whatever it is that you do to support thoughts that stray into past, present, or future. What does it mean to let go of support for thoughts? It varies. Your gestures of support may often be very subtle indeed, on the very fringe of your awareness. Very possibly you never considered thought to arise due to some identifiable support that you provide! All the more reason to be curious. If you simply open your attention, a thought, or more likely a stream of thoughts, will soon emerge. What did you do, or not do, to initiate this process? What did you do to maintain it? Look right into your experience with as little judgment or theory-spinning as possible.

By definition, a pith practice such as this emerges from experience and brings you into experience also.[70] This makes the practices especially valuable. Buddhist training traditionally involves hearing, reflecting, and meditating. Hearing includes reading and study; it brings understanding. Reflecting takes understanding deeper and makes it a personal felt-sense. It's a way to discover or recover insight into your own ordinary processes.

Again, a thought comes. Is there something that has supported it? How do you know? Once you have felt it, how do you let it go? And what happens when you do? You look into this, not to find answers but with light wondering, just to see what it is like. What you discover may be quite subtle, not showy at all. Whatever you find is enough to expand your visceral understanding. It's not a dramatic shift, but you are in new territory. It can help if you have someone to dialogue with, a friend who will at your request gently stop you when you get caught up in ideas and invite you back to what you actually did or stopped doing. Our everyday experience is composed of many tiny inner gestures that usually remain on the very fringe of awareness.

There is no predetermined "support" on which you are meant to land. No model to conform to. There is only your attention's open lens, to see what you can see. In my case I've found two things. First, a subtle trajectory of tension seems to light up at the beginning of an idea. It emerges as a pattern of slightly fizzy bits of energy. I might feel it kinesthetically in my chest or throat area, a subtle sensation and easy to miss. The location changes, but it's almost always associated with a specific place in my body, whether at the surface or deeper within. Discerning it might take a few minutes.

The point is, once identified, I'm at a fork in the road. I might be able to let it be, as the instruction suggests, in which case the thought stream dissipates. Or I might doubt that I've really identified it, and I continue observing until a clearer felt sense arises. Usually, before too long I am satisfied that I've let go of some sense of a support or catalyst of thought. That "something" is often hard to describe but easy to sense. Then I just sit back, as it were, and observe motion and stillness, as well as the wider horizon that this offers.

Another way I may notice a support, which is a little harder to catch, is the sense of a looker or thinker as central. The thought process has a center, and I am it. Like the support, it can seem to be part of my chest, catalyzing things from there. I'm less focused on the carbonated parade of thoughts than I am on the experience of being a kind of magnetizing center to and from which thoughts are broadcast. My next move is to sense this more closely, while at the same time (though it sounds paradoxical) the scope of my attention relaxes and opens a little, dissipating my sense of a magnetizing me. Something shifts, a constriction I didn't even know was there seems to lighten, I'm ready for a wider horizon. Again, this is just an example. What's important here is your own experience, no matter how different.

Once you've had a taste of how you support thought and then let it go, the next phase of this pithy practice is at hand. Jigme Lingpa's language is precise and evocative.[71] He suggests we be "wholly open" (kha yan), a term that most literally means "without a leash"—unbridled, not reined in, unconstrained. Free. Not led around by any old thought or reactivity that surfaces. His further suggestion is to be easy (glod), a vital Dzogchen instruction. My teachers would often gently intone this in the course of Dzogchen teachings, hlo, hlo, repeating it lightly, almost like a lullaby. It's an easeful sound, hlo, hlo (rhymes with sew, sew), an onomatopoeic induction in a gentle voice that soothes my whole being. This is key.

Longchenpa says that if we can't relax, we will always be in ordinary thought.[72] To relax doesn't mean that nothing is happening. Sensations, images, or memories may in fact become even clearer. My ocean is calm, yet colorful fish swim underneath. Some are slower than others, but there is no stopping such fish! The mind's dynamism is ever present. To my mild surprise, I learn that I can experience movement and stillness simultaneously. Wisdom, after all, is classically described as unborn and unceasing. These are not in contradiction! They relate to the larger horizon that emerged when I let go of a constricting "support" or "me-ness."

So, as much as possible, I don't fight or try to create any type of experience. To the extent that I remain unbridled by thought, I don't label and I don't judge whatever comes peeping through my horizon. They have permission to come or not. Active or still, awareness continues. I discover that there is indeed movement and there is indeed stillness. And being present to them in this freer and more easy manner is as simple as it is astonishing. Without my habitual way of supporting thoughts of the past, present, or future, and through focusing on my ongoing process rather than on reified parts of it (the kind of thing described by verbs rather than nouns), everything in my experience is included, since all gestures of mind are either moving or still.[73] The limited sense of a me who puts everything not-me on the periphery is no longer the show runner. Feeling this softens the imagined line in the sand that makes awakening in this lifetime seem impossibly distant.

This pith practice pivots toward Longchenpa's description of the dharmadhātu as the space in which things manifest;[74] that is, as the ultimate and all-inclusive field of our experience, home to all movement and stillness. Recognizing impermanence takes the shine off of saṃsāra, helps us let go and be free of it. Gaining such determination is crucial to the entire path and common to all the Buddhist traditions of India. From the perspective of Dzogchen, recognizing impermanence kicks open the door to seeing the actual nature of our mind.

Ordinary mind lassos its objects, limiting our awareness to one possibility, making a series of moments seem like a single unit of time at the expense of our openness and flexibility in responding to the moment. As the lasso tightens, ordinary mind grows increasingly insistent on things being one way and not another.

Attention that is simply present to experience without getting stuck in a particular part of it invites and allows us to taste wholeness. Wholeness means being present in a simpler way to the field of our experience and yields increasing freedom from ordinary mind and its reactivity. Swimming this open ocean, you are viscerally aware of your immediate surroundings, of currents eddying nearby, while still present to the wider horizon of ocean and sky. This is pleasurable. It heals some of our existential aloneness.

Repetition is part of mind training. We repeat the whole sequence of training many times. Perhaps we do a retreat, as Longchenpa suggests, of three, eleven, or twenty-one days on each training. In this way, our experience of the pith practices also grows, enriched by and likewise enriching the experience of the story-meditations and other elements of the seven trainings.

Having now considered the first pith practice in some detail, let's go back to the rickety boat, the better to appreciate how, with our mortal "me" literally at sea, we are finally facing our mortality. Our whole being is roused, finally awake to the truest drama of our lives. Desperate, we recall our home and the loved ones we will never see again. Our usual illusions of self-sufficiency, the raging conviction we have in the robustness of our own existence, are smashed. These illusions have fueled our entire journey. No longer afraid of our own fear, we cry out. Our cry is a recognition. We call on the vastness we have overlooked for so long. This cry is a turning point, it cracks open a new horizon that rearranges our entire experience of self. This is the real drama, not the waves.[75] We howl at the futility of what has come before, wide open for something new.

Clearly, touching into impermanence impacts every organ of knowing and sensibility. The simple practices just described engage cognitive, emotional, and somatic vitalities. Death is our mortality's ultimate fruition. Ernst Becker felt that denial of death is crucial to successful living.[76] For Buddhist practitioners, integrating with our realistic sense of mortality is liberating. A middle way between these poles of denial and despair is articulated by the late existential psychotherapist Irvin D. Yalom, whose contemporary perspective deepens our appreciation for reckoning with inevitable death.

Yalom discusses two ways of denying death: hoping for an ultimate rescuer and the feeling of specialness. The ultimate rescuer is an external hero, a superman who saves the day. Specialness is an internal ideation: I'm too special to die! (But I'm not the only one who has ever felt this!) Both prop up the idea that there's a me at the controls who will steer clear of the forbidding cliffs of this existential reality. In Jigme Lingpa's story, by looking squarely at our own terror, we get free of it. In Yalom's existential psychotherapy, we grow present to mortality and accept the reality of it. His extensive research concludes that this can free one from apathy or unsatisfyingly superficial life patterns.[77]

In our vignette, once we've tumbled over that cliff and been catapulted out of the boat, we find ourselves in a space greater than any available when we turned a blind eye to mortality. Entering this space is our teacher in the iconic form of Guru Rinpoche ("precious teacher"), who represents not an external hero but the ocean of our nature. When we dissolve into this, fear and wanting dissolve with it.

Even if wanting dissolves at the path's culmination, passionate wanting is important on the way. It keeps us moving into ever greater alignment with our purpose. Wanting headed in the direction of awakening is crucial. As Adzom Rinpoche said, all desire is not the same. Yet passionate purpose is not enough. Confidence and trust are likewise essential. The panic-stricken figure in Jigme Lingpa's tale is engaged at full throttle. Life is at stake. But it isn't just panic that prompts our cry for help. Such calling out, such prayer, is not a material transaction, a request for something to be given. It is itself transformative. It is our response to our own call, which arises from a personal ocean of longing, pain, and love. From the depths of our desperation, confidence, trust, and a sense of relationship rise to the surface.

Calling for help is opening toward something larger than yourself. It requires courage and strength. We fear losing an autonomy that has served us. But when a wave surrenders to the sea, does it lose itself or become vaster? Surrender portends an altogether new relationship with self and world. The significance of this shift and its relevance for personal transformation cannot be overestimated. Widely misunderstood and too often confused with superstition or gullibility, it is better recognized as a full-bodied integration in which the horizon of self expands.

Sacred traditions of many kinds are oriented to someone or something greater than oneself. Modern secular modalities such as Alcoholics Anonymous and other groups who seek to heal addictions make acknowledging a higher power central to their approach. Why is this so powerful? The English anthropologist Gregory Bateson, who studied AA's method, concluded that opening to a higher power of any kind changes the fundamental structure of self.[78] Acknowledging something larger than ourselves, something that is at the same time intimately part of us, completely rearranges our inner landscape. Existential aloneness finds relief. The ecology of self and responsibility shifts. We don't bear all life's burdens ourselves.

We long for something more expansive. We yearn so powerfully we must cry out. Will the cry be answered? Rumi says such crying is already an answer. In yearning there is already a taste of what we seek. And so, at this point in the story, we imagine how an empowering surrender to love would feel to us. This can't be forced. It doesn't happen at will. It's difficult even to invite it. Yet our imagining it ripens conditions for it. Shifts that occur when we are more fully at ease, or when we are pulled out of ordinary comfort states, can be moments of supreme self-dissolving. The story-mediations offer a controlled environment in which to face our fears at a pace and level that we can adjust as needed.

Jigme Lingpa's story-meditation and his culminating instruction to observe stillness and movement in your own mind are simple enough. Everyone's experience of engaging the story will be different. Most important to avoid is tossing that experience aside, judging it as insignificant or thinking it's not what it is "supposed" to be. Nothing is supposed! There are only instructions, intention, and, most of all, what actually occurs.

It is neither wise nor necessary to come to any conclusions about your experience. Just return to the training again and again to see what develops. We are not computers, where whenever you hit a key, an identical form appears. In practice, whenever you take up an image, a story, a challenge, or look at your own mortality, you react anew. Stay open, stay curious, and see what happens.

Stories we tell ourselves about ourselves can be annoying, inaccurate, or worse, but they persist. Our inner voiceovers try to link the disparate events of our lives. But once a narrative is in place, an increasingly immobile landscape grows up around it.[79] We can get stuck in our stories. Part of practice is to dissolve limiting narratives to gain a larger, more inclusive ambit of experience.

That's not the whole story, though. While we often get stuck in our stories, intentional use of the story can bring coherence to our complicated lives. I read Albert Camus' *The Rebel* in high school, and the only thing I remember from it today, which impressed me immensely the moment I read it, was his statement that the urge to write a novel—a long story—is the desire for a sense of unity in our lives. Jigme Lingpa offers a story-path to override our smaller stories, gives us a big tale in which everything has its place.

So if part of you rebels at practice, that is fine. Rebel. Resist. Recognize how you feel in this moment. And keep on with the process. Over the course of months, years, or a lifetime, you will get some surprises. You won't welcome them all. After all, again, these teaching stories are aimed at surrendering your usual sense of who and what you are. Of course you will resist that.

The psychoanalyst Emmanuel Ghent, in his classic work distinguishing surrender from submission, describes surrender as a "longing for the birth, or perhaps rebirth, of true self." Such surrender, not to be confused with submission, is aligned with longing for "something in the environment to make possible the surrender of our false self"[80] and open new possibilities for being. In the words of the famed psychoanalyst Michael Eigen, humans are drawn to seek "a way of experiencing which is undertaken with one's whole being, all out, 'with one's heart, with one's soul, and with all one's might.'" This kind of confident surrender harkens back to our experience as infants, when faith, surrender, and creativity all intersect for us.[81] We are infused with spontaneity, joy, and fulfilling vitality.[82] At such moments we are an integrated whole. This sensibility harkens back to a pre-verbal awareness that continues below the radar of our more active mind.[83]

Calls for help, coming from our depths, move us away from our ordinary sense of separateness and independence. We soften the contours of this separateness in other ways as well, exulting in nature, falling in love, or just feeling outlandishly happy for no reason. At such times, the full-on vitality of our being finds the story of our separateness to be false. It happens naturally. The potential for awakening has always been part of us: buddha nature lies within like butter inside milk, like a lamp obscured by a vase, to use two of Nagarjuna's famous examples of the constant and intimate presence of our buddha nature.

Is a reliably present buddha nature an attractive prospect? Well, not entirely. Our habitual face does not want to meet our real face, for that will put the former out of business. Yet our yearning is so strong that we cannot turn back. Even a touch of surrender to this longing will start to break the pattern.

Surrender brings you face to face with your most expansive being. It is a release, not to be confused with the loss of autonomy characterizing submission. Submission places you under the power of someone else. Surrender is not resignation. Resignation means admitting that you cannot get your own way; your separate will feels thwarted by something external to it. Sweet surrender connects with a trueness in you.[84]

Back to our story, where all this happens in a moment. Something new is arising as the old boat, the repetitive patterns steering our mind, is pulled out from under us. In a state of utmost receptivity, you, the practitioner, having opened to a different dimension, get a dramatic summing up from Guru Rinpoche himself:

> In the midst of all your cries and lamentations, your kind guru appears in the sky before you . . . Swaying in a gentle dance, he exclaims, "You have believed that saṃsāra is like a wish-fulfilling jewel, but it is painful by its very nature. This is what happens when you never think about your mortality. Your present perception that clings to things as real and solid stems from the ignorant belief in the notion of an individual self. The deceptively seductive man and woman you encountered are your innate and acquired ignorance. The ship is the aggregate of your defiled illusory body, fragile as a water bubble . . . If dying were just like throwing a stone down a well, all would be well and fine. But the acts you've accumulated will impact you without fail . . . What are you going to do?[85]

In this do-or-die moment, ordinary calculations are insufficient. Indecision tears us apart. How do we find that larger horizon? Paradoxically enough, we find it by acknowledging our doubt, regret, or paralyzing fear. We roll with the avalanche until it spits us out into space.[86]

Surges of healing can follow such surrender. In a retreat I offered on these topics, a brilliantly rational and successful professional, alternately brusque and touchingly open, was part of the group. We spent two days on the first training in impermanence. While reflecting on the story-meditation experience, this participant's eyes grew brightly moist—deep feelings had welled up in facing the story's mortal challenge, the typically stern face was visibly softened and radiant. Something had shifted. "The play's the thing," Hamlet said, and playing with the story-meditation experience had brought forward a capacity that was often simply hidden.

Giving ourselves space to perform fears that typically lie dormant is liberating. In our story-mediation, this is the potent moment when, filled with fear, you call out "with one-pointed concentration. And then, when you have no idea what to do, a whitish light pours forth from the guru's heart and touches deep into your own."

This connecting with Guru Rinpoche is a distilled guru yoga, a practice central to Tantra and Dzogchen. There, as in this story-meditation, you melt into Guru Rinpoche, into reality itself. While empty of any substantiality, you are shiningly present.[87] This distilled creation-phase practice helps resolve perceptions of separateness into a state of expansive, imageless knowing. Instantly freed from fear, you move to help other fearful beings gain freedom too.[88]

Guru yoga is the central practice of Tantra and Dzogchen and the trained imagination is central to it. It is intimately personal and also transpersonal. Guru yoga crowns the foundational practices, and every tantric practice centered on a deity is a guru yoga, a story-ritual in which one unites with the awakened mind of the teacher.

This is what occurs when, as we have seen, Jigme Lingpa's traveler dissolves into the guru. The old clothing of self is gone, if only for a moment. But in that pivotal moment, the traveler recognizes how all the trials of the journey were never really separate from the sky-like reality into which one now dissolves, and from which one emerges afresh. This is a distilled completion-phase practice, the culmination of guru yoga and an entry into the vast expanse of Dzogchen's view.[89] The essential Dzogchen tantra *Reverberation of Sound* says that "no matter what kind of behavior one engages in, one never leaves [reality,] the *dharmatā*."[90]

After the drama, it is a relief to let go. No story now, just sheer unencumbered awareness, an open secret that has been there all along. But without training, it goes unrecognized.

All knowing is not the same. The story-meditation moves from the not knowing of confusion, to the not knowing of stunned paralysis, to release from both. Now we let go of all fixations. Thought has no support. All thoughtless states are not the same. Being thoughtless is not the same as being thought-free. In the first case, something is missing, in the second, we are simply present, so transparent to the depths of our ocean that whether our thoughts are active or still, we do not react. Increasingly, everything is waves upon our ocean.[91]

This ocean is not an instrument of enrichment, as in the first story-meditation. It isn't something we use to get somewhere else. The ocean of saṃsāra is a threat, the ocean of wisdom is a place to rest. The fluidity of "ocean" as a symbol expresses the ebb and flow into one another of our thoroughly human and presciently awakened being.

• • • • •

All five pith practices, one each at the end of the first and second training, and three in the course of the third training, bring a distinctive Dzogchen orientation to these trainings.[92] Each is an opportunity to ease into an unencumbered state into which the grace-mind (*dgongs pa*) of the buddhas can arrive. Once we encounter these piths in the first three trainings, we continue to practice them alongside the other trainings, and also as a sequence of training all their own. In these ways, they will over time impact our experience through the remaining trainings, as we will see in later chapters. In view of this, we offer these five piths, one a time, as oases between chapters where you can pause and explore them for yourself in the different contexts of our text.

2. Second and Third Mind Trainings: Pretense Dissolved, Reality Revealed

Each of the initial three trainings offers essentials of sūtra, tantra, and Dzogchen. Each invites fresh dialogue between our human and awakened voices. In every case, a trained imagination helps catalyze the flow between them.

Jigme Lingpa's story-meditations train imagination in three ways. The pith practices invite us to drop imagining altogether. Since this is easier said than done, we often end up just imagining that we are not imagining! So the first thing is to recognize that, short of sitting in an objectless state of "unthinged" awareness, we are always imagining. Of all the reasons we need a teacher on the path, this is one of the greatest. We will listen only to someone we respect, trust, and feel comfortable with, someone who has our best interest clearly at heart, when they say, "You're still imagining. You haven't yet seen the real."

My long-time teacher Geshe Ngawang Wangyal, a complete original from Kalmyk country in Russia[93] who studied for twenty-five years in Tibet's great Drebung Monastery, stopped me in my tracks more than once with unexpected declarations. I had no permission to be there, he announced one morning, after I had spent a few days on my first visit to his Washington, New Jersey, retreat house. This was well outside town, far from any bus station; there was no way to leave unless he asked someone to drive me to a station. Early on in that visit, just as he was trenchantly noting, yet again, that I had not received permission to visit, the slamming of car doors and voices calling goodbye made it clear that a car on the property was about to drive toward town. I saw it from the window. He heard it from his chair. I didn't offer to go. He didn't tell me to. Existential paradoxes were a specialty of his. Fast forward to another visit. Late one afternoon I was setting the table for dinner. I was looking for napkins. Still very much an on-the-fringes newcomer, I didn't know where they were. Nonetheless, thanks to my unflagging judgmental narrator, I felt that I should know. So I was embarrassed to ask. Suddenly, Bakshi appeared out of nowhere and boomed, "Stop pretending." I was the only one in obvious earshot. I froze. I had barely enough presence of mind not to blurt out, "But I'm just looking for napkins, sir!" And then, no doubt impacted by the force of his presence, I wriggled free of robotic self-judgment. For once I was curious instead of worried. Why did he say this? Why now? Was I pretending? Pretending what? To know? To not know? To be helpful? I didn't know! I asked myself this question on and off for decades. Over the years, reflecting on many other similarly provocative moments with Geshe-la, I felt I finally understood. I was always pretending. Eventually, as a fledging Dzogchen practitioner, I recognized that anything short of real knowing is contrivance, pretending and pretentious. I had found the launching pad for all my other troubles. But I was stuck on it.

Nevertheless, I saw that this involuntary pretending would resolve only to the extent that I balanced my untamed mind and cultivated a trained imagination to take me around my blind corners. The story-meditations In Jigme Lingpa's trainings, as we have seen, expand the scope of what we can imagine ourselves doing under unusual or dire circumstances. As in many practices in the Tibetan tradition, imagination has an important function.

SECOND MIND TRAINING

The second training teaches the difference between fleeting and lasting happiness. And Jigme Lingpa frames this as a teaching on karma and becoming free from karma. The third training, which we shall discuss next, focuses on how compassion arises when we recognize the suffering living beings face. Jigme Lingpa's key instructions in both these trainings include story-meditations and pith instructions.

In the opening scene of the second training, you again find yourself in unfamiliar territory, with no idea how you got there or where to go. This time you are approached by eight young men. You do not know them. They too invite you on a journey, this time to a jeweled island, warning that you must be ready to overlook all the difficulties the journey will entail. You agree. By the time you finally reach the island, your hair is white and old age is upon you. Overjoyed at the island's treasures, you load them up and head home. But three days from home, bandits snatch away your treasure, bind and stab you, while taunting, "If you have a guru, supplicate! If you know any God or Ḍākinī, call out for help! At the very least meditate on death."[94]

With enormous grief you realize that you've focused all your attention on enriching yourself in this life, only to find yourself in the hands of these murderers. As you wail, torn open and beseeching, Guru Rinpoche appears before you. Light radiates from his body and drives away the assailants. This light then absorbs back into the Guru who seals the occasion by explaining its import. Your obsession with fleeting happiness has brought you to this, he says. His words move you. And you see now that it is your own ordinary mind that has misled you. The eight men you didn't recognize are your eight consciousnesses—mind, five senses, the afflicted consciousness, and the mind basis of all—that "seduces you away from the wisdom of your own awareness."[95]

Intense regret for this waste of your precious life, the real treasure, wells up. Desperate and broken, you howl mournfully. Light pours out from the guru's heart and touches your heart as you are instantly reborn in the guru's pure land, an awakened guide for others. And then, once you have completed this imagining, Jigme Lingpa offers the second pith practice.

Settling naturally, your consciousness is restored to ease.[96]

Such resting is free of effort. Mind "settling naturally" means that you don't pretend to be an agent controlling how things go here. Nor does settling occur through any external agent. Indeed, the category of "external" seems to melt away. There's little or no trace of inside-outside boundaries.

After experimenting with this instruction, one practitioner reported, "For me the ease comes with stepping away from reaching out to the experience and allowing it to come to me." And so, from the perspective of this second pith practice, we recognize something more about the first.

To relax, especially in that first pith, eases the limiting contours of ordinary mind, the sense that something is "inside" or "over there." There is just settling. According to the first pith practice, your unbridled *kha yan* state is free and open, like a balloon floating freely, not tethered to anything. Elsewhere, Longchenpa uses this term to denote an unobstructed state, a state with no bias in any direction, beyond the orbit of ordinary rubrics of is and is not.[97]

The open state of this first pith practice is like riding a horse without reins, or as Tibetans say, "a horse with an empty mouth." There is intermittent movement and stillness; the only constant is awareness. You are observing (*bya ra*) whatever arises, whatever subsides, while also just letting be.

And it may be that movement and stillness come to free themselves. There are affinities between this natural freedom and the uniquely Dzogchen practice of dawning and freeing (*shar 'grol*). However, the pith practice of observing motion and stillness in a state of unbridled openness, as Jigme Lingpa phrases it, differs from actual dawning-and-freeing as well as from the key Dzogchen practice of cutting free (*khregs chod*). In these Dzogchen contexts you are not attending to movement or stillness, you are simply present to mind-nature. At the same time, this first pith of easefully observing motion and stillness clearly helps develop the capacity to simply be with one's own nature in the way Dzogchen emphasizes.[98]

The relative strength of "letting be" or "watching" in the first pith will vary. The instructions themselves don't determine where you will land. Depending on your training and affinities, the amount of ease that accompanies "watching" will vary and the degree of settling will also vary. Sometimes there are harbinger experiences where we touch into something quite beyond our usual. After all, says Jigme Lingpa:

The consummation of the teachings is
when the entire range of instructions,
the doctrines of sūtra and tantra,
are understood in a single sitting.[99]

Hence, again, the need for contact with a qualified teacher who can help the practitioner discern the delicate distinctions in one's own practice.

In light of this, we appreciate how the second pith practice invites us to restore ease of mind. By simply letting our consciousness be, we unmoor ourselves from the push-and-pull of thoughts, just like Geshe Wangyal's startling accusation of pretending popped me out of my usual orbit. We taste some freedom. The simplicity of the second practice further relaxes how we are. Here we have no focus. We are resting in complete ease, *ngal gso*, a distinctively Dzogchen term that also titles one of Longchenpa's most famous trilogies.[100] We still think in terms of contradictions like yes and no, holding tightly to the line that divides them, but with this openness we are riding a sunbeam to the sun.

Along the path, dualism softens. Our sense of inside-outside is one basic dualism we experience. When it softens even a bit, as can happen in almost any practice—for example, in the unbridled openness of the first pith practice, or in the ease that the others invite—it impacts us. With softening there can be a physical loosening as well and we may therefore interact more fluidly with others, partly because we can attend to them better once our body and mind are relaxed.[101]

Intentionality, focus, and endeavoring—hallmarks of the karmic narrative—allow us to become permeable to Dzogchen teachings. In Dzogchen itself there is nothing to do. You cannot make a crystal more transparent than it already is.[102] In the *All-Creating Majesty*, an important Dzogchen tantra discussed by Longchenpa, we read:

Given that awakened mind (bodhicitta) is your true nature ...
when you try to achieve something through meditation,

that is ordinary mind:
you are abandoning natural mind.[103]

Easy spontaneity is a hallmark of Dzogchen practice. The ultimate ease is resting in the dharmadhātu, fundamental arena of our experience. Longchenpa likens settling into this primal arena to settling comfortably in our own bed.[104] A state you aren't trying to tinker with or fix.[105] Being natural, alas, does not seem to come naturally while the reins of old pretensions hold us. Jigme Lingpa's simple instructions invite ease, openness, and settling.

THIRD MIND TRAINING: BODHICITTA AND THREE PITH PRACTICES

A unique feature of Longchenpa's mind training is that all seven are trainings in bodhicitta, awakened mind. Garab Dorje writes:

> The first training in bodhicitta will turn your mind away from saṃsāra, the second will make you repulsed by suffering, the third will arouse the prerequisite of faith, the fourth will allow you to engage the guru's instructions, the fifth will give you resolve in meditation, the sixth will keep you from engaging in negative activities, and the seventh will cause your meditative concentration to develop.[106]

How exactly are these trainings in bodhicitta? The word *bodhi* comes from the Sanskrit root *budh*, "to awaken." *Citta* means mind. In translating *bodhi*, Tibetans articulated two crucial elements of awakening, purification of negativities (*byang*) and the furthering of good qualities (*chub*). The term *byang chub* is used throughout Tibetan literature to translate the Sanskrit term *bodhicitta*, which in English is rendered simply as "mind of enlightenment" or "awakened mind."

Tibetan grammar justifies translating *bodhicitta* as a "mind intent on enlightenment," in accord with the karmic narrative's gradual development of bodhicitta.[107] Tibetan grammar also supports translating *bodhicitta* more simply as "a mind that is awakened," in accord with Dzogchen understanding. In brief, Tibetan and Sanskrit grammar justify understanding bodhicitta either as "a mind that aims at enlightenment," in accord with the karmic narrative of gradual progress on the path, or as "a mind that is awakened," meaning that wisdom, or the potential for it, is already present and need only be revealed, [108] in accord with wisdom narratives. Emotionally and physiologically, these are differences that make a difference. We feel and behave differently when we assume our goal is far away and when we feel it is ready, waiting for us to see it.

The eliding of bodhicitta with one's own nature is already described in the *Perfection of Wisdom in Eighteen Thousand Lines,* a sūtra that probably first circulated in India about two thousand years ago. There Subhuti explains that "a bodhisattva is so-called because *bodhi* ('awakening') is itself one's state of being (*sattva*)."[109] To identify wisdom in one's own experience is the essence of the wisdom narrative.

In the karmic narratives of Buddhist traditions, and throughout much of the Indian Great Way or Mahāyāna tradition, awakened mind—bodhicitta—is an object of aspiration and inspiration. It is cultivated over lifetimes. In Dzogchen, awakened mind is reality itself. Practitioners start from the very human perspective of needing to activate bodhicitta intentionally, and grow into recognizing it in their own sheer presence. The shift from karmic to wisdom narrative is a shift from an ordinary human perspective to an awakened perspective that has always been an open secret awaiting discovery.

On our way to wisdom, karmic traps abound. In the third training, Jigme Lingpa gives us a guided tour through the six realms of saṃsāra, showcasing their particular sufferings. In this way he dramatizes the connection between the recognition of pain and the development of compassion.

His brief descriptions of the hot hells are vivid and unbearable. Finally, the guru arises in your mind-space, symbolized by the sky in front of you. He explains that your own actions are the source of this pain. But that is not his main point. Rather, he emphasizes that "if you have the courage to take on others' pain, you may be able to free yourself."[110] And he relates the famous story of how Shakyamuni Buddha in a long-ago life developed boundless compassion in one of the hot hells:

> Shakyamuni was born as the strong man Pakshita in hell, where he had to pull a wagon. His companion at the time, Kamarupa, aroused the wrath of the guards by not doing his share of the work. The enraged guards beat him on the head with iron hammers. Seeing this, Shakyamuni felt boundless compassion for his friend. Pakshita asked that his friend's harness be placed around his own neck. The guards beat him senseless for this, and in the next instant he is liberated.[111]

Hearing this, you grow even more intent on awakening to the ultimate kindness that is bodhicitta. As a result, light bursts from the guru's heart, the two of you merge, and you instantly become an awakened guide for others. And for the first time explicitly in these vignettes, light emanates from your own heart, emptying all the hell realms.[112]

Escaping from the hot hells and once again an ordinary being, you find yourself in a vast burning desert, wishing it were just a little cooler. That wish takes you instantly to the cold hells. Reminded once again by Guru Rinpoche of how actions lead to suffering, you experience intense compassion for all those who, like you, have brought themselves to this state. You aspire to free them, and in the next moment you yourself are awakened and free.

Looking into the face of your own heated experience takes courage as well as wisdom and creativity. It means looking right at it without denying, embellishing, judging, or rewriting the raw experience. Above all, without handing over your sense of identity to that experience. You simply feel it, pleasant or unpleasant. If it's too much, place it further away in time or space, or reduce its intensity by half or 80 percent or more. Don't start with your worst nightmare or most delirious exultation. Be gentle, and do what you can to gather the support you need and the space and time, as well as friends in practice.

In short, selectively imagine according to your capacity. Stop if it is overwhelming, and seek supportive guidance. The path to wisdom requires wisdom. And it is part of wisdom to know limitations, so be kind to yourself. This is not a selfish gesture; kindness to yourself will support your kindness to others.

Kindness to yourself has many faces. Looking at the sky is kindness. You can see it from everywhere. Or stand near a tree and enjoy the sound of the wind through its leaves, the sound or sight of hopping birds, feeling the light changes. Can you separate your seeing from the sky you see? Your hearing from birds' call? Most succinctly, can you separate anything you know from your knowing of it? What might this have to do with the ease with which you offer kindness to others? The ease with which you navigate your life? Investigate this for yourself, and in that light, consider what some of the great texts and adepts have to say.

One thing Longchenpa and the Dzogchen tantras say over and over is that nothing you sense is ever outside your own experience or your own nature. This is a true home, as comfy and safe as your own bed in times of peace. Just like the nature of any wave is water, the nature of pleasurable and painful experiences, or wisdom and ignorance, is your own sheer awareness. Can these experiences be separated from your awareness of them? If not, does recognizing this make it easier to feel less alienated from your experience and thus to live even a little more fully, intimately, and also courageously with the problems, as well as the sparkling promise, of this world? In other words, consider whether the intimacy with movement and stillness observed in the first pith practice, or with happiness and pain in the third, make it easier to be at home in the world.

Ultimately pain and happiness both arise through the natural dynamism of knowing itself. When two waves rise in the same body of water, does it make sense to acknowledge one and not the other as water?[113] Once we lean into knowing as such, as we do in the third pith practice, we take a big step toward seeing how all experiences arising from our field of sheer knowing are in fact identical in nature. It doesn't mean we don't treat them differently—you might surf one wave and not another, choose one desert among others, but unlike in the case of the ordinary choosing mind, we don't see these as fundamentally different. It's a profoundly interesting challenge.

For Longchenpa, the third training is a chance to focus on the unreliability of saṃsāra in order to motivate oneself toward wholesomeness such that compassion for all types of living beings manifests in you. Jigme Lingpa makes the third training an opportunity to visit all the realms of saṃsāra and their varied sufferings. On our tour through the hells, we saw and vicariously experienced the terrible pain of hot and cold hells, and understood these as the result of actions done by the persons suffering there. We have held the karmic perspective very close. We were instructed to meditate on this "until you become extremely dejected and disheartened."[114]

Such is the karmic perspective. And it is powerful. You don't rest in dejection, however. Once again, at the height of the drama, the guru appears right there in the hell realm and sums things up for you:

> Child, understand that your suffering is karma, and rejoice that it is being exhausted. With a feeling of intense compassion, take on still more to relieve the suffering of others."[115]

The moment you commit to this, compassion burgeons and your own suffering is indeed exhausted. Your karmic baggage is gone. The compassion you felt in the face of karmic trauma now unites with wisdom as you instantly become a guide able to lead others And now, as if to seal this very reckoning, comes the third pith practice:

> Looking into the very face
> of whatever happiness or pain dawns,
> your consciousness settles down in its natural state.[116]

It is no accident that Jigme Lingpa situates this pith right in the middle of exploring the worst sufferings known to saṃsāra, right as we are training to acknowledge our own and others' pain while remaining free of hope or fear. This training reinforces Longchenpa's succinct summation of our human situation in his *Precious Dharmadhātu Treasury*:

> Pain, happiness, are sheer presence dawning.
> To either grab or discard them binds you to the world.[117]

The third training and this third pith dramatize the interface between karmic and wisdom narratives. The karmic river has utterly dissolved into the ocean of wisdom, the mind's own natural state. Having given you a taste of calm in the depths of saṃsāra, Jigme Lingpa continues the tour so you can observe the karmic fruits of miserliness, the uninterrupted suffering of hunger and thirst. This is the lot of the *pretas*, or hungry ghosts. Profoundly moved, you cry out in anguish and, again on the advice of Guru Rinpoche, declare yourself ready to take on all their pain. As a result, rays of light pour forth from your heart and heal them completely. And then immediately, the fourth pith practice:

> Examine, the doer of movement and stillness.[118]

The doer that initiates movement or stillness is the heart of the matter, not the movement or stillness. This is simple yet puzzling. Something isn't right. Obviously movement and stillness occur. How will you discover what is going on here? A wider field of presence may be the only way forward. Are movement and stillness simply different waves in the originary waters of your doing, or your knowing? And exactly where or what is that watery field? Well, there is nothing for it but to look more closely. Is the mirror the origin of its reflections? Does it create them? Do they come from somewhere or pop up from nowhere? Again and again, we look.

This practice is associated with "searching out the mind's defect" (*sems kyi mtshang brtsal ba*), a trope well known in Dzogchen contexts. Such searching results in "demolishing the rickety shack of the mind" (*sems kyi khang bus debs*).[119] You are, potentially, undermining mind-structures that get in the way of recognizing your mind's real nature. That is the point of this practice. You are not yet looking at mind-nature, you are moving in that direction. You might even land there, or nearby. You are no longer watching thoughts analytically. You are letting be. You are getting out of your own way. The rest depends on karma and connection. Again, consultation with your teacher is essential.

The Japanese Zen master Dōgen (1200–1253), a patriarch of Soto Zen, famously observed that after awakening he felt the flowing of the mountains and the stillness of the river. Longchenpa describes a great ocean of being in which mountains and rivers share the same flowing nature. Why not? Mountains can burst with dynamism and rivers can abide in stillness. But the point is not really the mountains or the river. The point is learning about our own mysterious processes of perception.

The great twentieth-century Tibetan poet Gendun Chopel (1903–52), born into a Nyingma family and recognized as a Nyingma tulku, who became one of the most illustrious recent masters of Geluk textual traditions, wrote:

> Without pursuing perceptions,
> When you look directly at the perceiver itself,
> You will see your own inexpressible face;
> The path to Buddhahood is not far.[120]

Here we get a hint of where the pith practices' observation of movement and stillness can lead. No need to pursue perceptions! Your newfound recognition brings ease, allowing a more flowing state of awareness.

There is pain and pleasure. There is movement and stillness. Something happens, or something does not. In this verse from Jigme Lingpa's autobiography, we get an especially impactful sense of where his pith practices can lead:

> Child, mind watching mind
> isn't awareness of knowing's essence.
> Child, let such knowing be uncontrived and
> without wandering, simply be.

Child, in mind states that bother about anything,
the key points of meditation are incomplete,
so child, be in the freshness of simply settling and
being unbothered, just let be.

Child, to say stillness is the measure of meditation
misses calm and special seeing's unity,
so child, within states of stillness or movement, erasing or
    placing,
be free of focus, be unbridled in sheer knowing.

Child, this foretells seeing your face,
Samantabhadra's unceasing mind of grace,
so child, in fresh depths free of hope or fear,
let be in the great unfixed, unfound. [121]

These words are brimming with a confidence that may be contagious.
And yet, short of full awakening, hope, fear, and doubt do emerge.
Large or small, my inner contradictions vie for space on a daily basis.
Eat what I love or think about health? Be polite or sing my heart song?
The many choice points along the trajectory of our lives threaten to
divide us from ourselves. Recognizing that all of them are waves in our
ocean, our habitual sense of separateness and alienation, can slowly
resolve. A view that includes and is larger than all the competing factors starts to seem more possible. Even when we chose one direction
over another, as eventually we must, we remain present to the larger
field in which everything happens. In a real sense, nothing changes.
Like everyone, we chose to do this and not that. At the same time, as
the Dzogchen master Namkhai Norbu used to say, our life can grow
lighter.

And now Jigme Lingpa's tour of saṃsāra continues in the animal
realm, revealing the suffering of its furry, gilled, or feathered inhab-
itants. Seeing this, you again feel such tremendous compassion
that you swell with the courage to offer up your happiness and take
on their suffering. Instantly, your fear vanishes and you awaken,

emanating light to all species, causing them to become *rigzin,* holders of awakening.

Can you really make fear vanish by facing the terrors around you? This is the premise here. It is a process, not a moment's one-step cure. It involves much face-to-face engagement with what moderns might call the "psychological self," what Buddhists frame as our karmic traces, and what Geshe Wangyal brilliantly reframed as our own unstoppable pretending. And now follows the fifth pith practice:

> Finally, cut through the threads that weave thought. Let your mindfulness and awareness ease into unbridled openness.[122] This distills what you have been moving toward all along.

In the first pith practice you explored unbridled openness and the interweaving of stillness and movement in your experience. In the second, there was simply your consciousness at ease. Informed by these, in the third pith practice you looked at whatever happiness or pain was dawning, and let consciousness settle in its own home ground. The Tibetan term Jigme Lingpa uses here for such settling, *rnal du dbab,* could also mean "settling into reality" and is the name given to one of the practices for approaching the famous Dzogchen practice of cutting through (*khregs chod*). The affinity with Dzogchen is there; it always remains for practitioners to discover their own real face. Any experience short of awakening to this reality is imaginary.

In the fourth pith practice, you discover what it's like to inquire directly into whatever might lie behind stillness and movement, undermining the hovel of a house you have been occupying all this time. Neither texts nor oral traditions fully describe what we might discover for ourselves, and these discoveries are among the most magical, enlivening gifts of practice.

Elements from the previous four pith practices are present in the fifth. The ability to let go the support of thought and find unbridled ease in the first pith practice fosters the fifth pith practice's cutting through the threads holding the weave of ordinary mind together.

The first pith's instruction to let your mind be easy (glod, pronounced hlö) is also present in the fifth pith practice: mindfulness and awareness together ease into unbridled openness. Unlike in the first pith practice, your mindfulness in the fifth no longer has an object. Also, this fifth pith practice pairs your objectless awareness with a more global and careful awareness (shes bzhin) along with unbridled openness (kha yan).

What do you do, or not do, when you sit with this pith practice? You're familiar with mindfulness already, and you're growing more familiar with unbridled openness. You are unbridled in the sense of being unencumbered by any object. Now, however, your mindfulness and your awareness have no focus. They just are. And even if nothing is there to put your finger on, would you describe it as nothing at all? Knowing is there, is it not? The field of your experience, however unencumbered, is not nothing. At the same time, it is not exactly anything. As Longchenpa says:

> Empty essence, unceasing nature.
> Nothing's there, yet everything comes forth.[123]

You seek to sense awareness itself, not mind-cum-object. Again, what do you do, or not do? Whatever gestures you discover will be helpful in virtually all practices going forward and foretell much of what Dzogchen itself invites. These rivers flow to that great ocean.

This is the last of the pith practices. All of them remain helpful throughout the course of these trainings and indeed constitute a training in themselves. Practicing them enriches virtually all other tantric and Dzogchen trainings as well.

In terms of Jigme Lingpa's movement through the seven trainings, we are still in the third training on compassion, and how you hold your attention there may already be impacted by these pith practices. Jigme Lingpa does not mention them again. We will return to them, however, since much of the path as a whole grows from the basic dispositions of mind that they help make familiar.

The third training's tour of saṃsāra continues so you can recognize the inevitable suffering in the human and divine realms. Guru Rinpoche does not appear again; perhaps by now he is understood to be a constant presence. Jigme Lingpa simply exhorts practitioners to beware the trials of ordinary existence and determination to dissolve them with compassion. What follows from this?

Even if you are just stretching out your arm, says Jigme Lingpa, make sure that it is a wholesome activity.[124] This is a really practical instruction. Reaching for a napkin? Opening a car door? What if you imagine or intentionally pretend—in the very best sense of both words—that just through your intending it, these movements are creating auspiciousness and happiness for you and everyone?

Would you climb a mountain if you hadn't already imagined what it will be like when you reach the top? Likewise, long before we get there, we intuit or imagine that Dzogchen's wisdom offers a view truer than what we see right now. Intuition feeds imagination. Your ability to imagine as you read and to practice story-meditations brings the path to life. And so we do well to distinguish our trained and intentional imagining from other kinds of fantasy-building that only whisks us away from our presence. What we intentionally imagine can be experientially transformative. This is the premise for a wide spectrum of sūtra and tantric practices (and, in modern times, for training in everything from sports to self-assertiveness).

Imagination is an important subset of thought. It's included in the long arc of "conceptuality," as Buddhist theories of mind understand this. "Conceptual mind" is everything from hard analytical cranking to the most subtle imaging possible. However delicate and vivifying, imagining, like all conceptuality, falls short of direct experience.[125]

This spectrum of conceptual engagement is classically detailed in the sixth-century Indian works of Dignāga and Dharmakīrti, and in many later Tibetan elaborations of them, including in Tibet's famous tenets and mind-awareness presentations,[126] which are central to Tibetan training in the causal or karmic narratives of Buddhism.

Classic Buddhist literature says that thought is always in error. Even when thought references something externally verifiable—a mountain, a squirrel—it conflates its image of the squirrel with an actual animal, imagined joy with actual joy. This is also what makes imagining so powerful. One of the reasons we love to daydream, to imagine what pleases us, is because such ideation seems to bring it right to us. This error is intrinsic to thought and to all imagination. But all imagination is not confused in the same way. Confusion means imagining something that isn't, like water in a desert, or denying something that does exist, like cause and effect. In both cases, we are involuntarily imagining something that is not the case. In these trainings we see how a trained imagination that aligns with what does, or can, exist helps counter errors and bring to experience what we have already accepted cognitively, such as the fact of impermanence. It's a skill rarely discussed and definitely presumed as a basis for much of Tibetan-style practice, including the story-meditations Jigme Lingpa has offered us here.

Imagination goes to the heart of our capacity to remain aware of our human possibilities even when they seem most at risk. Consider what we call "thinking." What do you actually do when you think? Or when you worry, or hope, or remember? How much do they engage your imagination and impact your immediate experience as well as choices for the future?

The storied imagination and the pith practices in the first three of the seven trainings enrich bodhicitta. In Adzom Rinpoche's words, "Bodhicitta destabilizes the very ground of our grasping at 'me'" and, in the process, expands our capacity for all good things.

3. BODHICITTA:
IMAGINATION AND PITH INSTRUCTIONS

E VEN IF intentional imagining dissolves confusion, such dissolving isn't necessarily easy or even appreciated. For one thing, we feel our perception is correct. We see something out there. It definitely seems to be there and not here. But is it? This is not a simple matter. Or perhaps it is *such* a simple matter that our complicated minds obscure it.

When we are attracted to someone or something, from where does this attractiveness emanate? For most of us, most of the time, the beauty, utility, or other pleasing quality seems objectively present out there. It doesn't feel like it's in the eye of the beholder. Such "out-thereness" is part and parcel of our sense of the thing itself. Indeed, we want it to be out there so we can enjoy it. That "over thereness" is a good part of what excites us. We want to get at it, and we want to bring it from *there* to *here*. Our insistent wanting something is predicated on the feeling of being separate from it.

An over-active imagination can exacerbate error—I am the worst person in the world, I am the most special—whereas intentional imagining helps loosen up such fabrications. This is how we make our personal turn toward wisdom. Wisdom is free of images, which gives it the freedom to imagine anything at all.

Tantric imagining is creativity on display. It helps practitioners bridge any apparent distance between ordinary experience and mind's real nature.[127] Imagination moves right to the cusp of that nature before dissolving into its own wisdom-space, undisturbed by imagery. This can happen in the guru-dissolving part of the story meditation, or in any guru yoga practice, or as the fruition of Jigme Lingpa's pith practices.[128]

Solidity and separateness seem real and reliably true. We regard them as givens, not as imagined. We do not consider who or what gave rise to them, they are just there. This is what Buddhist philosophy calls inborn ignorance. Luckily, inborn doesn't mean inevitable! Our ignorance is an error from which mind can get free. And Dzogchen always reminds us that our human errors can never stain or even touch our real nature, also called our buddha nature.

A big part of practice is learning to see simply. Simple seeing is clear seeing. It is simple seeing of what is, without story or labels, without even the story of seer, seen, and seeing. The seen is just part of our experience! In the *Bāhiya Sutta*, from the early Indian Pali tradition, Buddha famously advises a student:

> In reference to the seen, there will be only the seen. In reference to the heard, only the heard. In reference to the sensed, only the sensed. In reference to the cognized, only the cognized. That is how you should train yourself.[129]

Stop pretending. Stay with what is. Get rid of confused imagining. Feel the power of mindfulness and insight. Focus on the present, get to the real.[130] Yet all imagination, confused or not, is part of reality:

> Awakened mind, source of all that is, creates everything—
> however these appear, they are my essence;
> however they arise, they are my magical displays.[131]

As you read are reading this, you are imagining something. Imagination is pretty much always at the ready, flexible and creative. Imagining you can succeed. Imagining you can't. The list is endless! Using imagination to magnify confusion so you can identify it. Imagining what release from anger feels like in your body. Imagining moving through your day with boundless love, and what that would be like for you.

The human imagination is an unflaggingly generous resource. While imagination can be an obstacle, it is also a gift. It can be at the heart of what binds us, and also, as in these trainings, a vital catalyst for getting free of these bindings. For Dzogchen, imagination, an expression of mind-nature, shares with reality an unstoppable creativity. You want to meditate, relax, or grow kinder? Your imagination can help. It is indispensable. All paths to freedom require it and most of life's challenges demand it. Imagination participates in cognitive, sensory, and embodied somatic learning. Thinking and imagining intertwine on the path, as Jigme Lingpa shows.[132] Thought's erroneous conflation of object and image works to our advantage in poetry and ritual.[133] Thanks to that capacity, the aspirational surrounds we imagine in the story-mediations—rising as an awakened being—are intimately part of us. Images matter.

Indeed, Longchenpa gives much space to the imagistic metaphors of sun, sky, and ocean, devoting a third chapter of his *Precious Dharmadhātu Treasury* to them. More concrete than abstract description, images enter easily into the spaces of our imagination.

One thing is clear. We all want, and therefore imagine, an impossible stability. We don't want to feel that impermanence applies to us. Such resistance is part of the confusion these trainings address. But our confusion isn't wanting to be addressed! No matter how much we aspire to the path, we also like our status quo. Erroneous or not, we find it irresistible.

Confused imagination errs either on the side of overreach (*sgro 'dogs*), imagining what isn't there, or underestimation (*skur 'debs*), denying what is there.[134] Much as exercise engages different muscle groups, release from confusion requires training. Gradually, we are able to relax a wide spectrum of well-worn habits that govern our mind, gestures, and even the play of our senses. Imagination remains in play until, through fearless intimacy with sheer and naked knowing, it facilitates its own dissolution.

Our confusion starts with sensory experience. Things look pretty stable and we regard them as such. As long as things are going reasonably well, we don't look to revise this perception. We want stability! But there is no stability except what we imagine. At some level we know this but look the other way.

To overcome our inevitable resistance to correcting this error, practitioners reflect on impermanence and causality. We notice how the things around us are impermanent. We story-meditate our way through the horror of how things fall apart. And, finally, we look into our own mind, appreciating its unceasing nature—while not really anything, which means it can never fall apart, is also definitely not nothing, which means it can be known and that knowing it will make a difference.

Buddhism teaches what life also teaches. Even without meditation, as we grow older our impermanence becomes more apparent. Still we resist! Jigme Lingpa writes:

> Near death, yet craving home, clothes, and wealth;
> my youth gone, yet not turned from this world . . .
> Lama, free me from such ignorance.[135]

Not everyone wants to hear about impermanence. We feel we have too much at stake. We don't reckon with what's at stake in *not* bringing our attention to it.

TANTRA

Tantra is a ritually choreographed performance of transformation, and until actual realization arrives, intentional imagining is its life force.[136] This intentional imagination is not the free-wheeling imagination of modern art. It is a full-being process that integrates attention, emotions, physical gestures, and bodily presence.

Is it possible to attain something that we have not yet imagined? Guru Rinpoche, in calling attention to the pitfalls of saṃsāra and demonstrating the flow and glow of awakening, is asking us to vividly imagine a situation or experience very different from our habitual range. What is prayer but an opportunity to imagine, and then to feel, that something more is possible? Not a guarantee, a possibility.

The imagining invited through practice instructions is not idiosyncratic or random in the way of daydreaming, yet it is even more personal and potentially impactful. Guru Rinpoche's appearance, for example, is precisely described, his basic iconography settled for centuries, yet everyone's experience and actual imaging is different.

In Jigme Lingpa's stories, the luminous lama dancing in space before you at the crushing low point of your seafaring journeys marks the shift to tantric imagination. Here, as in more extensive forms of guru yoga, an awakened being appears and offers unconditional love and guidance, someone you feel close to in a very personal way *and* an expression of your own nature, which you are in the process of discovering. This is the ultimate guru and, in Dzogchen understanding, it is a wholeness that is the opposite of loneliness, no matter where you are.

The luminous lama in the form of Guru Rinpoche is also in essence your own teacher, someone you know well who also knows you well and who has earned your trust. Someone, in short, to whom you feel connected in a very personal way. The feeling of intimacy and comfort can be very profound. In Tibetan culture, one need only say "teacher" or "my lama" and everyone understands the depth of feeling associated with this. Traditional practice texts tend to emphasize Guru Rinpoche's appearance, and for modern practitioners such descriptions often bring a focus on the technical skill of imagining to the fore. But even if the figure of the guru appears clearly, this is not meant to be like seeing a video image or some "thing" in your environment. It's more like a display from your heart's inner sanctum. And this, in fact, is how a really accomplished Dzogchen practitioner experiences the entire world.

At the same time, like any relationship, the relationship with your teacher and with the reality of your own nature has karmic and emotional dimensions. The emotional patterns we carry into life and our relationships do not disappear in our relationship to wisdom. If we tend to be mistrustful in general, mistrust will likely manifest in the teacher relationship as well as in the ritual practices of guru yoga. We may fear being overwhelmed, left out, manipulated. These responses are good information! They help us discover more deeply how we are at this time. In the midst of this very human predicament, we practice.

Bringing to mind the face of the guru has physiological as well as emotional meaning. A large percentage of the human brain is for the purpose of observing faces, and the ability not only to observe but to mimic a human face is present in infants in the first hours of life. In our first experiences of receiving care in this body, we recognized and responded to our nurturer's face.[137] We also, from the very first hours of life, were able mimic facial expressions we saw.[138] Guru yoga draws on this formative human experience to help us connect with the face of reality.

Prayer is also part of guru yoga. As in monotheistic traditions, heart-felt prayer furthers a sense of personal relationship with the one to whom we pray, whether Christ, Yaweh, Muhammed, Guru Rinpoche, or reality itself. All are at once humanly available and transcendent. In the more mystical strands of monotheism—the Gospel of John, the Kabbalah, Rumi, or Sufism—the division between human and divine grows thinner. Tibetan tantric teachings, in principle, dissolve this line altogether. In actual Tantric or Dzogchen practice, we move back and forth across it continuously.[139]

Our human and our awakened processes are simultaneously in play as our ordinary flesh-and-bone body becomes, to our own experience, a body of light, no different than the iconic awakened being who previously seemed so very different from us. Such imagining has a distinct kinesthetic quality. It is an embodied imagination, entrained through this same practice.[140]

Every part of this practice thrives best when attention is relaxed and clear. Being a bit playful helps too. In the story-meditations, even in the face of death and impermanence we have space for something other than dread or despair; imagination is not constrained.

Giving play to luminous imagining—your body no longer flesh but lucent—trains our kinesthetic awareness, and using your kinesthetic imagination to send light through your body is a key element of tantric practice. There is no separating your imagination from your energetic sensibility, your sense of contact with what you imagine. The light streams have color that is seen in the mind's eye or felt somatically, or both. The point is that our sensory dimensions are connected such that sometimes experience is no longer locked into a single sensory dimension. For example, you may experience a swapping out of sensory functions, seeing sound or hearing color. Or a vital attribute, such as intensity, can be experienced visually, viscerally, aurally, tactilely, and through the sense of smell as well; it can can be felt by one or more senses sequentially or simultaneously.

Such sensory experience harkens back to the way we experienced the world when we were infants. Our surround was not then divided into individual objects separate from ourselves. Rather, we sensed it as an ongoing stream of what Daniel Stern calls "vitalities and intensities" available to any or all five senses.[141] There seems to an experiential or felt-sense similarity between this and the many ways Longchenpa describes so-called sense objects as not separate from one another, or from ourselves, in the way that they seem.[142]

Felt experience is always in the present. Trained imagining keeps us alive to the possibilities of freshly felt experience as we go about our lives. To sense the feedback loop between what I intentionally imagine, such as light flowing from my heart, to my actual feelings about those I encounter as I walk in my neighborhood, may be a gentle surprise. My sense of separation feels like it is softening.

When such experiences newly emerge, in formal practice or otherwise, it is meaningful to give them a little space, to simply to rest in that discovery. Your entire organism feels the impact, however subtle. After a bit, look again at your knowing's origins. In this way, you can experiment with moving through one or more of Jigme Lingpa's pith practices in a single session. This is best done after you have had good experience, for weeks, months, and more, with each of the pith practices individually. Without attachment, appreciate whatever insights or experiences might arise.

WHAT IMAGINATION IS NOT

A sense of wholeness is not an idea. It is a "felt sense," to use Eugene Gendlin's term, and a "lived experience," to use a term common in the emerging field of micro-phenomenology.[143] In Indian-based Tibetan

Buddhist philosophies of mind, mind is a knower that is either conceptual or nonconceptual, cognitive or sensory. The conceptual mind always involves images, however abstract.

When we as children learn names such as "cat," "car," "shirt," and so forth, the name we learn doesn't adhere only to the specific instance of the four-legged calico charmer that your mother tells you is a cat. The name syncs up also with an image in your mind that, in an instant, excludes from thought everything that is not a cat. This is what allows you to recognize small and large calicos or monochromatic furry four-leggeds as cats.

Compared with direct experience, such images are quite generic, imprecise, and abstract. Just part of a furry flank, a single whisker, or simply the letters spelling out "cat" is enough to exclude all images other than cat.[144] These images—mere flashes of color and shape with varying intensity or vitality—don't so much represent anything as eliminate everything not included for you under the rubric of "cat." But they do connect you to the thing you're thinking about. This is why reflecting on and then imagining impermanence can facilitate a full-on direct knowing of impermanence that is emotionally and somatically impactful.

What is imagination? Above all it has to do with our relationship to the images that arise in our mind and the meanings they carry. Bring to mind your mother. In a moment, there's an image that connects you. But if you were able to paint or take a snapshot of that image, it wouldn't necessarily be anything someone else would recognize as your mother. It's an image unique to you and your relationship to her. A certain pursing of the lips or an arrangement of hair may be all that comes to mind, or a kind of undefinable felt sense that is, all the same, precisely aligned in your mind with your mother. Difficult to describe, this fleeting visual leitmotif nonetheless sets your mother apart from anyone else.

Whatever their representational properties, these images are not *felt* abstractly. Memories of your mother are tied into networks of embodied sensations and emotional presence.[145]

Perhaps right now you are sitting in a room you know well. What if you close your eyes and bring to mind something you know is in the room? This takes only a moment, and you might let it sit for another moment. Then open your eyes and look at that very thing. Are the two identical? What differences do you notice?

For example, are there details apparent to your eyes that did not come to mind when you imagined the thing? Is there more specificity in color, shape, and detail? Such are the differences between thinking and direct sensing. This is how the great Indian logicians Dignaga and Dharmakirti describe key differences between thought and direct experience.[146] Now you know them directly.

All paths move toward direct experience. Thought is always just the beginning. The late Daniel Stern, who does not seem to have had any connection with Buddhist traditions, concluded through his own research that lived experience alters us in ways that thinking alone cannot:

> Change is based on lived experience . . . verbally under-standing, explaining, or narrating something is not suf-ficient to bring about change. There must be an actual experience . . . An event must be *lived*, with feelings and actions taking place in real time, in the real world . . . in a moment of presentness.[147]

How does your trained imagination differ from mind-wandering? First, it is intentional and teachable. It can expand your range of cognitive and felt experiences. This expansion in turn helps free us from bondage to habits of reactivity encoded in how we think, the constant reiteration of which is our true saṃsāra.

Training the imagination can bring resistance. For example, you might resist the import of impermanence or feel you are not open to the sense of connection that underlies guru yoga. Our challenge is to be aware of resistance without either smothering it by sheer willpower or jumping right on board with it.

Direct perception is full of freshness. It does not generalize and it does not presume. When we see our mother or friend with our own eyes, when we hear their voices or touch their hands, we sense infinitely more detail than what the thought "mother" will bring.[148]

For example, the world seems neatly divided into self and other, here and there. Is this the way it really is? If you place your attention on your breath, or on a flower blooming in front of you, can you separate your attention or sensing from your breath or the flower that you see, touch, or smell? If none of these are outside your knowing, can you say you and they are truly separate?[149]

The fact that our mind participates in or supports what seems to be outside us means there is already an overlooked intimacy with everything our senses touch. This intimacy is an essential discovery. As Toni Morrison has said, "Attentiveness will always yield wonder."[150] Awareness, some degree of attentiveness, is always there. Can you ever look at anything, much less your own mind, except through the lens of consciousness? Scientists have referred to this as the "problem of consciousness." For Dzogchen, this so-called problem is actually a profound insight into how things are. Your knowing is in fact inseparable from every other aspect of your experience—it is the ground of all your experience, just as a mirror is the ground of all its reflections. Everywhere you look, whatever you see or touch, you experience it through your knowing. Dzogchen, as we have seen, takes this further, saying that all knowing is supported by wisdom. Hence wisdom is everywhere.

Secrets animate us because they make us wonder. Wonder bubbles forth unbidden and effortlessly. It is living proof that our minds are not stuck, but curious. Wonder is a fruitional state, uncultivated, and it joins up with other vivifying states such as bliss, easeful poise, and compassionate responsiveness.[151] We practice to access these, yet none can be had in their fullness through calculation or effort.[152] Wisdom, the heart of how we are, is the antithesis of calculation and the ultimate awakened mind or bodhicitta. Longchenpa writes:

> Self-sprung wisdom is
> the very essence of awakened mind.

Stay right with it and it shows up.
So don't look elsewhere, look right there.[153]

This wisdom is in every part of our experience. Nothing to do and nowhere to look for it except inside our own knowing. Or even in our not knowing! Because it is beyond true or false, right and wrong. This, like much of what is essential in wisdom narratives, cannot be fully appreciated by our ordinary mind. Acknowledging the resistance we feel teaches us much about what our ordinary mind finds essential to its own comfort. At the same time, essential wisdom does not take leave of basic ethics, compassion, or common sense. That is why the seven trainings as well as traditional foundational practices, or *ngöndro*, are so crucial as approaches to Dzogchen.

For example, what does it actually feel like, in the first pith practice, to let go of whatever we experience as a support for thought? One practitioner described this support as a sense of "something to latch onto, whereas before I looked it was just an unlabeled sense of seeing. Once I latched on, there was a sense of dualism, and then a name and then a judgment. Before that, I was just with my sensation, without connecting it to any idea or even an object." This succinct story distills three aspects common to so much of our ordinary experience: dualism, naming, and judgment.

Another practitioner commented: "It felt very fresh. And when I realized it didn't matter whether there was stillness or movement, that there were no mistakes however it went, I felt very free."[154] Indeed, an element of surprise or freshness often accompanies such insights. There's no pretending when we're in a state of wonder, freshness, or feeling free. Pretension is leaning into what isn't actually there and won't bear us scrutinizing it as if it were. All is froth on the ocean of your experience. Such is the perspective of primordial wisdom, essence of awakened mind.

This is a taste of what the seven trainings and five pith practices can be like. We just need to sit there and take note of how it is for us.

Even when we can't really say how or where or what it is, to bump up against the inexpressible is also a learning. As Longchenpa says:

> What's magically born from an unborn arena
> is impossible to determine or disrupt.
> Can't point to it as "this," no sign of a thing!
> Panoramic and sky-like by nature, it's unborn.
> Just there; not before or after, not a start or end.[155]

To be aware that awareness is always there yields a trustful intimacy quite beyond that of ordinary thought.[156] Imagination provides a rich liminal space—neither fully thought nor yet naked, direct experience—in which the drama of practice unfolds.

In 1984 I was living at Harvard's Center for the Study of World Religions when Sam Gill came there to speak. Among other things, he described a Native American bear-hunting ritual. In this ritual, performed prior to an actual hunt, the hunter imagines encountering a bear, addressing it with respect, and explaining with regret and humility the need to take its body. The bear in turn responds graciously. The two parties come to a kind of contractual agreement and the killing becomes a mark of the bear's generosity, as well as the people's respectful gratitude, transforming the ordinary hunter-prey paradigm. Prof. Gill proposed that this ritual was a way of living out an ideal, the way a thing should be. In expressing respect and appreciation for the bear, the community was not in denial about the cost of their actions to another being. Very likely they carried out the hunt with minimal cruelty in order to live as close to ritual ideals as they could. Very likely this resulted in more careful stewardship of the bear's gift of meat and thus reduced the number of bears killed long term.[157]

And while we might cynically say that the bear died anyway, we can also appreciate that the ritualized respect was genuine; wanton killing for sport never became part of native cultures. The bears were included in the relational circle of the tribe itself; they were not a commodity to be objectified. Ritual reminders of a deeper relationship, human and divine, were always at hand.

Tibetan ritual, which more than likely has some shamanic roots in common with some Native American performances, is also a way of joining imagination with ritual protocols that bring home a more complete state of wholeness. Such rituals, involving music, song, and often dance, have a richness of affect and impact that is absent in thought alone and is most explicitly modeled on ancient Indian rituals of hospitality to humans and divinities.

The Tibetan word I translate here as "imagine" (*dmigs byed*) literally means "to take as your object." It is often translated as "visualize," as in "visualize a deity." But this term tends to make people unproductively nervous about the details of what they do or don't "see" in the mind's eye and to get lost in thought about that.

To imagine that Guru Rinpoche stands in front of you is a creative moment in which you align your own unique gestures with ritual intention and artistic traditions. Ritual engagement is simultaneously part of a larger discipline and an occasion for the emergence for your own distinctive experience.

Buddhist and Tibetan practices offer countless variations on how light is imagined in connection with the body.[158] These practices become a full-bodied, whole-hearted engagement. Our kinesthetic sensibility registers their combined effect on the body. Daily repetition brings a wide range of sensations and insights, and fresh discoveries. Longchenpa notes that we are unaware that "excellent primordial wisdom abides in the body."[159] Indeed, wisdom suffuses the entire body[160] and is the final nature of everything; the easiest access to it is through the heart:

> Supreme primordial wisdom is there of its own accord
> in the precious unbounded mansion of your heart center . . .[161]

This is why the imaginal gestures of guru yoga and tantric practice as a whole give special attention to the heart. Everything evolves and dissolves there. Depending on the practice, one or infinite buddhas dissolve into you, or you, as a luminosity of a certain color, dissolve into a buddha or send light into a field of many buddhas, who graciously return it back to you, or you bless infinite suffering beings into their own light of awakening. Finally, the luminous whole melts into your own heart center and into space, and then rises again.

Sometimes, as in the seventh training, the body's whole interior lights up as you bring kinesthetic awareness to your energy centers (*cakras*) and to the channels through which the energies flow. Sitting with that kind of energetic sensibility makes it easy to feel that light shines from your heart or crown or fills the universe. In all these variations, the light of your awareness shines everywhere. Where would alienation find a foothold? And while initially this may sound exotic, in the end it sheds light on how everyday human experience is also miraculous in ways we haven't noticed yet.

Feeling the sun warm your skin means you directly feel a warmth emanating from an orb 92 million miles away. Whatever your senses touch, they touch intimately. Wisdom too is as vast as it is intimate.

Your awareness touches everything in your experience. Acknowledging this unlocks the wholeness highlighted in Longchenpa's gnostic orientation, a great completeness from which nothing is excluded. To dissolve into light, and then as light to melt into infinite space, as occurs in so many practices, is practicing wholeness. Even when all imaging vanishes there is awareness. Sheer, naked, undisrupted awareness, the deep and creative sanctum (*sbubs*) of all consciousness.

Ordinary thought categorizes and makes distinctions. Wisdom exists everywhere, goes nowhere. Dzogchen practitioners seek the radical inclusivity of their own nature. Breaking through unreal ideations of permanence, untangling the tempting attachments that constrict us, opening one's heart to all six realms—all these elements of the first three trainings conduce to a vast completeness. Longchenpa often cites ancient tantras such as *Six Expanses*, which give first-person voice to this reality:

> I manifest as undivided and indivisible
> Since my objects, actions, and conduct
> cannot be differentiated from me . . .
> I am not an object. I am free of any concept or underlying bias.[162]

The wisdom ground of everything[163] is not separate from what knows it. Though it cannot be imagined as it really is, imagination connects us to it.

Just as water is the nature of all waves, the wisdom ground, the all-suffusing dharmadhātu, is the creative source of all images and also their actual nature. Nothing is excluded from the horizon of our own unbounded wholeness (*thig le nyag cig*). We are not possessors of wisdom, we are wisdom. Only wisdom knows this.

The more profound the teachings, the more likely the resistance. Resistance makes for good storytelling. It can also be a sign that the message is getting through. We resist because we recognize wisdom teachings as a shot through the heart of how we ordinarily hold body, self, life, and love. We want to defend against it with all our might.

One edifying scene of resistance has come to light in a previously untranslated Great Way scripture that opens with Buddha requesting Mañjuśrī to teach about the serene source and arena of everything, the dharmadhātu.[164] Whereas the *Heart Sūtra* famously provoked objections with its litany of things that don't exist and its insistence that all phenomena are emptiness, Mañjuśri taught that the stainless dharmadhātu exists in everything. When Buddha first asked him to discourse on this everywhere-present dharmadhātu, Mañjuśri, the coalescence of the wisdom of all past, present, and future buddhas, demurred:

> But, Blessed One . . . since all phenomena are the nature of the dharmadhātu . . . [this] cannot possibly be a topic of discourse or study . . . how could I begin my teaching with this?[165]

The Blessed One seemed to agree: "Mañjuśrī, if those who are possessed of excessive pride hear that teaching, it will frighten them." Mañjuśrī seamlessly picks up this thread, noting that "while those who grow fearful likewise have the nature of the dharmadhātu, *the dharmadhātu does not become frightened.*"[166]

Buddha and Mañjuśrī seem to say that Mañjuśrī's job is to reach the part of his listeners' mind that does not take fright, so that they can see their dharmadhātu nature for themselves. How will he help them, and us, around that resistance? Because if the stainless dharmadhātu, which is also our buddha nature, is already part of everything, and, even more radically, is therefore already in us, why bother with practice? Moreover, Mañjuśri tells his listeners that even the afflictions have the nature of the dharmadhātu.[167] In that case, why curtail afflictions? Once again, it seems Mañjuśri is throwing away the very heart of the Dharma. Such is the radical inclusiveness of the dharmadhātu in the sūtra known as the *Teaching on the Indivisible Nature of the Realm of Phenomena*. On hearing this teaching, we are told, one hundred monks were liberated.

Others were not liberated. In fact, they were offended. Why strive for anything if the goal is already here? That is a profound question! But it is also a protest. The monks who felt offended walked out. For them, practice is about cultivating something we don't have. They could not hear it was also about recognizing something they do have, any more than I could believe buddha nature was a story having anything to do with me. After all, the *Heart Sutra* famously closes with the famous mantra *gate, gate, paragate, parasamgate, bodhi svaha*. *Gate* (pronounced ga-tay, rhymes with "ma say") is cognate with "to go," and *para* means beyond. It means gone, gone, gone beyond, gone way beyond, awake.[168] How is the path not a journey to some other place or experience?[169]

But Mañjuśrī is not done. He goes on to converse with Śāradvatīputra, who gets right to the point: "Mañjuśri, is there, then, never any mind that is liberated at all?" Mañjuśri responds:

"Venerable Śāradvatīputra, if there were a mind to be observed inside, outside, or in between, then there could also be a liberated mind. However, venerable Śāradvatī-putra, there is no mind to be observed inside, outside, or in between, and therefore there is no bondage or liberation whatsoever."[170]

Nonetheless, two hundred monks have had enough of this teaching. They "do not understand it, are not interested in it, and do not believe in it." As a result, "disapproving and disconcerted, they then left the gathering." They did understand something, however. They definitely recognize that Mañjuśrī's sword of wisdom aims to destroy the sense of self and purpose that they find precious. They don't yet see that he is lifting the curtain hiding what's really precious.

Why train if there is no liberation? But Mañjuśrī never said there is no liberation. He said there is no mind to liberate, much as in the Madhyamaka analysis developed by Nāgārjuna and Candrakīrti, and this is a theme Dzogchen will also run with.

Mañjuśrī now goes to meet the protesters, disguising himself by taking the form of an ordinary monk. He engages them in conversation, asks how they felt as they left the teaching, and gradually returns to the question of a liberated mind. He asks them, does mind have color or shape? No. Any kind of form or appearance? No. Does it dwell inside or outside? No, they all respond. Can a mind without any form or appearance, that does not dwell inside or out, and so forth, can it be liberated? No, they respond. Mañjuśrī can now bring home his point:

It is the observing mind that goes forth, makes a vow, and becomes a monk.

Yet the mind that practices the path has no intrinsic existence, is not real, and does not occur. And that which is non-existent, unreal, and non-occurring knows neither arising, disintegration, nor remaining. That which neither arises, disintegrates, nor remains cannot be bound and cannot be liberated. It knows neither attainment nor realization. Venerable ones, it was with this in mind that youthful Mañjuśrī said, "Within the nature of the realm of phenomena [dharma-dhātu] there is neither affliction nor purification. Nobody ever attains anything; there is no realization and no liberation."[171]

Heralded here is the utter boundlessness of the dharmadhātu, and a clue to why Longchenpa, in *Precious Treasury of Philosophical Systems,* makes it his focus at the very outset of teaching the bodhisattva path, as well as central to his opening chapter in *Precious Dharmadhātu Treasury*. This nature is the quintessential human inheritance (*rigs, gôtra*). Free of afflictions, it is so unrestricted that it doesn't exclude or defend against anything. Nor can anything exclude or defend against it. It is as naked as naked gets. Because it's not really anything. This is reality, and at the level of the heart, it is the omni-generosity of heart known as bodhicitta. "No room for form, with love this strong" is how Rumi describes the intimacy of souls unencumbered by bodies.[172] Free of the pride of self, exulting in the boundlessness of an open heart, ultimate bodhicitta is a boundless heart intimately fused with the wisdom of ultimate truth. In the perfection or sūtra schools of Mahāyāna, this is the bodhicitta one develops. Adzom Rinpoche, citing Maitreya, describes bodhicitta as "the ultimate purpose of all our practice and training."

In Dzogchen, bodhicitta is a synonym for reality itself. The sheer presence known as *rig pa* is an open awareness forever united with emptiness, luminosity, and the tender responsiveness of compassion. Nothing, not even the vilest behavior, can close that heart forever. This is the heart to which Longchenpa's third training in bodhicitta opens. Even to imagine it can be overwhelming, and yet inspiring at the same time. Confidence and courage will be needed. The fourth and following trainings help develop these.

FIRST PITH PRACTICE

Leave your thoughts of the three times to themselves, without support. Be wholly open and at ease. Then, whether your mind is active or at rest, simply maintain a state of mindful awareness.[173]

དུས་གསུམ་གྱི་རྣམ་རྟོག་ཐམས་ཅད་རྟེན་མེད་ཁ་ཡན་དུ་གློད་
ལ་འཕྲོ་གནས་སོ་སོའི་ཐོག་ཏུ་དྲན་པ་བྱ་ར་བཞག་གོ།

Mani stone at nuns' practice grounds,
Adzom Gar, Sichuan

4. WHOLENESS ON THE PATH:
CONFIDENCE AND INTEGRATION IN
THE MIDDLE MIND TRAININGS (4-6)

WISDOM IS A natural maṇḍala. It suffuses everything by being intrinsically present everywhere. Four principles address the nature of human being consistent with Dzogchen's wisdom-centric perspective:

1. Wisdom is a feature of reality rather than a means to it.
2. Wisdom is inseparable from its spacious source and stainless matrix, which is everything, the dharmadhātu.
3. Dzogchen is a fruitional path—the wisdom at its base is also the wisdom of the path's completion and completeness.
4. The body has a natural access to wisdom—an esoteric position that anchors the seventh training.

THE FOURTH TRAINING

The fourth training is a turning point. Things cannot continue as before. We will die. Everything we feared or hoped for will evaporate from our experience. We must let go of empty pursuits. An identity crisis! Who will we be if we take this turn?! If living meaningfully becomes your priority, what follows? Longchenpa's fourth training, with the whole weight of the Buddhist lineage behind him, rousingly proclaims that we have no time to waste. Jigme Lingpa furthers this observation by emphasizing that meditation training is essential, and that a teacher is therefore necessary. His fourth training opens with this conviction: I must get key instructions from a teacher.[174]

Why, you might well ask, do we need a teacher? We can read. We have search engines galore. We are independent thinkers and don't need someone else meddling with our process. Still, we may be curious about why Jigme Lingpa and the tradition overall support this view. For starters, what kind of a relationship would I have with such a teacher? And why? Longchenpa's brief instructions do not elaborate. Jigme Lingpa does. He says this fourth training is "not just a matter of reading books."[175] Learning takes place in relationship, and we know from the sūtra tradition that the Buddha's students were people who sought to connect with him directly, largely by asking him for advice.

Relationship has always been core to human experience. Why would spiritual connections be any less important? Relationships with others mediate our relationship with ourselves. And our relationship with ourselves is the template for how we connect with others. What goes around really does come around.

Jigme Lingpa describes three categories of human teachers: the outer teacher who helps us cut through misconceptions, the inner teacher who gives us instruction on secret mantra, and the secret guru, our Dzogchen preceptor, who points out our mind's real nature. Finally, there is also "the natural guru of the ground—reality itself shows you your own mind's purity."[176] Reality is the ultimate teacher. The purpose of the relationship with your human teacher is to recognize this.

What does it mean to teach? The term we translate as "teach" or "teaching" (bstan pa) literally means to show, share, or communicate. How best to do this is a frequent theme in Buddhist texts and is clearly on Jigme Lingpa's mind as well. He recommends that before closing a session, the teacher should condense and summarize the essentials of what was just discussed, distilling it into pithy points that can be cultivated in meditation. He cites from Tantra of the Clear Expanse a description of the internal landscape and the physical posture of the teacher[177] and then concludes:

> Uttering pleasant words, lucid and clear
> Explain by interweaving examples, their meanings,
>   and rationale

In a step-by step manner, teach the spiritual vehicle and
   approach
That best matches the capacities [of your listener].[178]

Moreover, the teacher should abandon "thorns to the ear, such as speaking too slowly, too quickly, or unclearly."[179] And until students reach a certain definitive orientation to wisdom, they must be carefully introduced to the karmic narrative.

We can feel here again Jigme Lingpa's and his entire tradition's confidence in the fruitful partnering of conceptual with experiential learning. Such consanguinity is a hallmark of Tibetan training and has deep roots in Indian Buddhist theories of the intertwining of conceptual thought and direct experience. Both are helpful. Still, effortful learning has its limits. Jigme Lingpa's own first taste of bodhicitta came not through study but through seeing a little boy, his own age, beaten and treated harshly by a monastic disciplinarian.

THE FOURTH TRAINING:
RESISTANCE AND THE HOWS OF WHOLENESS

Meeting a teacher is a chance to feel and then gain freedom from patterns that blind us. When I first came to meet Geshe Wangyal at his wooded property in rural New Jersey, I was terrified. I'd heard he was always ready to scold and send students away. I felt it would take all my courage and energy to gain permission to spend time at his newly established retreat house where a few lucky students were able to live and work with him, and (we realized many years later) get re-parented in the process. I had heard many stories about his scolding, his inscrutability, his powers of observation. Much as I wanted to meet him, I was frozen with doubt. What could I possibly say to such a person? I had no idea. I just hoped that somehow things would take care of themselves.

He once described himself as having eyes in the back of his head. Everyone who lived there felt this was true. He seemed to know everything that was going on anywhere on the property. Hearing this, I relaxed a little. He already knows what I'm thinking! What a relief. I won't have to say anything. He will just know. In keeping with this plan, while others gathered to talk with Geshe-la in his room during one of my first visits there, I sat quietly in the living room, away from the pressure to say or do the right thing. At some point I hear Geshe-la shout, "What's wrong what that girl? Why doesn't she say anything?!" The game was up. I would have to learn to show up, to risk nonacceptance and survive scoldings. I would have to have to speak up.

It wasn't all roses. For one thing, I had to give up my convenient and self-serving idealization of Geshe-la as all-knowing and all-fixing and confront my various anxieties and self-judgments. I learned that my neophyte's brand of idealization did not bring me confidence. It created distance. On the other hand, a naturally emergent heart connection, basic human kindness, which Geshe-la also displayed in great measure, built trust. I needed to see for myself how dialogue with such a spiritual friend, a supportive community—participating rather than hiding—would in the long run be deeply nourishing.

My blighted idea to become a model student by saying nothing was actually a form of resistance. As it turns out, the teacher-student relationship often catalyzes resistance. The resistance that can come through meeting a teacher is, however, nothing compared to the resistance that comes when meeting oneself, which is the purpose of practice. Friendships, partnerships, and marriages fall apart because of it. Dedicated, accomplished practitioners fall away from their paths due to it.

Serious practice always meets resistance. To recognize resistance as such is one of the biggest challenges in practice and in life. When resistance is not recognized for what it is, we call it something else. Like the monk who said he "wasn't interested" in Mañjuśri's teaching, we say we are too busy, too tired, the teaching doesn't make sense, the teacher isn't interesting.

This is a critical moment on the path or on any trajectory of personal revisioning. The most crucial moment to connect with a teacher (or a therapist, or a close friend) is when we most don't want to. Resistance signals that wisdom knocking at our door. The message is partly getting through but we're not ready. Part of us understands very well that the way we are is under threat. It's no small thing to recognize resistance, give it space, and crack open the door to something else anyway. Only to find that what we seek has been hidden behind it all along. It's neither an idea nor an ideal. It's us.

Repetitive self-judgment is neither creative nor helpful. It masquerades as intelligent rationality, but the judgmental superego is in fact wildly irrational. It won't lead us anywhere new. Much more promising is to touch precisely into the actual experience of the moment. The fact that I recognize, for example, how clumsy or ineffective my prose is as I'm writing means I already have an idea of how it could be better. Denying the possibility for improvement gets me nowhere, and feeling despair about current inadequacy leeches the energy needed to move forward creatively. Both prevent me from dealing with the emotional, somatic, and psychological analogues of what Buddhism calls the two extremes—reifying and nullifying. It's much more fun and fruitful to move forward.

Possibilities for change are woven into our being. The flux of impermanence identified by Buddhists, the brain plasticity identified by neuroscientists, our own experience of changes in mood, weather, and polity all point to fresh possibilities. Buddhist and scientific perspectives and our own life experiences agree that change is part of our condition.[180]

In wisdom's light, there is no real obstacle in mind, and no real mind either. Our nature is free of these, and wisdom is our nature. Therefore refuge cannot not lie outside us. There is no such outside where it could reside. As a famous Zen saying colorfully puts it, "If you meet a buddha on the road, kill him." Kill the idea that buddhahood is outside. Our admiration of the great qualities in awakened beings should not distract us from seeing that our very admiration means these qualities are somehow already part of our horizon. Otherwise we couldn't see them, we wouldn't value them. To praise such qualities is, as Rumi says, to praise our own eyes. Calling on and praising a teacher's good qualities is done very much in this spirit.

Once I realized I had something to learn from Geshe Wangyal's refusal to accept my distorted ideas about relating to him, I could appreciate the kind, wise teacher he was, interested in seeing me shift perspective in a deep way and capable of helping me do it.

Relationships bring forth our most powerful feelings. The stronger and more trusting and dynamic the relationship, the deeper the possible learning. From this perspective, the traditional instruction to see your teacher as a buddha begins to make sense. But we must be sensible about this.

On a languid summer afternoon during my third or fourth visit to Geshe Wangyal's retreat house, he was relaxing on a wooden chair in the dining area while a few of us sat on the floor in bantering conversation. The mood was light and relaxed. The low afternoon sun gave the wood table and chairs a light golden sheen. The instruction to see your teacher as a buddha popped into my mind and I decided to try it! I stared at Geshe-la, imagining a buddha there with all my might, especially the yellow-gold-reddish glow of Buddha's face as rendered by artists through the ages. Of course, Geshe-la's very interesting face and gestures did not change, but I was perceiving them more clearly and, perhaps, more openheartedly. Though to my eyesight he remained the same, something in my experience did change, whereas I had been feeling mildly tense and cautious, I now felt gently aglow and simply happy.

This was one of my earliest experiences of realizing that what my eyes saw did not govern and was not the fullness of my experience. Intentional imagining is impactful. The tantric elements of Jigme Lingpa's story-meditations also involve the ability to imagine, to see what your eyes do not behold, to respond to a scene in ways that change your habit of being totally identified with ordinary states of body and mind.

Once we have observed a teacher for a good amount of time—classic texts suggest five or seven years—and they have our respect, Tibetan traditions have the practice of seeing them as a buddha. Seeing the teacher as a buddha is part of an arc of practices by which one trains to see all beings as buddhas; in fact, as in the story-meditations here, we help them become buddhas.

Again, practice is a first-person process. It is we who are perceiving them in this way; it is our habits of perception we are training. This is not the same as objectively stating for one and all that so and so is a buddha. The point is that you train in order to wean yourself away from ordinary mind states. Can we maintain pure appearance without losing our minds, without confusing tantric practice with the kind of simple-minded idealization I initially imagined?

Mañjuśrī famously advised Tsongkhapa that we have to give some credence to appearances. Things are not what they seem, but the way they seem is not totally irrelevant either. We don't try to eat a chair or sit on our vegetables even if we recognize that neither of them are 100 percent what they appear to be. Conventions have power. My earlier idealization, culminating in the absurd idea that I need not speak because Bakshi was omniscient, undermined the conventions of human behavior. Geshe-la himself was unconventional in many ways, but he trained his students to pay attention to the conventions required for a balanced life.

We are built for relationship, primed for mimicry. Very young infants, as we have noted, will imitate the face of an adult who leans over with a smile or sticks out a tongue. Why should wisdom be any less contagious? In fact, wisdom is very communicable! This is why the relationship with a teacher is stressed. When things work well, the hierarchical yet mutually collaborative connection between student and teacher optimizes communication. For the student, a genuinely supportive teacher is as important as a loving parent. The ability to hold and be held in loving trust is crucial for cultivating compassion and other essential human and awakened qualities.

A telling experiment by Patricia Kuhl at the University of Washington found that infants who took face-to-face lessons in Chinese learned much more swiftly than infants who attentively watched the very same lessons on video. Reporting on this, David Brooks writes, "They paid rapt attention, but learned nothing."[181] Kuhl found that the social brain of those in the first group became activated through direct eye contact with the teacher, and this facilitated their swift learning. Similarly, Suzanne Dikker of New York University found that when classes go well, the students' brain activity syncs with the teacher's brain activity. Teachers and students regulate each other. The Tibetan traditions' construction of ritual, especially in tantric transmission, understands direct transmission from the teacher to be an essential catalyst for spiritual growth.

After months and years of basking in the wondrous qualities of a teacher, there comes the sunrise surprise that we are developing those qualities ourselves. This is the real reason we are advised to "regard all the guru's actions as the actions of a buddha."[182]

Finally, we understand that our praise of buddhas is praise of our own future. My teacher of forty years, Khetsun Sangpo Rinpoche, hearing my earnest thanks for a particular teaching, gently dismissed this and said, very slowly, with an unforgettable kindly fervor, "One day, one fine day when you really see, that's when you'll truly thank your teacher."

Guru yoga is not actually about the guru. It is about exploring the depths of our own possibility. The teacher already knows that awakening is possible, and that the feelings that drive us to distraction do not ultimately define or limit us. From Dzogchen's perspective, they are part of an untiring dynamism whose true import we have yet to discover.

We learn best from people we trust and love, people who know and care for us, warts and all. This insight is crucial as we consider the role of the teacher. Hierarchy can go awry. Admiration can become slavish yea-saying. The tradition is aware of this, and that is why students are advised to scrutinize a teacher well before committing to that teacher. In modern contexts this rarely occurs and, partly for this reason, severe problems have developed. Sometimes the parties have to part. Sometimes enormous energies toward healing and regrouping are required. And still, a student's heart connection with a teacher is as crucial as a child's trust in her parents.

As children, and as students, what we admire is what we become. Relaxation of the heart requires trust. Parental success is measured by a mature child's independent flourishing. Spiritual teaching is measured in the same way: students grow confident and have enough trust in themselves and in the world to forge their way through it with kindness and insight.[183] Trust and relaxation yield personal integration. The fruit of this integration is confidence: I can make a decision, carry it out, and experience its fruits. Even a small aspiration successfully carried out makes a big difference. It greatly reduces the distance between action and aspiration.

There are caveats. Jigme Lingpa reminds us that these exhortations toward devotion and his advice to follow a teacher's instructions will apply only if you are sure the teacher is not demonic! Instructions to see your teacher as perfect, and distortions of the training-practice of seeing your teacher as a buddha, have led to very difficult and even tragic and traumatizing situations in Buddhist communities in the West.

Can we recognize wrongful behavior in a teacher while also seeking the ultimate in them and ourselves? Not easy. Clearly, harm needs to be stopped and the harmed need a way to heal. Only then does it make sense to consider afresh how, while doing our part to avoid harm to ourselves and others, we can find our way to the larger horizon that brought us to practice in the first place. This large challenge lies at the heart of skillfully addressing our human reality as well our awakened potential.

Most of my own teachers were born in Tibet. All of the many Buddhist teachers I studied with were impeccable in their behavior; I studied with them closely, was sometimes alone with them, and there was never a hint of sexual or other untoward inclinations. However, I know from friends and students, as well as the psychological literature, how the hurt that comes from wrongful behavior by someone whom we regard as a spiritual inspiration or authority is pernicious and heart-wrenching. The pain must be addressed, and measures taken to prevent it. When and if they are ready, practitioners can *also* understand this kind of experience as a ratcheted-up instance of our attempts in practice to recognize that the way things appear is not the way things are. Reflecting on this is *not* a substitute for acknowledging the pain, addressing it, and taking steps to cease the wrongdoing. Reflecting on the illusory nature of things is also, most certainly, not an excuse for any perpetrator, nor an invitation to deny the pain of survivors. In the best of circumstances, recognizing the difference between how things are—impermanent, insubstantial, and illusory—and how they seem—permanent, substantial, and very real—takes months and years of patient practice. These are worthy goals that inspire humility, certainly not cudgels to use against self or other.

In the right context, practices of pure appearance, such as seeing oneself and others as buddhas, help us open to our own great potential. This is a broad-stroke description. However, practice is not done in broad strokes but in deep conversation with whatever emotional or cultural history the student and teacher bring to the situation. As appropriate, there is the invitation to be porous while not losing oneself in fantastic idealization or fixating on stubborn denial that turns a blind eye when boundaries are breeched. To discern the difference between a devotion that is nourishing and a rigid conformity to the idealizing language of traditional texts is especially vital for contemporary practitioners. It is not a simple matter.[184]

Since the early 1970s I've studied and practiced closely with Tibetan scholars and meditation masters who grew to adulthood and completed their training in old Tibet, some of whom became like family. None of them emphasized what I'd call severe obedience (though such was part of Tibetan monastic life, sometimes abusively). My teachers in fact often tried to save overzealous students from themselves. Perhaps this was already an adaptation to Western ways, and if so, in my view it was skillful.

Texts on the student-teacher relationship suggest that one must do everything a teacher says and also do one's utmost to further the dharma. There is no doubt that Tibetan monastics and committed lay practitioners take these precepts very seriously. In 1980 I was able to spend two three-month periods studying at Drepung Monastery, established barely a decade before in South India. During the several months between my two stays, a monk named Monlam, whom we had come to admire for his kindness and devotion to his community, had nearly lost his eyesight. What happened, we asked him? He had been working night and day on preparations for an upcoming visit by His

Holiness the Dalai Lama. He was responsible for overseeing much of this work, and as it had to be completed by a certain date, he had refused to take time out to see a doctor. He had eye-drop medicine for glaucoma but did not even take the time to use that. He expressed no regret as he matter-of-factly reported this to us. Serving his teacher took precedence.

At the same time, I have seen traditionally trained Tibetan lamas visiting the West take traditional admonitions more lightly. In 1974 at the University of Virginia, my partner Harvey Aronson and I were walking with Khetsun Sangpo Rinpoche to his late morning class. The sun was high, shadows everywhere. The texts admonish students never to step on the teacher's shadow. Harvey chastised me when he noticed I had stepped right on the silhouette cast by Khetsun Rinpoche. I stepped away from it immediately, only to hear Rinpoche laughing heartily at us both, and in his charming way saying, "Please don't worry about this." I didn't.

Fresh inspiration is a keynote of the fourth training. During his teaching, Adzom Rinpoche's spontaneous song marked the occasion for us, and the next trainings likewise carry a spirit of exuberant commitment.

The Fifth and Sixth Trainings

Longchenpa tells us that the measure of success in the fifth training is understanding that meditation is essential. "Devour procrastination and conquer sloth!" urges Jigme Lingpa.[185] Getting on with practice is the focus of the fifth training. In the sixth training, Jigme Lingpa reviews the ten unwholesome acts that must be abandoned for practice to succeed. He encourages trainees to address whatever unwholesomeness predominates.

In the sixth training,[186] Jigme Lingpa here also extols refuge as a practice that allows you to be joyful when sick and happy when dying. Let people say what they will about you, he chides, act as if they are talking about a corpse. Yearn to be totally on your own, without even song birds to keep you company. Meditate on your teacher's

instructions. And he lands these points further with these words from
Guru Rinpoche:

> Alas, how sad! The mind that thinks this life's
> wealth and prosperity is wonderful and lasting,
> the mind that thinks the mind of the most immature being
> is stable and fine—
> who in this world could be more foolish than that?
> No one in the past and no one in the future![187]

To overcome such foolishness, conceptual training is viewed
as insufficient. Something else is needed. As Śāntideva famously
observed, the ultimate is not an object of the ordinary mind, especially ordinary conceptuality. Jigme Lingpa picks up and expands on
this in his *Wisdom Chats*:[188]

> Śāntideva, seer of the real, said:
> If analysis analyzes,
> then the analyzed
> [also gets] analyzed.
> It's endless.
>
> Once you analyze analytically,
> there's no basis for analysis.
> There being no basis, [analysis] is unborn.
> Exactly this is called "nirvāṇa."
> ...
> In our main meditation practice
> we focus on tantra's method path[189]
> to extinguish karmic winds.
> Understand this practice!

One of the most important pivots of the tantric path is its turn to the
body. In the process, one is introduced to the gnostic sensorium that is
key to Tantra and Dzogchen. The seventh training utilizes the subtle

human and gnostic resource of bodily sensing to untangle the karmic energies on which mind rides. These energies will now be trained to take a different route through body to enable an optimal flow of wisdom. The human body is perfectly arranged for this to occur.

CONTEMPLATIVE INTERLUDE:

SECOND PITH PRACTICE

Settling naturally, your consciousness is restored to ease.[190]

ཉེས་པ་རང་བབས་སུ་དལ་བསོ་བར་བྱའོ།

Detail of mani stone at nuns' practice grounds,
Adzom Gar, Sichuan

5. SEVENTH MIND TRAINING:
WHOLENESS AND THE SENSES

THE SIXTH TRAINING culminated in a wholehearted commitment to practice and awakening. The seventh training gives instructions on how to accomplish the three classic meditative experiences of bliss, clarity, and nonconceptuality. Meditative experience (*nyams*, pronounced "nyam," rhymes with palm) is by definition transient. It fades away like morning mist. In this it differs from realization, which is stable and continuous.

In the seventh training, one gains familiarity with two types of meditative experience: the union of bliss and emptiness and the union of clarity and emptiness. Simple nonconceptuality is itself a meditative experience, leading to actual realization of reality. As Longchenpa says of the seventh training, "Bliss is the skillful means that gives rise to the wisdom of emptiness." When bliss and clarity unite they continue all the way to buddhahood. Buddhas are blissful! The final nonconceptual training here is not just a meditative experience but is itself a nonconceptual wisdom observing reality.[191]

The seventh training engages the body to ripen the wisdom introduced through the story-meditations and pith practices. It offers distilled channel-energy practices of the type usually kept secret, because doing them without close supervision can be harmful.[192] With the expectation that these practices would be undertaken only with a suitable teacher, Adzom Rinpoche's elaboration of the text's instructions clarifies the body's role in a path to wholeness.[193]

This training makes explicit use of the body's energies. First, one cultivates bliss-emptiness through a focus on the central channel. Second is cultivation of clarity-emptiness, which involves holding winds in the navel region. Third is the training in nonconceptuality. In

Dzogchen itself, says Longchenpa, energies naturally enter the central channel without being forced there. [194]

Our ordinary sense of bodily solidity is embedded in a dualistic framework of inside and outside. The seventh training softens this framework, this solidly embodied "me" that we have pulled out of thin air. What will happen when this sensibility dissolves? Will we allow ourselves to find out? We might like the idea of a radiant wholeness. But do we really want to give up the seemingly solid "me" at the center of everything we know? What if we land in desolate nothingness?

Welcome to the seventh training. Buddhist practice overall moves from distraction to attention, from effort to ease, from conceptual to nonconceptual. Each of these trajectories involve somatic shifts in the body. [195]

Our ordinary sense of being a person who can do things, our sense of agency, is built on twoness. We won't give it up easily. Which makes it vital for us to consider the seventh training. Here we focus first on its traditional context and then on a few telling examples from recent scientific studies. These are the two main sections of this chapter.

TRAINING IN NONCONCEPTUALITY

Channel-and-wind practices are held quite closely in Tibetan Buddhist traditions. The texts elaborating them are restricted and oral instruction is offered only to persons who have already moved through several stages of practice, including completion of the foundational practices. Yet in Longchenpa's and Jigme Lingpa's work on the seven trainings, an introduction to the essentials of channel-and-wind practices are openly available. Adzom Rinpoche did not detail them in his public talks, but generously responded to my questions and gave permission for his responses to be included here.

This three-part somatic training yields nonconceptual states of bliss, clarity, and reality. The three practices of bliss, clarity, and nonconceptually knowing reality integrate body, energy, and mind.

Since mind rides on energies in the body, shifts in one create shifts in the other. The shifts are bilateral: energy affects mind, mind affects energy. Placing attention on key points of the body, especially on hubs of energy circulation known as wheels, or *cakras*, is what gives tantric practice its particular power. Not relying on reasoned logic (*gtan tshigs*), these practices catalyze more powerful shifts in experience, says Longchenpa, than is possible through thought alone.[196] Placing attention deep in the belly, for example, efficiently stabilizes the mind by allowing the energies it rides on to settle deep in the body. Likewise, lightly sensing into the central channel is a valuable companion for virtually any practice. Longchenpa's briefly summarizes how to train in bliss-emptiness:

> Pull your energy up from below while pressing down from above and fix your mind on a white *ah* at your heart.[197]

Jigme Lingpa expands on this instruction:

> While practicing the four applications, press the upper energy down and draw the lower energy up. Imagine that this causes fire to blaze forth from the *ah* syllable at your navel, causing the *ham* syllable at the upper opening to melt. This, in turn, produces a steady flow of nectar that streams down and permeates the four chakras and all the minor channels, triggering the wisdom of bliss-emptiness. Finally, fix your mind on a white *ah* syllable at your heart-center, cut the thread of discursive thought, and rest one-pointedly. This will produce the wisdom of emptiness, the knowledge that utilizes the skillful-means bliss. Until you have familiarized yourself with this state, train in short, frequent sessions.[198]

The four applications are the stages of inhaling, holding, rotating, and expelling the breath. The oral tradition through Adzom Rinpoche adds these helpful images: (1) pull in your breath like a rope, (2) send it down to your belly, (3) swirl it around your belly, and (4) send your breath out before you like an arrow.[199] These four steps are meant to force the afflicted, dualism-inducing energies from the side channels into the pure world of the central channel. The channel itself is experienced somatically and through intentional or spontaneous imagining. You might feel that you have a light inside you, or are followed by light, or see this light in dreams, or perceive a tunnel.[200]

Full engagement with the four applications are part of the bliss-emptiness practice. Jigme Lingpa's instructions invoke them in the first part of the practice, whereas Longchenpa introduces them in the second part of the practice when attention is simply on the white *ah* at the heart. In this way, Jigme Lingpa gives more emphasis to the vase-breathing exercise than does Longchenpa. In both cases, you hold the breath until you need to breathe again. Adzom Rinpoche tends to emphasize Jigme Lingpa's instructions, clarifying that this holding takes place after the channels are filled, not while the nectar is descending.[201]

Adzom Rinpoche also points out that whether we are walking or sitting, gently relaxing your belly and filling it with the energy of the breath is in and of itself very useful. This is also a way to grow familiar with the gravitational pull of the navel center. Your navel center is where the main three channels come together (*rtsa gsum bsdud*). Known in Tibetan channel-wind literature as the "channel of emanation," this center is described as four finger-widths below the actual navel and four finger-widths inside the body. This is where karmic winds enter the central channel. It is also where the fire of Tibet's famous heat-producing practices resides. We can also say that the mother essence is there (the red drop received from the mother).

One of my teachers pointed out that possessing such channels is a very great gift of the human body; we are shaped in such a way as to be able to use these special methods of practice. The channel-wind practices are part of Highest Yoga Tantra and often practiced to high art by Dzogchen practitioners, even though Dzogchen itself does not emphasize forceful methods for bringing mind into the central channel.

Unique Features of Channel-Wind Practices

Jigme Lingpa writes that the essence of speech is wind.[202] Ordinary speech rides on winds of delusion—its energies move through the 72,000 channels of the body, but winds of confusion never enter the central channel. The movement of wind is the clearest explanation for why wisdom is described as inexpressible.

The opening line of Rāhula's famous *Praise of Mother Wisdom* is: "Beyond talk, thought, or story."[203] Jigme Lingpa elaborates on this opening line, explaining that this line distills three ways that ordinary expression fails to encompass the state of wisdom: the winds of speech and thought are unlike the winds of wisdom. Jigme Lingpa's point is that wisdom cannot be talked—speech cannot say it—because ordinary speech rides on winds of the side channels and cannot enter the wisdom channel.[204] Wisdom can't be thought because thinking, which is never as precise as direct experience, concretizes and generalizes what it brings to mind and therefore cannot get at wisdom or flow through our central core. Finally, telling a story, or describing wisdom, inevitably means that the speaker is different from what she describes, thus belying wisdom's native wholeness.

The energy of ordinary speech—of ordinary life—bypasses the central channel and thus precludes the experience of a wholly engaged and holy wisdom. Even though, as Longchenpa has told us, wisdom abides throughout the body, it cannot be experienced as such under most circumstances. Through practices like these, we take our own gnostic turn toward a new kind of embodied completeness.

TRAINING IN THE NONCONCEPTUAL UNION OF CLARITY AND EMPTINESS

Longchenpa gives these instructions:

> To train your mind in the nonconceptuality of clarity-emptiness, begin by expelling the stale breath three times. As you inhale, imagine that all external appearances and

objects melt into light, merge with blue space, and then completely fill your entire body.

Usually the body feels dense, weighty. How might it feel, even for a moment, to sense your body as nothing but blue space? Perhaps we find this delightful. Perhaps the body-mind pushes back, saying no! I have weight, I am too important to vanish into space. Perhaps a little of both occurs. The transparency, limpidity, and open space that in this practice supplant the weighted body offer no landing place for our usual sense of "I." Our ordinary gaze and knowing don't find a place to land here either. The whole field of our experience is nothing but clear, restful, and radiant.

East or West, practicing with the body brings access to deeper states of experience. All three nonconceptual states are facilitated by sensing deep into the body in a way that also vanishes its corporeality. Jigme Lingpa adds an interesting detail, saying that your body should be clear and empty like the interior of an inflated balloon. An improbable image, striking in its freshness.

We grow up hearing that our insides are full of squishy, fleshy, pumping organs. We see pictures of open-heart surgery. Do you think these images have no impact? I certainly wasn't aware of carrying any such images around with me. To my surprise, therefore when I first sensed into my body as an empty balloon, I was immediately struck by how very different this that was from the images that, in fact, I was carrying around with me, without ever realizing they were there.

The instruction is to feel that, within this spaciousness, your central channel rises from your navel center. Fire rises from the *ah* at the navel center, its heat melting the white upside *ham* at your crown. In Sanskrit *aham* means "I." Here, our sense of I, as well as its close companions, me and mine, are literally melting into essential sweetness, a nectar that descends from your crown to suffuse your central channel and all subsidiary channels throughout your body. In this way, bliss-emptiness arises.

In the "Vajra Heart Essence" of his *Precious Treasury of Philosophical Systems,* Longchen Rabjam writes:

The first step in formation of the physical body occurs when the causal factors from father and mother, white and red bright orbs . . . become inseparable from the subtle energy and mind of the being who is thus conceived. With this, two extremely tiny, clear cells form, about one-tenth the size of turnip seeds; these will become the convergence of channels in the navel center. From this starting point, once the body becomes fully formed and is born, and for as long as it lasts, the subtle vajra body has three channels, four chakras and so forth."[205]

This gives us a context for Longchenpa's own succinct instruction in his seventh training: "While [the nectar is descending] pull up the energy below and press the upper energy down, and fix your mind on a white *ah* in your heart"[206] whereby bliss gives rise to an empty wisdom. Bliss is a method for experiencing wisdom.

Many contemplative traditions teach meditators to rest attention at the navel center. Chinese traditions refer to it as the *dantian,* Japanese call it the *hara,* and Sufis the *kath.* Tibetans refer to it simply as the *do* (*mdo,* rhymes with doe). The point is that it makes a difference *where* in the body you place your attention. Tickling feels different in different parts of the body, does it not? Why would there not also be variability when we tickle with our attention?

According to Longchenpa and Tibetan embryology, the navel center is a meeting ground between the material body and more ethereal sources of human being. The entire body grows forth from here in the mother's womb. It makes sense that focusing here would bring a different impact than directing attention to the heart, the crown, or the movement of breath.

Longchenpa gives further background on the body's significance.[207] Because our buddha nature is enmeshed in our ordinary physical body, he writes, we are described as "embodied beings." Because buddha nature is enmeshed in the ordinary mind, we are described as "ordinary beings." Because our buddha nature gets overlaid with karma and habit patterns, we are described as "obscured." Because the thing that obscures us is a state of not recognizing our own nature, we are also called "benighted." In these remarkable descriptions. Buddha nature is placed at the center of every level of our existence. Embodiment refers not simply to a physical configuration but to the fact that buddha nature is experienced there.

The central channel is unique in that it never gets "enmeshed" by the fleshy body. Because it is not made of flesh, it does not degenerate along with the material body, nor is it available to ordinary sight or touch. Surgeons opening the chest will not find it. The energies that move through it are not afflicted with dualistic perception; the wisdom-mind that rides those energies does not conceive of itself as "inside" or separate. It participates only in awakening, not in our ordinary humanness, even though it's at the core of our human body, mind, and sensations. Conceptual thought rides on winds of the side and other channels in the body. It cannot enter the central channel.

With this practice, our presumed boundary between mind and matter lightens, or even dissolves, to our own experience. The luminosity and brightness of the central channel is now shared with the entire body, and ultimately with our entire field of experience. The familiar somatic and cognitive makers are gone. Awakening never seems more possible as when we see for ourselves that it is possible to grow free, even briefly, from our habitual sense of self:

> At the very core of the bodies of all beings
> lies the precious and immeasurable mansion of the heart center,
> from which come many thousands of channels.
> In particular there are four supreme channels.
> Riding on subtle energy, awareness dwells particularly within
> these four channels.[208]

Presence in the central channel brings familiarity with the sacred, secret body in which all awakening, birth, and dying take place. The central channel is the locus for a state of nonconceptuality that culminates in awakening. But wisdom has not been newly created.[209]

Uniting the nonconceptual mind with bliss and clarity are special methods for escaping the orbit of materiality, a misleading solidity that supports our sense of separateness and self. Weight weighs in too. Research suggests that the sensation of our own weight or the weight of objects we contact helps structure much of our psycho-emotional experience. Holding a heavy or light clipboard, solving puzzles whose pieces were rough or smooth, and touching hard or soft objects influences our impressions and decisions. Rough objects and coarse clothing have been found to make social interactions feel more difficult, while holding hard objects tends to increase rigidity in negotiations.[210]

Each training prepares one to let go a little more of increasingly subtle holdings and to grow increasingly at rest in nonconceptuality. Thus, in taking up the second of the three nonconceptual practices, uniting clarity and emptiness, the holding and releasing is done a little less forcefully than in the bliss-empty practice, and one does not swish the "air sandwich" around in the belly. And it keeps getting simpler.

Training in the Nonconceptual Primordial Wisdom of Reality (CHOS NYID RNAM PAR MI RTOG PA'I YE SHES)

At this point in the seven trainings, Longchenpa says:

> Relax your body and mind from deep within. Without moving your eyes, meditate in a state free from all the proliferation and dissolution of though activity. By meditating in this way, you will be able to concentrate on whatever you direct your attention to, after which you will be able to rest for longer and longer periods in a nonconceptual space-like state. When this comes to pass you have mastered this practice. In the process, bodhicitta grows greater.

This meditation is accompanied by a very relaxed expression of the four applications. According to oral tradition, there is no holding the breath or rotating the belly here. However, your relaxed state allows your belly to expand as breath-energy descends.[211] There is no bumping up against objects, no hint of a bounded arena. You have thinned out proclivities that thwart such boundlessness, allowing freshness and wonder. This is a refreshing respite from what modern psychology calls "invariant representation" or "expectational bias"— seeing sameness instead of the vibrant and constant unfolding of surprises for the senses. Hence, more freedom, presence, and potential for creativity. This alone is transformative.

Wisdom is a state of imageless presence. Simple, free of frills, no display of any kind. But as Longchenpa observes, being free of elaborations is not sufficient! Mind is like space, but it is not space, it is suffused with wisdom. If reality were *just* an empty primordial purity, nothing would happen or be known.

This view of an intrinsically luminous ultimacy contrasts with the total absence emphasized in Tsongkhapa's and other Geluk descriptions of emptiness, based on their reading of classic Indian Middle Way sūtras and commentaries.[212] Dzogchen's view of reality includes a radiance expressed through the spontaneous dynamism of sheer awareness, unmediated sheer seeing. Such dynamism furthers responsiveness, the moving love maṇḍala of Jigme Lingpa's refuge and bodhicitta's deep resolve to awaken all.[213] This flow unites your own empty essence and luminous nature.[214]

What might this look like in a real human being? Exceptional practitioners I have met, especially my own teachers, were as different from one another as human beings can be—wrathful, playful, witty, serious. I watched them closely over the course of many years. Of course I can't know their experience, but all were, it seemed, ingeniously creative. Another quality they seemed to have in common was their immediate responsiveness to any situation that came up. At the moment of encountering just about anything, they neither pushed it away nor fused with it, yet seemed to take it in completely. They focused as necessary, yet at the same time seemed continuously integrated with their whole surround and ready to play with whatever showed up. Also, throughout whatever was going on, they seemed fed by something invisible to me but incredibly sweet and sustaining to them. No matter what happened externally, some inner seemingly changeless state prevailed, even as their faces were as changeable and expressive as any human countenance I've ever observed.

To cultivate the meditative experiences of bliss, clarity, and non-conceptuality is to ride clouds of mist. There is no point in getting attached, they will come and go. Some underlying sameness, which one might eventually access through the nonconceptual recognition of reality, will abide. That is realization, not fleeting meditative experience (*nyams*).

Meditative experience can be very impactful. Once tasted, it's impossible not to hope you'll experience bliss or clarity soon again. So the practice becomes a gradual process of learning to rest in actual experience, letting go of anticipation for a different or more extended state. This is like catching the scent of your favorite food when you are famished, and not running toward it. We are told so much about the downside of being attached to these experiences that we sometimes fail to allow our own appreciation, a joyful gratitude that has nothing to do with pride, to surface. This is also not wise. For joy, as Adzom Rinpoche says in his commentary, is mightily helpful. It energizes us. We often find ourselves oscillating between a state free of reactivity, and back inside it. For example, we may experience a state of bliss and then find ourselves either in resistance or attachment to it. This is the sort of thing to explore with trusted spiritual friends or teachers.

Positive meditative experiences are like the good smell of food starting to cook. There's something to enjoy, but nothing to sink your teeth into. Something is happening, your meditation is having an effect. However, unless our nonconceptuality actually touches into reality, it is just another fleeting meditative experience that lacks the stability and impact of actual realization. It quickly vanishes, like mist before the sun. We can't help wanting it back, yet our attachment halts our progress. Realization of reality, on the other hand, is not fleeting. Longchenpa has said:

> Unless you can distinguish between experience and
>   realization,
> you will mistake habit-based experiences for realization.

Realization is constant, and unchanging, getting neither better
nor worse.
As you train in this, good qualities will arise as experience.[215]

Realizing reality is beyond mere nonconceptuality. It is the actual
nonconceptual primordial *wisdom* that knows reality (*chos nyid rnam
par mi rtog pa'i ye shes*).[216] When ordinary thoughts dissolve in the
luminous sky-field that is home and source of all experience, reality
is revealed. This is an instruction. It is also a description from experience about an experience that may arise for you.

This sky-field, our mind-nature, is beyond cause and effect, it
doesn't change.[217] This field is not an idea, it is a lived experience, a
complete reorientation of our mind, body, and senses. And we are
reminded again that while mind-nature is like the sky, it is not the
same as sky. In his autobiography, Jigme Lingpa writes:

Mind-nature is like open space,
yet superior, for it has wisdom as well.
Luminous clarity is like the sun and moon,
yet superior, for there is nothing material.
Sheer awareness is like a crystal ball,
yet superior, with no blocks or cover.[218]

Shenphen Dawa Rinpoche writes:

Our mind and our memories flow through these subtle
channels (throughout the body). We believe that our memory resides in the brain, but in truth it flows through the
entire body. The brain is like an engine, and the subtle
channels the network through which our memory flows.[219]

MORE ABOUT THE BODY

Discovering your own body is a big surprise. I say this as someone who
spent nearly seventeen years of Buddhist practice working mainly

from my head, entirely blind to my body's crucial role in practice. Including the body and the senses in practice is essential to reckoning with being human. It's a reckoning I managed to overlook for the first seventeen years of my connection with Buddhist practice. My first visit to Tibet woke me up to it, and since then I value it as a vital element of every part of the Buddhist path. In brief, I hold very, very dear how practice integrates and impacts the bodily senses. This impact is particularly obvious in channel-wind practices, but in fact every practice integrates mind with body—from watching the breath, to exploring impermanence, to the challenges of opening to a heartfelt sense of love.

Because it is such an important matter, I have also found it helpful to look at the body through select Western lenses. It's part of a process of seeking optimal integration of all parts of us into practice and into life as we find it in the twenty-first century. We begin here with the Danish Dzogchen teacher Jes Bertelsen, who includes the body among five areas of natural human expertise that he convincingly maintains are relevant to contemplative practices throughout the ancient and modern worlds. I then bring forward observations from the world of science on the experience of weight, agency, and the widespread inclination generalize at the expense of meaningful detail, even among scientists who are, by definition, dedicated to precision and detail.

Five Gateways: Body, Breath, Heart, Creativity, Consciousness

Jes Bertelsen describes five areas of universal competency. His point is that all human beings possess these competences and that this is meaningful because they are found in different forms in a wide variety of practices throughout the world's cultures.[220] Each is a gateway. As a curious reader, you might now ask yourself, in terms of your own experience, what are five areas of competency that you and everyone else has? Take a moment, if you like, before reading on. A hint: these are not competencies that require any training. They are basic. At the same time, training can enhance them significantly.

Body, breath, heart, basic creativity, and consciousness are five gateways available to everyone. Each has a place in the seven trainings. Bertelsen writes:

> Consciousness of the body consists simply of the ability to sense one's entire body. The ability to spread one's attention evenly over and throughout the whole body. Experience shows that people who work on this continue to return to . . . the image of completely filling out one's body. That the body is a form that consciousness can settle into and fill in as comfortably and completely as possible . . . For most people it is easiest at first to sense the body more completely when it is relaxed and at rest. But in time it will be important to train dynamically, that is to say, to maintain contact with the body also when you are on the move.[221]

Body, breath, and imagination are vital aspects of the seven trainings and have particular significance in the seventh training when, for example, one holds or rotates breath in the belly, or transforms the experienced fleshy body into light, or brings luminous attention to the heart.

Dzogchen traditions say we access wisdom most directly at our heart center, at the center of our torso. Feelings of love, trust, and gratitude are also most easily sensed in this center, in the middle of the chest, the heart of practice. The heart in turn is supported by the navel center, the root of our bodily existence.

Consciousness is the field of all experience. Everyone knows something about their own consciousness, just as everyone knows something about their own breath, heart, and way of expression. In Dzogchen practice, consciousness—from ordinary to sheer basic knowing—grows more and more familiar, until it is finally so transparent it reveals its nature to itself. In the meantime, mind and body transparencies support each other.

To know your mind's natural transparency means you are not limited to a focus on mental contents, as is ordinarily the case. Rather, you give attention to consciousness itself. Likewise, in Jigme Lingpa's pith

practices, and in the nonconceptual meditations of the seventh training, it is not the mind's contents but the tone or state of mind that is
central. Being concerned with *how* the mind is rather than *what* it contains is an important shift in awareness.[222] Thoughts inevitably float
by—they are part of the *what* of our incessant creativity. We let them
be and sit at the confluence of all five gateways of human experience.

Basic creativity is ingredient in our responses to everything
around us. Dzogchen sees reality, and therefore real human nature,
as infinitely creative, a constant source of wonder and amazement.
Adepts like Milarepa and Adzom Rinpoche are famous for their
spontaneous heart songs. Dzogchen retreats traditionally close with
inspired participatory performances—song, dance, witty repartee,
and the like—deliciously enjoyable after the formal structure of
retreat.

Weight, Hapticity, and Light

Our body's kinesthetic sensibility is alive to the feel of everything we
contact, especially to weight, or hapticity. Recent studies clarify how
this and other felt-sense factors impact our perception and experience.[223] Most important here is that basic tactile sensations influence
higher social cognitive processing.[224]

The seventh training, like all tantric-based practices, engages us in
a new type of kinesthetic experience—a weightless body of colored
light. These practices are powerful because our perceptions of self
and separation are inextricably bound up with our own body-sensing.
Lightness of weight and the light of illumination come together in
practices dissolving the solidity and boundedness of ordinary self-
experience. Cultivated over long periods of time, these practices tend
to shift the somatic and cognitive senses of self.

Yet the body feels so solid, so real! And yet we know it is not.
That itself is astonishing. How can that be? Is it meaningful from an
objective or scientific perspective to shift from our habitual sense of
a bounded, solid body to one that is boundless and wave-like? Two
contemporary scientists—Neil Theise on cell theory and Larry Barsalou on what he calls "the vice of nouning"—looking at very different

matters, get to the heart of how and why such a shift might elude us. Most especially, both speak to the slippage involved in our otherwise prodigious human capacity for knowing. And what they discover is amplified by what Daniel Stern has to say about how we saw the world when we first entered it as infants.

Neil Theise on Cells

The foundational paradigm of Euro-American medicine is cellular structure.[225] The idea that the body is composed of cells means material cells. End of story. Or is it? Neil Theise helpfully places cell theory in a larger context that teaches us much about how our minds clamp onto categories that are more arbitrary than we recognize. From the perspective of Buddhist contemplatives seeking a knack for not clamping, the more we can understand about it the better.

Cells were so called, Theise observes, because they seemed to be definably bounded areas recalling the empty surround of a monastic or prison cell. Ancient Greeks, however, likely influenced by their Indian partners in cultural dialogue, saw the body as an endless fluidity, not as something divisible into cells or constructed by them.[226] Similarly, tantric systems, and specifically our seventh training, see the body as the organized yet open playing field for currents that carry felt-sensory information throughout.[227]

Cell theory is under challenge in Western science. This is partly because much of what defines the boundary of a cell has to do with interactions that occur on its outer layers. But a layer is just a conglomeration of molecules, and modern procedures can now cause a cell in the bone marrow to become a liver cell. The only way the two can be construed as categorically "the same" continuous cell is by tracking its genome. Theise, of course, says this best:

> Neither I nor any of my colleagues would have had trouble saying that the cell in the marrow had become the cell of the liver, despite the fact that most, if not all, of the phenotypic and molecular aspects of the cell had changed in the process of engraftment. The only way we could say it was the

"same cell" was by marking the genome ... In other words, the cell was defined in such transplantation experiments by its genome ...[228]

Most of the cell's own particulars have changed. Where is its defining boundedness now? The narrative of continuity depends on the genome and other elements of the cell, not on the cell itself. Theise further observes:

> With the genome as the point of view, then, the cell becomes defined not as a structurally bounded box, but as a *field* of molecular organization in space and time ...[229]

If we reify the cell's identifying boundaries, it is like a box. If we don't reify them, we can recognize that the cell's periphery is malleable and can vary over time. Theise's further point is that even the paradigm of cell theory itself, crucial as this has been to advances in medicine, may obstruct an appreciation of healing mechanisms based on other paradigms. He is identifying how an ingrained inclination to reify, helpful as it is in context, can also obstruct the growth of understanding. Acupuncture, for example, sees the body as a complex field of interconnected points. A field is different from a cell. Waves are different from particles. Energy is different from matter. Subject is different from object, and self is different from other. The elements in each of these pairs do differ from each other in meaningful ways. However, from another perspective, these same dyadic elements are inseparable from each other. For example, objects only exist when subjects exist. Physical phenomena that appear as waves can also appear as particles. And today the brain-cell narrative at the center of neuroscience is making accommodations with an equally powerful narrative of networks of communication not only within the brain, long the bread and butter of neuroscience, but also between brain and body via, for example, the vagus nerve.

We already know that the movement of colorful energy streams is a core element of tantric practice. The experience of such energies runs counter to our more usual sense of a more solid body, a more substantial self. The challenge here is not unlike the challenge Theise describes in calling on cell theory to make way for the new paradigm of unbounded fields in the body. In science and in contemplative practices, as in life generally, biases toward familiar structures are hard to overcome. Part of practice is allowing and acknowledging our resistance so we can appreciate what biases and reifications are obstructing the reorientations toward which practice moves.

Our everyday experience of embodiment includes experiences of vacuity (empty stomach), fluidity (drinking, spitting), and solidity (sitting, standing). In tantric practice, it also includes emptiness, flowing light, and light forms stabilized as luminous embodiment. Such differentiations at one level do not stymie interaction at another. Waves and particles both exist, neither can be denied, but neither alone captures the fluidity of the actual situation; together they challenge ideas of simple continuities. Only a narrative that accounts for both is comprehensive. For Dzogchen, however, what is most important is cognizing the source from which these multivalent phenomena emerge. That itself, in its view, renders a state of wholeness known experientially, not just cognitively.

We are in many ways estranged from our experience, and therefore from the wholeness that it exhibits. Thinking can never experience wholeness fully or directly. Our thinking grabs us powerfully, so much so that it is easy to confuse with feeling! Yet thinking is very different from feeling, sensing, and living. Thought feels precise to us, but it is not! Mental images or verbalized thoughts deal in generalities, and they capture our attention in ways that keep us unaware of nuances of experience, including our ability to sense into others' experience. The digital universe is vivid and precise in certain ways, but it does not give us the full surround of lived experience coming through all our senses, emerging through our own imagination, and tempered by the world around us, nor does it supply the simplicity of resting still in the open air. All this influences our encounter with Dzogchen's invitation to wholeness. Next is another fascinating description of how we resist that invitation.

THE VICE OF NOUNING

Buddhist philosophy and contemporary science agree that our tendency to exaggerate the solidity of things and feelings has deep roots and comes in many forms. Making choices based on assessments of good or bad, casting judgments shaded with emotions, wrapping our sense of identity around a cause, flag, corporate culture, or favorite color—these are all instances of reification. It doesn't mean we shouldn't have opinions, relationships, or causes. Not at all. It means that our identity need not collapse into any one of these. Our sense of what we are can, in Buddhist perspectives, encompass a larger field that more localized senses of identity can obscure.

The historical, genetic, and other contributors to anyone's identity are a tale beyond thought. Our collapsing into an identity apparently apart from all these is regarded throughout Buddhist traditions as a core source of pain in our lives that manifests in infinite variety as desire, hatred, jealousy, and pride. Uprooting this is the central orientation of Buddhist practice. On the other hand, modern psychology does well to point out that some coherence of identity is vital. Buddhist traditions implicitly agree; by far the majority of their teachings are addressed to persons who think and behave like coherent selves. Nonetheless, even this becomes a basis for afflictive behavior.[230]

Erroneous or not, reification is instinctively attractive. It makes us feel powerful. It supports our deceptive but undeniable sense that we are independent agents and self-governing individuals. Our expressions of agency make us feel weighty, substantial, and just plain there. We find this both reassuring and real. This preference persists even after extensive contemplative training, or keen scientific instruments, show us with certainty that no such reified stability exists.

Why is this illusion so persistent? It seems that our bias toward reification meshes with our biases toward simplicity and generalization. Though these processes are different, both support the sense of solidity that we are craving. Prejudice toward a particular group of people, for example, is a brutal outcome of simplification and generalization. Yet it has wide appeal because it aligns with a powerfully felt false sense of certainty that, even if wholly contradicted by neutrally observed facts on the ground, can make one feel in control. Such prejudice wreaks havoc for individuals and societies.

One reason we get pulled into such illusions, says Larry Barsalou, is because most of us "gravitate toward essentialist ways of thinking that simplify and objectify mechanisms."[231] Barsalou's work suggests that the powerful urge we have to grab onto anything and hold it as real— wallets, watches, feelings, and ideas—contributes to what Buddhists regard as the mistaken idea of a self. Histories around the world show that it is much easier, especially in stressful times, to simplify the complex and intensify the solidity of good or bad than to reckon with the multivalent causality of events and reactions.

Barsalou is curious about why this bias toward simplification intrudes even among scientists, a cohort dedicated to precision and sensitivity to context. Yet scientists are also human and will unintentionally subsume detail and generalize in order to achieve a more coherent, larger picture—what we might consider a whole with holes in it, a pseudo-wholeness.[232] This bias seems exactly counter to the orientation of scientific inquiry. So where does it come from?

Barsalou connects this tendency with the "more general and basic phenomenon of coercing processes into noun concepts."[233] He suggests that it stems from inclinations already present in childhood. He points to evidence from developmental psycholinguistics that the kinds of object-categories associated with nouns are typically acquired earlier in life than the process categories associated with verbs—words descriptive of behaviors or of physical and mental events. [234] He notes that the words we learn most easily as children are nouns identifying concrete and specific things rather than abstractions or processes.[235]

Verbs point to processes, nouns point to objects. Barsalou notes that processes, unlike objects, lack clear shape or boundary. This makes them more difficult to categorize, just as the paradigm of robustly defined cell shapes may overshadow perception of the more dynamic genome structures.[236] The intersecting rainbows of our sensory experience are not eminently noun able. They don't turn into "things," and therefore the self-sense that emerges from them is neither stable nor reified.[237] Then, imperceptibly, we move toward what Suzuki Roshi called a "gaining idea"—that is, one that gains us the impression of a more solid, dependable sort of me-ness.[238] Suzuki Roshi even goes so far as to say that "to be a human being is to be a buddha." This throws us back into the quagmire of our questions about both! It also disrupts the projected solidity and separateness of both.[239] In this way, a stable, concrete, robustly contoured self is what we usually conjure as core to our lived experience, even as the gestures by which we do this remain on the edge of our awareness.[240]

These gestures, the very things that seem to hold us together in ways we find reassuring, disrupt a deeper and more natural ease. We use this over-reified core as a launching pad for leaning into what we want and pushing away what we don't want. These push-pull moves become entrained as patterns that keep us reactive and restless. They support our sense of separation, not just from others and the natural world, but also from our own experience of being what we are.

The pith practices help bring these self-ing gestures to experience.[241] With the awareness we cultivate through them, the whole superstructure of nouning may lighten up.

Our First Unified World

Our ordinary, disjunctive ways of structuring our human selves, most of all as real and separate, creates on the fringes and in the depths of our awareness a persistent boundary between "me" and everything else. This sensibility is both powerful and ineffable. It undermines expansive states of being, such as are ascribed to buddhas. Many yogis, mystics, and saints describe ways of knowing that do not comport with separation and solidity. Interestingly, based on his famous studies of infants, Daniel Stern reminds us that our capacity for experiencing our surroundings as an uninterrupted dance of vitality, the way we did as children, never completely disappears.

Stern convincingly finds that infants have a wholistic way of processing information, and that although this ability ebbs as we grow, it nonetheless remains throughout life. He says that descriptions of this way of perceiving are best "captured" by dynamic, kinetic terms, such as "surging," "fading away," "fleeting," "explosive," "crescendo," "decrescendo," "bursting," "drawn out," and the like.[242] These vitalities are not locked into any one sensory track or modality, such as seeing or hearing. Stern refers to them as a-modal. For us they constitute a fresh lens through which to observe how we support our thoughts, or how we relax, or what movement feels like—key elements of the pith practices.

Stern points out that as infants we experience such dynamics as "qualities from within"—that is, very much as part of our own orbit of sensory experience and not so much as arrivals from outside. When, as infants, we saw our mother or caretaker reach for a diaper or bring over a blanket, we did not see these as actions that had a particular intention or purpose; we felt them as differing registers of vitality, a "rush," a "push." These keenly impact the sensorium and yet seem to bypass narratives of separateness, or even agency. But they allow us to recognize our mother through her distinctive way of moving through our space.

Experiences that emerge through the pith practices, or in any of the story-meditations described here, may revive some of the keenness of vitality sensing, as if emergent from a vastness that is perennially part of us. Such experiences are apparently always on the horizon. Many mystics and meditators, as well as anyone who has had an unbidden insight or intuition, may be nodding in agreement here. To our Buddhist imagination, they may even suggest an open corridor of communication between our human and more buddha-like selves.

Stern's work calls attention to a significant way station in our practice. Ordinary experience is often heavily weighted toward what we feel we can get our hands on or put our minds around. In other words, we like what we could call the noun-able known. The pith practices agilely undo the warp and weft of those solidities for a potentially fresher, more easily flowing way path through our lives.[243] This has everything to do with the body.

The seventh training puts us in touch with a capacity for profound rest through bringing awareness to the body's deep interior. We are introduced to the subtle variations that occur as our sensibility and energies grow more subtle and clearer to our experience. We are training to feel and also to shift the winds or currents that move through our body.

The seventh training's combination of the imaginal and the kinesthetic will, in time, dissolve the solid-seeming sense of self that is a bedrock for dualistic experience and supports conceptual journeys of all kinds. Adzom Rinpoche has already described the somatically sensed *prāṇa* carefully held in the belly and flowing through the central torso as key to the seventh training. The felt-sense of this movement is catalyzed by the practitioner's trained imagination. An ability to engage our subtle interiority is honed by the traditional trainings Longchenpa and Jigme Lingpa describe. In addition, Jigme Lingpa's pith practices prepare us for new subjective nuances associated with these very states in ways that enhance our encounter with wholeness. Together, these offer a path to wholeness through the body.

From the perspective of wholeness embraced by Dzogchen, our sense of twoness is illusory. It conceals how we really are. Wisdom practices are primed to dissolve this illusion. Small wonder we find ourselves resistant to them. They might even make us want to cling harder to our me-ness. Jigme Lingpa puts this beautifully in these lines from his *Wisdom Chats*:

> This view can't be said, thought, or expressed.
> When you move past thought and really see,
> you feel frightened, and so
> you contrive
> and contrive,
> you tighten and
> you tighten.
> You think, "This is the authentic path," but
> you've gone off in the direction of the crazed and heretical.[244]

Separateness frightens us; we want to bridge the distance. It also gives us the illusion of power; we want dominion over the distance. Either way, feeling distance or trying to bridge it, we are not at ease. A path to genuinely satisfying wholeness requires that we look straight into our ordinary face until we find our wisdom staring right back at us. We do this symbolically by gazing into the eyes of Guru Rinpoche as we call for help and as we melt into the fulness of our nature, to which the pith and story practices introduce us. Longchenpa paves the way for this kind of seeing with the gnostic turn toward wisdom he makes very early on in his layout of the teachings. This is the turn we take in our next chapter. A pith practice will bridge us to it.

THIRD PITH PRACTICE

Looking into the very face
of whatever happiness or pain dawns,
consciousness settles down in its natural state.[245]

བདེ་སྡུག་གང་ཤར་གྱི་རང་ངོ་ལ་ལྟ་ཞིང་ཤེས་པ་
རྩལ་དུ་དབབ་བོ།

Carved stones at nuns' practice grounds,
Adzom Gar, Sichuan

6. Awakening and the Turn to Wisdom

OUR URGENT THIRST for more and better is intrinsic to the karmic narrative. But the fundamental paradigm of the wisdom narrative, the one that so shocked me in my initial encounter with it, is "something better is here already." There is nowhere to go and no one who is going. Once wisdom and awakening are recognized as natural essence, they cease to be goals and become intimate conversation partners. This is nonsense to our ordinary mind and a beacon to our sheer knowing.

How is it, we asked early in this book, that Longchenpa's trainings, the essence of all foundational practices, bring one to a great completeness? How does the karmic narrative melt into the wisdom story, and how do we come to see that the two have always been part of one unbounded wholeness? Here we traced this shift by noting how Longchenpa himself pivots toward wisdom. We called these pivots "gnostic turns" because they align practitioners with Dzogchen's unique view well before one reaches the stage of formal Dzogchen practice.

The pivots we discuss all relate to the serene arena of the dharmadhātu, which is also the centerpiece of one of Longchenpa's most famous writings on Dzogchen, *Precious Dharmadhātu Treasury*. We start here with pivots to Dzogchen found in Longchenpa's description of the sūtra bodhisattva path, which in classic Indian texts focuses on cultivating the love and compassion culminating in bodhicitta.

Longchenpa's choosing to emphasize the dharmadhātu in the context of bodhicitta is significant. After discussing why this is so, we conclude with showing how Longchenpa's principles are also core to Jigme Lingpa's nine-vehicle refuge and his framing of the bodhisattva's awakened mind, which Dzogchen will reveal as the actual nature of everything. His pith practices create a foundation for compassionate expression to occur even while free of a dualistic sense of giving and taking.

Jigme Lingpa's instructions, the story-mediations and the five pith practices, encompass the entire gamut of the path. In sūtra traditions, bodhicitta is something we strive to achieve. In Dzogchen it is already in the fabric of everything. Like waves and particles in quantum theory, these two states are different and yet not different. For sūtra practitioners, bodhicitta is something to attain, a way out of the karmic jungle. In Dzogchen, bodhicitta is simply the way things are, the nature of your own mind, ready to be discovered. As the real nature of everything, bodhicitta is profoundly akin to the dharmadhātu, the spacious and stainless source of everything.

THE KARMIC NARRATIVE'S BODHICITTA

Śāntideva's *Guide to the Bodhisattva's Way of Life* teaches a fourfold method for developing bodhicitta that culminates in a mind intent on awakening for everyone's benefit. His descriptions of love and compassion are the source of Tibet's famous *tonglen*, or "giving" (*tong*) and "taking" (*len*), practices. The rhythm of giving (or offering) and taking (or removing and receiving) is also at the heart of tantric ritual and is distilled in Jigme Lingpa's story practices.

Indian-based instructions on the bodhisattva path center on how to cultivate love or compassion.[246] All would agree with Asaṅga that

wisdom is the mother for developing buddha qualities.[247]

Tonglen practices exemplify how compassion, ultimately unified with wisdom, makes us whole. We are not pushing anything away. We are also not running after anything in the manner of grabbing something for ourselves. We just give out and take in, as naturally as breathing. Step by step, we cultivate love and compassion until we discover an actual awakened mind. United with wisdom, ultimate bodhicitta frees us from the karmic swirl of suffering.

Seeds of the wisdom narrative are found early in Indian Buddhism. For example, the famous *Luminous (Pabhassara) Sutta* says:

> Luminous, monks, is the mind. And it is defiled by incoming defilements. The uninstructed run-of-the-mill person doesn't discern that as it actually is present, which is why I tell you that—for the uninstructed run-of-the-mill person—there is no development of the mind.
>
> Luminous, monks, is the mind. And it is freed from incoming defilements. The well-instructed disciple of the noble ones discerns that as it actually is present, which is why I tell you that—for the well-instructed disciple of the noble ones—there is development of the mind.[248]

This suggests it is not enough to fight off bad habits, as emphasized in karmic narratives; we also need to tap into and allow what is already intrinsically and effortlessly present to present itself. Asaṅga, writing in the fourth century, offers a similar perspective:

> Mind, we see, is always luminous in nature
> Contaminated [only by] adventitious flaws.[249]

If this weren't so, practice could not succeed. A naturally luminous mind means awakening to a process that is natural to our organism. Mind is like space but is different from space because it has awareness. Mind gives rise to thoughts. What happens to the mind when thoughts come? Does its nature change? Are thoughts to mind like fish to water? Ice melting in the sea? Radiance from the sun?

Jigme Lingpa's third pith practice explored the relationship between thoughts and their sources. In this practice, we simply let consciousness settle. We are curious about how such settling feels, how it might be similar or different from letting go or growing calm. And we look into the very face of whatever dawns, whether it's happiness or pain. Ideally, we don't label it but only feel into it. Some shift in how we experience that very act of sensing may occur. One long-time practitioner, soon after being introduced to this practice, wrote me: "In looking at pleasure and pain directly, I am finding that no matter whether it is pleasure or pain, all my experiences of either tend to resolve into a single unified field of experience. I'm not sure how else to describe it."

It's a small yet big thing to discover that a specific experience of pleasure or pain can resolve into an intimate, unanticipated sense of wholeness. This helps us appreciate Longchenpa's introducing the bodhisattva path by describing the all-inclusive wholeness of the dharmadhātu. In other words he does not, like Candrakīrti, Śāntideva, or Tsongkhapa, open with a description of goals or proclaim the importance of love and compassion. He doesn't mention compassion until close to the end of his section on bodhisattvas. His first priority is to draw attention to the natural potential that makes awakening possible. He opens by noting that this potential or inheritance for awakening is by nature a crucial support (*rten*) for practice:

> If one understands that this essential disposition (*khams*, *dhātu*) is spontaneously present in oneself and others, one will feel enthusiasm, understanding that there is nothing to prevent one's mind from gaining liberation.[250]

This basis needs no causes, it is already perfect. In calling this natural capacity a crucial support for the path, Longchenpa aligns with the whole arc of his *Precious Dharmadhātu Treasury*, where he calls bodhicitta "that which contains everything and is the true nature of everything,"[251] and shows it to be the actual ground (*gzhi*) of everything.[252] And he cites a passage from Asaṅga's *Sublime Mindstream* in support of this:

> Utterly luminous mind-nature is unchanging, like space.[253]

Understanding the dharmadhātu as your own inevitable inheritance is what Longchenpa is emphasizing here. He invites us to see our inborn potential for awakening, less concerned with describing the feel of compassion than that it is intrinsic to your buddha nature, and makes clear that this is a brand-new way to appreciate what you are as a human being.[254] This real realm known as the dharmadhātu, he explains in the context of Middle Way philosophy, is not only pure by nature, it is ultimate truth, and as such it springs forth of itself, a primordial wisdom:

> ...when it is stained, it is called "spiritual inheritance," "the basic constituent of being," or "buddha nature"... when it is stainless it is called "awakened" or "gone to suchness."[255]

This unchanging nature is perfect and complete, just as it is. From here it is an easy pivot to Dzogchen's own view that the dharmadhātu, the source-space of everything, is inseparable from primordial wisdom, a recognition that is is central to Longchenpa's poetic evocation of Dzogchen in his *Precious Dharmadhātu Treasury* and his bravura commentary on it.[256]

In tandem with this, already in the context of sūtra, Longchenpa names wisdom as the way things actually are. He does this in almost the same breath as he names dharmadhātu the ultimate truth of the Madhyamaka Prāsaṅgika school—in contrast with the overwhelming emphasis in Tibet on naming emptiness as the ultimate for that school. Both of these points, again, are powerful pivots toward Dzogchen because they open directly to the secret that wisdom is not the path's goal but the path itself. And while there is much about Dzogchen that is uniquely Tibetan, this pivotal principle has its roots in Indian Mahāyāna. Enriching this point, Longchenpa draws again on Asaṅga's *Sublime Mindstream*:

> There is nothing whatsoever to remove from this, nor anything in the slightest to add.[257]

Dust doesn't alter a mirror. Clouds don't change the sun. Exactly like that, our defilements do not alter our unchanging nature. We address defilements because they are not good for anyone and, though they do not affect our nature, they block wisdom's light from our eyes.

The pith practices, without ever telling us what to experience, seem often to bring forward experiences that resonate with buddha nature as Dzogchen understands it. The mirror is neither separate from its reflection nor stained by it. Your grief and happiness are not separate from the ground in which they appear. Or, as Asaṅga puts it, the wisdom associated with stainless buddha qualities is inseparable from the state of an ordinary person who has mental afflictions. And by the way, he adds, this wisdom is inconceivable.[258] For Longchenpa this point pivots directly to Dzogchen, wherein primordial wisdom is both carefully distinguished from ordinary mind and recognized as already present in every mind-state.

Why is this so important to Longchenpa's understanding of bodhicitta and bodhisattvas? Longchenpa again turns to Asaṅga:

> If you did not have that crucial buddha element,
> you would not be dissatisfied by suffering, nor
> seek out or take interest in freedom from it,
> or even aspire to that.[259]

The essential perfection of our mind is at the very foundation of our messy and mistaken patterns. This is another important thing, but because I didn't know it, I scoffed at the notion of being anything like a buddha in any sense. I hadn't yet heard that everything is either wisdom or a distortion of it. In either case, its nature is wisdom. Becoming Guru Rinpoche, a beloved and powerful practice from Adzom Rinpoche's *Luminous Heart Essence* cycle, contains these lines of refuge:

> Right in the middle of my mistaken seeing, my saṃsāra,
> I bring forth a union of refuge and awakened mind.[260]

Our two faces—our beleaguered activities and our intrinsic wellness—are, from the first, inseparable. All path processes, from impermanence to final recognition of reality, acknowledge our two faces. In the end there aren't really two faces, but for our experience until then, there are. Our wisdom face, finally, sees itself in our ordinary face. Our ordinary face sees its true condition and melts into the mirror of wisdom. There is no first meeting between these two. They are in each other all along. We are always in the world and yet not entirely of it. And our responsibilities, our burgeoning love and compassion, include both our own and others' human needs and potential for awakening.

That is the ultimate message of the story-meditations too. In dissolving, we do not simply fade away. We come back to meaningful action in the world. And yet this is action with a difference. Wisdom is different from ordinary mind. It is less hampered, more agile, transcendent in its very immanence. Our ordinary minds cannot encompass this, but our potential for more expansive seeing can.

Wisdom is responsive, not reactive. It does not behave like our ordinary mind, even though it's right there with it. Nothing actually happens to wisdom as we progress on the path. We just grow more familiar with it, and that makes all the difference. It's the difference between recognizing your dearest friend on the road or walking right past the very one you were looking for. Failing recognition, you feel alone, beset. Finding your friend beside you, everything changes. Wisdom is just such a friend, the dearest of dears. This is surely why Sufis speak of the friend as true knowing, and why they and other traditions speak of the divine, or one's own soul, as the eternal beloved, the heart's ultimate bride. Like the sun, loving wisdom lights up your sky. This is not contradicted by clouds passing through. Everything in human experience is an expression of wisdom and potentially a path to it.

And so it is that Longchenpa introduces the principle of the two purities, a paradigm unique to the Old School, the Nyingma. The first purity is the primordially pure sky of your nature, the second is the purity achieved when all obscuring clouds—our reactivity, our unwholesome responses to the world—have dissolved into our expansive dharmadhātu.

Elegant descriptions of the dharmadhātu are all very well, but what

Longchenpa wants everyone to understand is that we ourselves can recognize it. That is the central thing he wants us to know about the bodhisattva journey. That it's possible. And, again, he draws on Indian wisdom to make this clear, specifically Asaṅga's *Sublime Mindstream*:

> Like a treasure and a fruit-bearing tree,
> this spiritual lineage has two aspects:
> a beginningless, naturally abiding aspect and
> a sublime aspect, genuinely matured.[261]

Jigme Lingpa's *Wisdom Chat* subtitled "The Wealth of Possessing the Two Purities" emphasizes the importance of understanding the first of the two purities, the primordial one that is always with us.

> The quintessential Dzogchen instruction is
> to take fruition as the path!
> So is the truth of primordiality
> a cause-and-effect sequence?
> Or is it a reality that
> transcends rejection and remedies?
> Is it utterly pure?
> The term "pure from the beginning" (*gdod nas dag pa*)
> teaches variations on the theme of primordial purity.[262]

There is nothing to add or remove regarding primordial purity. The ḍākinī foundational practices, centered on Yeshe Tsogyal, another Dzogchen sādhana revealed in Adzom Rinpoche's *Luminous Heart Essence* cycle, tells how best to relate to reality.[263] We are asked to "rest, neither erase nor place." There is nothing to add or newly place in our nature. We come to awakening just as we are. Given the chaotically insalubrious nature of many of our thoughts and actions, this is a stunning prospect.

The primordial sky is always there to be lit, and the sun is always there to light it. What are clouds in the face of these cosmic powers? Our sun is hidden by clouds, but not diminished.[264]

Though the two are not alike, ordinary mind is not something other than wisdom. A sun-like glowing dynamism is part of our nature.[265] Failing to recognize this dynamism augurs the chasm of duality and the gamut of problems that bring us pain.

Of course, we don't expect to grow transparent to suffering just like that. But we can see that the possibility exists. This galvanizes to do whatever we can to serve the world. Meanwhile, sickness is sickness, sorrow is sorrow. They are there, never to be ignored. But they are no longer the end of the story, the bottom line of who we are. We glimpse a larger horizon. Even right in the middle of experiencing unbearable sorrow, there is something else that holds us, a kind of cushion. It takes a great deal of practice and patience to find that ineffable cushion. We remain very humble in the face of this challenge, and in the face of whatever progress we make. To the extent that we see that pain is never all we are, we feel even more compassion for all who suffer. We do not dismiss others' pain. On the contrary, it is all the more poignant for being an illusion.

What would it feel like to watch through thick glass as a child screams for her mother, small body shaking with fear, while you are unable to communicate that mother has just stepped behind a curtain in that very room and is even now holding out her hand to lift it? The more we understand the pain around us, the more tenderly we regard all human and creaturely suffering. In this way, wisdom lights a fire under our wish to help. May we grow wise enough to respond so brightly! Until then, we help any way we can. We march peacefully. We join collectives that support all of us coming together. We find the suffering of oppression and injustice ever more unbearable.

Images impact us. The great ones, like sun and sky, are worth thousands of words. As Rumi says, "The sun has no tomorrows." For another five billion years, any creature lucky enough to walk this earth will look up and see the sun as we do today. Sometimes its face will be hidden, sometimes it will shine more fully. But it is still our sun. Two faces, two purities, two situations, and everything in between, but the sun always shines. It has no tomorrows, not because nothing changes but because it shines through all change.

Naming wisdom, rather than emptiness, is our mind's nature, reminds us of this steadfast sunlight. Putting wisdom at the heart of things is also the heart of Longchenpa's pivots from Middle Way to Dzogchen's great completeness.[266] Wisdom suffuses experience entirely. To rest in this is to rest in wholeness. Rest is your organism recognizing that there isn't anywhere else to go. It's here. "Don't seek elsewhere!" says Longchenpa.[267]

Change obscures the changeless but does not alter it. Everything we see is animated by reality itself. This is offered not as dogma but as a message from the deep experience of a long line of practitioners looking at our human situation straight from the heart. A line commenting on Jigme Lingpa's *Great Mother, the Great Bliss Queen* reminds us:

Because there is birth from the birthless,
living beings are confused.

Birth is movement and change. The birthless is still. Unceasing vitality emerges from it.[268] Jigme Lingpa's first pith practice acquaints us with the dance between them, which Dzogchen will explicitly address. With the second pith we practice letting consciousness relax without focusing on an object. In the third, we learn to look pain and happiness in the face and find right there a transparency through which we move. With the fourth pith we investigate the doing that initiates pain and pleasure, again landing in an open horizon that is neither, while at the same time we become intimate with both. In the fifth pith, we cut the threads that are the warp and weft of all thought,[269] and again find ourselves, as in the first practice, mindful and radically open, but now without any particular object.

All this helps us work with what seems an impossible contradiction—birth from the birthless. But it turns out that this is only a contradiction when we forget the larger dimension in which all perception takes place as the unborn and unceasing make each other possible.

Longchenpa's writings on Dzogchen include many descriptions of the primordial wisdom that suffuses the dharmadhātu, and that depict this dharmadhātu as the ultimate dance floor for all flux and focusing, birth and cessation. The first chapter of Longchenpa's unsurpassed evocation of Dzogchen, *Precious Dharmadhātu Treasury*, expresses this:

> ...swirl and peace, dawning of their own accord *(rang shar)*,
> never depart the serene arena (dharmadhātu)
> that is their very source...[270]

What seems paradoxical or incompatible dance together, the swirl of saṃsāra (unceasing motion) and the peace of nirvāṇa (unborn stillness). The sevenfold training and five pith practices open us to this dance. Practitioners must find this for themselves.

The dharmadhātu and the primordial wisdom that suffuses it are birthless. Everything arises from them. Jigme Lingpa's pith instructions to observe, in turn, what is still and what moves, or happiness and pain, or the originator of these, or simply to let be, somehow and sometimes summon experience of a wholeness in which all these participate. I don't mean that every pith-practice experience is precisely what Dzogchen points to. But they do begin to undo clear-cut separateness. In this way wisdom itself is compassion, the heart of the bodhisattva path.

PITH PRACTICES IN LIGHT OF LONGCHENPA

Longchenpa's pivots turn to the most intimate, fresh, and inspiring birthplace of all our experience, the dharmadhātu which, as we have seen, he introduces in the context of sūtra bodhisattva practice, and which his Dzogchen writings describe as an ever-luminous mindspace, our only place for genuine rest. Anything less shrugs off our vital inheritance.

With this in mind, we consider again Jigme Lingpa's third pith practice. He inserts it into his discussion after the story-meditation in which you witnessed the terrible suffering of the cold hells and were exhorted by Guru Rinpoche to feel a compassion for its denizens so intense that you are ready to take on all their suffering yourself just so they will be free of it.

When you awaken to this radical compassion, you immediately become a guide who frees others. And at this precise moment, having just shifted your human imagination from a painful hell-prison to the acme of freedom, Jigme Lingpa suggests that you let your mind rest naturally, simply observing the true nature of positive and negative experiences. [271] Seeing our nature flows into the restful openness of simply being.

When Jigme Lingpa says "simply observe," he invites a way of being that neither grabs nor pushes away. Become transparent to all that occurs is part of finding genuine rest, which Longchenpa sometimes describes as mind resting in its own bed, at home in its own nest.[272]

The essence of wisdom is compassion. When we are deceived by appearances, when it looks to our simple senses as if the moon has fallen in the lake, we never find rest. The unresolved space between subject and object—the space of separation—is inevitably experienced as a contested space. How much of it do we control? Attachment and hatred roil, trying to get what we want and dispatch what we don't. According to Buddhist cosmology, we live in the desire realm. The reason we are so avariciously needy is because our minds are restless, distracted. The culmination of Jigme Lingpa's verse for cultivating bodhicitta is "so all may rest in their clear mind-sphere," the dharmadhātu. In this way, the practitioner segues from karmic to wisdom trajectory.

Many Buddhist practices invite observing thought, mind watching mind. The famous pre-Mahāyāna scripture known as the *Foundations of Mindfulness Sūtra* teaches focusing on breath, then on various aspects of mind. It is an iconic Buddhist practice, yet different from the transparent observation Jigme Lingpa invites in his pith practices. Classic Buddhist mindfulness is watchfully apart from and aware of its object. Jigme Lingpa's pith practices also begin with watching and ultimately invite dropping the mind's distancing mechanisms—letting go thoughts, easing into openness, cutting threads—in other words, disassembling every part of the rickety house that still obstructs our view.

And in this light, we note again Jigme Lingpa's own pithy observation of what can then occur:

> Child, mind watching mind
> isn't awareness of knowing's essence.
> Child, let such knowing be uncontrived and
> without wandering, simply be.[273]

The pith practices offer a kind of contemplative oasis between the "mind watching mind," which, as Jigme Lingpa explains in the verse above, is not Dzogchen's way, and simply resting in the sheer face of awareness, *rig pa*. To be without flux or frills, change or conceptuality, means there is no sense of a watching mind looking at a watched mind, there is simply one's knowing nature. Everything else is frills. Frills means thought, which Dzogchen always associates with effort. Wisdom is by definition free of frills. The watched-watcher divide fades into an open state of intimate yet expansive knowing.

Jigme Lingpa's special instructions, the pith practices, are deceptively simple. I enjoy them very much. They open up to a different sort of experience, paying attention to the how of seeing and knowing. Objects may be vividly known at the expense of reckoning with the expanse they inhabit. What about resting in knowing itself? Pain remains distinct from pleasure, but knowing does not get stuck in either. It finds an untrammeled mind-space in which all of this occurs.

In the first pith practice, staying in awareness of movement and stillness may yield a sense of a larger mind-space, harbinger of the dharmadhātu, just as looking at a mirror image brings you right into the mirror if you don't get hooked on the images reflected there. But we are usually too distracted by the images to notice the mirror. Curious? Gaze into a mirror with senses open to the whole mirroring, not just the image of your face. This is just an analogy, yet it points to how Jigme Lingpa's instructions orient practitioners toward the Great Completeness perspective that nothing you sense is ever outside the mirroring field of your own experience.

For Longchenpa, as we well know by now, the true nature of pleasurable, painful, and every other kind of perception is wisdom. From here it is an easy pivot to recognize that "awakened mind is the actual ground of everything."[274] That place of rest is always available and frees us from the provocations of our own actions. Karma, and the karmic narrative, can simply dissolve there. With practice, a new felt-sense becomes available.

Longchenpa's genius opened a historicized and profoundly visionary Dzogchen horizon in fourteenth-century Tibet. He drew from a vast corpus, including early Dzogchen tantras and the Dzogchen lineages associated with Guru Rinpoche and Vimalamitra, which he organized and commented on in his famous *Fourfold Heart Essence* collection. In the eighteenth century, Jigme Lingpa drew from and extended this body of literature.

Longchenpa and Jigme Lingpa both cite Indian sources; neither draw on Chinese texts. Still, conversations with early Chinese Chan in the eighth century were also part of the very early period of Dzogchen's development in Tibet. Here too we find harbingers of, or at least resonance with, Longchenpa's important gnostic turns.

In the *Platform Sūtra*, the early formative document of Chan, we find the famous narrative of the sixth patriarch's awakening.[275] An unlikely candidate, this poor and illiterate monk outshines the poetic efforts of the presumed future patriarch. He recites a verse that skillfully tilts away from the karmic and goes straight to a wisdom narrative. Is one to polish the mirror of one's mind or recognize that it is already bright with wisdom? Is the path about knowledge or wisdom? Shenxiu, the head monk and heir apparent, famously wrote:

> The mind is like a clear mirror.
> At all times we must strive to polish it
> And must not let dust collect. [276]

But his poem did not win the day. Huineng, the future sixth patriarch, was himself illiterate and so dictated a poem that another monk wrote out for him:

The mind is the Bodhi tree.
The body is the mirror stand.
The mirror is originally clean and pure;
Where can it be stained by dust?[277]

In Tibet these two positions are reflected in the difference between sūtra paths, which emphasize the need to purify afflictions, and Dzogchen or Tantric paths, which emphasize that the fruit, awakened mind and primordial wisdom, are in essence already there.

In terms of our human experience, it is not as if the wisdom narrative ever grows entirely unmoored from the karmic one, any more than, from Dzogchen's perspective, our afflictions become unmoored from their nature as wisdom. This is what familiarity with Jigme Lingpa's pith practices suggests. Let's say someone has spoken to you harshly and you are feeling sad or angry about that. Understandable. Yet if you look into that sadness or anger, the looking itself is not sad or angry. And the sadness or anger is not separate from the looking. As you become able to focus on the sheer knowing that is present, it's possible you'll discover—not intellectually, but in a visceral experience that may surprise you—that this knowing, not your reactivity, is most fundamental to your experience. This is part of what it means to understand that sheer knowing, *rig pa*, is what supports the not knowing we call ignorance. Ignorance does not provide support for *rig pa*. Therefore the sheer seer of wisdom does not collapse when ignorance collapses, "just as the ground remains even though a house has been destroyed."[278]

Much patient practice is required for Dzogchen realization to flower into fulsome experience of the wisdom that's already there. Hence the seven trainings. Those trainings, and the related but distinctive foundational practices, are all backlit by a growing sense that the wisdom sought is right here.

Our confidence that this is so does not come from either believing we are fully buddhas now or that we are only human and need to develop the path from scratch. Most important is to have confidence in seeing that your mind nature is buddha, meaning that you have buddha nature in your system already. This is very helpful for meditators, making it easy to introduce this nature as a focus of meditation.[279]

As Asaṅga points out in commenting on his *Sublime Mindstream*, even ordinary folk like us have positive qualities associated with a wisdom inseparable from our afflictions.[280] Most everyone needs training before this emerges. Hence the developmental path. Slow is often faster.

What is Dzogchen's relationship to prior forms of Mahāyāna and Tantra in Tibet? Scholars of early Tibetan religious history generally agree that Dzogchen emerged as a distinct form of practice in about the tenth century.[281] The practices Jigme Lingpa describes in the first three of the seven trainings follow what is now a traditional trajectory for Dzogchen practitioners, reflecting on one's situation as a human being with its opportunities and brevity, its uncertainties and pain, while also developing a heart-felt relationship with a personal teacher in order to recognize the mind-nature you have always had.

A work attributed to Padmasambhava divides tantric practice into three phases: creation, completion, and great completion, or Dzogchen.[282] Dzogchen was on the one hand a further phase of the completion phase of deity yoga, and also a potently simple way of being present. It is easy to see how in the course of practice sheer presence would emerge as a kind of culmination of guru yoga, and, in retrospect, understood to have been present all along. All deity yoga is also guru yoga.

Sam Van Schaik observes that in the ninth-century text *Questions and Answers of Vajrasattva*, the correct way of practicing deity yoga was described thus:

> In the ultimate deity yoga no subject or object is perceived. Because there are no difficulties or effort, this is the highest deity yoga.[283]

Adzom Paylo Rinpoche's *Luminous Heart Essence* sādhanas on several occasions describe the real or authentic teacher (*don gyi bla ma*) as reality itself. With this in mind, we again appreciate Jigme Lingpa's way of topping off his story-meditations with practices redolent with Dzogchen's direct encounter with intimate reality.

The loving responsiveness that Dzogchen says is already part of the threefold nature of our ground—empty essence, luminous nature, and all-suffusing love—manifests in the karmic narrative through intentionally cultivating love and compassion. There is a subtle but day-and-night difference between feeling that you are allowing something intrinsic to manifest and feeling that you are starting from ground zero to build up a compassionate heart. Though often presented as dialogically antithetical, in practice these perspectives intertwine and support each other. Likewise, the nine vehicles complement one another.

NINE WAYS OF REFUGE: PATH AS HOLOGRAM

The wisdom narrative grows increasingly prominent over the course of Nyingma's nine pathways. The pivots Longchenpa makes toward Dzogchen when he presents the bodhisattva path and Middle Way in his philosophical writings provide background for Jigme Lingpa's path perspective. We saw that Jigme Lingpa, following the story-meditations, provides distilled tantric creation and completion practices wherein one merges with Guru Rinpoche and then dissolves into space, followed by a segue into Dzogchen territory through Jigme Lingpa's pith instructions. In this way, each of the story-meditations and its segue takes one through the entire nine-vehicle path, moving from thought to increasingly subtle and wholistic experiences of wisdom.

This inclusivity is a hallmark of Dzogchen's open state, its view of reality, and the practices that bring one there. All are omnidirectional (*phyogs ris med pa*)—that is, they do not lean in any one direction to the exclusion of any other directions This is the very picture of completeness. The term may also be rendered as "not biased," describing the open-minded and nonsectarian movement in Tibet, of which Jigme Lingpa is an important forebear.[284]

Jigme Lingpa's opening homage to Samantabhadra in *Stairway to Liberation* turns on the importance of this inclusivity:

> The consummation of the teachings is
> when the entire range of instructions, the doctrines of sūtra
>   and tantra,
> are understood in a single sitting;
> uniting with the wisdom mind of the dharmakaya, free of any
>   effort or strain,
> is the unique richness of Dzogchen, the Great Completeness.[285]

Jigme Lingpa sees the entire range of instructions, all nine pathways from sūtra to Dzogchen, as an inclusive whole. A ladder's lower steps don't vanish as one ascends, but continue to support the climb. The lower vehicles do not evaporate as you move to the higher ones. For Jigme Lingpa a stairway or ladder is an expression of everything being there. This is also how he understands the practice of refuge.

In a mere four lines, among the most admired of his entire corpus, Jigme Lingpa offers a refuge that encompasses all phases of the path. By taking refuge in all nine vehicles, it signals Dzogchen's relationship to each of them. Although the nine vehicles are generally presented as a hierarchy, with the practitioner moving up from one to the other, from within the maṇḍala of practice itself the image is more of a hologram, with Dzogchen at the center, surrounded by the other eight vehicles, each a portal to Dzogchen, while Dzogchen in turn perfumes all of them with its perspective. They are all part of it, just as the whole mountain is a passage to its peak.

Longchen Rabjam, in the penultimate twelfth chapter of his *Precious Dharmadhātu Treasury*, tells us that at the heart of its key instructions are three main points: essence, nature, and heartfelt responsiveness.[286] These same three are the heart of Jigme Lingpa's famous verse of refuge:[287]

> In Three Real Jewels, three root Bliss-Filled Ones
> Channels, winds, bright orbs—this bodhi-mind

Essence, nature, moving love maṇḍala
Until full bodhi, I seek refuge.[288]

Refuge means security, safety, and help when we need it. In everyday life we constantly look for something larger and more powerful than ourselves to shield us from what we fear. We find one kind of refuge in family, politics, and fame. All are temporary. Buddhists train to find refuge in what is stable.

The Three Jewels are Buddha, Dharma, and Saṅgha, refuge of those practicing in the first three vehicles. In the outer tantras, Buddhists take refuge in the Guru, Deva, and Ḍākinī, who are, respectively, the sources for blessings, power, and activities. Practitioners of the inner tantras take refuge in the potential of the body's own channels, energies, and bright orbs, elements so subtle we would not notice them except through practice. Dzogchen practitioners take refuge in all the above and also in mind-nature—the indestructible and unimaginably intimate nature that is always with us. That is, one takes refuge in one's own sheer knowing presence.[289]

These four refuges are sequential and cumulative. The difference between the first and the last is like the difference between looking at an exquisite sunset and feeling the colors light up inside you.

Dzogchen understands sheer knowing, *rig pa*, to have three aspects: empty essence, luminous nature, and ubiquitously responding compassion.[290] One important source for this triadic reality is *All-Creating Majesty:*[291]

My nature, spontaneously there, without being sought,
is the three buddha dimensions, heart of all the majestic ones.
My uncontrived nature is the sheer buddha dimension.
My uncontrived essence, the full, richly endowed joyful
  dimension.
My manifestly present responsive compassion, the emanation
  dimension.
I show that these three do not come about through being sought.
I, all-creating majesty, contain the three buddha dimensions.

> The nature of each and all phenomena, however they appear,
> are the uncontrived triad: nature, essence, and responsiveness.
> I show these three dimensions to be my suchness.[292]

The trifold essence, luminosity, and flowing compassion ripens into the buddha dimensions of sheer form, bright form, and formed form, respectively.

Moving love, mind-nature's intrinsic compassionate responsiveness, emanates from the union of empty essence and luminous nature. This is described in the third line of the refuge verse, where we find a standard Tibetan word for compassion (*thugs rje, karunā*). Here however it means a spontaneous state of responsiveness that is the natural activity of the emanation-dimension buddhas. Buddhas don't ask what can I do to help, their compassion, free of concepts and dualism, simply knows where it is needed and flows there.

Moreover, as Longchenpa's *Precious Dharmadhātu Treasury* and Adzom Paylo Rinpoche's *Luminous Heart Essence* cycle makes clear,[293] these three—emptiness, luminous nature, and moving love—and the three buddha dimensions into which they ripen, are the real source and nature of everything that exists.

The Humanness of Awakening

In this way, Jigme Lingpa's refuge verse teaches us the fundamental DNA of a practitioner's outer, inner, and secret knowing. Its poetry and melody offer a deep seat in the intimate expanse of one's own nature.

The verse offers refuge for every level of practitioner. Whatever our everyday experience, or our path status, we are integrated with awakening. More and more, our human and buddha eyes see themselves mirrored in each other until they can melt into one unbounded seeing. They have been in each other all along.

Expansiveness, the softening of inside-outside boundaries—mystics often talk like this, but this is not talk for mystics only. The actual content, impact, and images vary widely, but many different types of people feel on occasion that very personal doors of perception have opened to a knowing they never knew before. Intuition, for example, is a knowing that seems to arise without evident cause. In this way, it bears analogy to Dzogchen's perspective.[294]

Drawing from writings and live interviews about the "unexpected emergence of an idea," Claire Petitmengin discovered that the experience of intuition is strikingly similar for artists, scientists, and others, even when the content of their intuition is very different. Her pioneering study focused on the structure of intuition, the *how* of intuition's arising. She found a number of cases in which a person's sense of agency is altered—the feeling of being a distinct "I" becomes "lighter" and even disappears just prior to the arising of intuition. "An idea is coming to me," or "is given to me," they say, not "I have an idea." For us, this is reminiscent of the sensibility associated with the story-meditations, when one's body becomes light in both senses before it dissolves.

Just prior to the arising of intuition, numerous persons interviewed also reported they felt a greater permeability between themselves and the outer world. "In such moments, there are no longer any barriers between me and things. It is as though I no longer have a skin." The boundary separating self from outside or from other softens. This is a fairly common experience in many types of meditation. There is also a spatial element to the shift that often immediately precedes the arising of intuition, such as that described by Marcel Jousse, who finds that at that moment his body is a "flexible and living mirror" that feels the movements of nature within itself:

> I can sense very well inside myself, in my trunk, the river flowing, or the poplar standing up straight towards the sky . . . I feel the river flowing in me. I feel the poplar standing up straight.

More recently, the Zen teacher Henry Shukman recalled an experience that surprised him on a beach in Argentina when he was nineteen years old, before he'd even heard of Zen or meditation. He was so young, and so astonished, that he could only refer to himself in his journal in the third person:

> A young man, a beach, a boat on the water. . . He could have been any young man in any century, gazing over any water.
>
> And the water was fascinating, blindingly white yet completely dark. Scales of brilliance slid over darkness, so it alternated between thick matt black and blinding light. . . What was he actually seeing?
>
> As he pondered this question, suddenly the sight was no longer in front of him. It was inside him. Or he was inside it, as if he'd stepped into the scene and become part of it. He could no longer tell inside from outside . . . He was made of one and the same fabric as the whole universe. It wasn't enough to say he belonged in it. It was him. He was it.[295]

Experience suggests that the things mystics and practitioners spend their lives cultivating are in a meaningful way natural to the human organism. All the more reason not to exoticize buddhas as unreal, as too other to hang out with or emulate. This is an important way of appreciating the human potential that we are talking about here. At the same time, unique structures and intertwined practices allow these fleeting portals of experience to be vastly furthered.

Longchenpa has his own way of rendering awakening as separated from present experience by the merest sliver. That sliver of a difference lies with how we regard our own buddha nature. If we don't recognize it right there in our own most fundamental nature, our core sanctum (sbubs), ordinary mind takes over. If we recognize it right there, just as it is, we are awakened. That's the only difference! In the first case our nature is obscured by our own ordinary experience. In the second, we are buddhas. In principle, though, we are neither. It's a vivid reminder that the human and buddha in us do not cancel each other out. In fact, part of our path is to move back and forth between relatively more or less degrees of clarity and obscuration regarding our nature. Both are the nature of the dharmadhātu. In that sense, they don't occupy different universes. Buddha was, among other things, also a human being. This helps clarify how we can already in a meaningful sense be buddhas, even if we don't yet look the part. I wish I'd read this in high school.

How do you recognize you are empty in essence? From my teachers, from the pith practices, from many different experiences in and out of practice, it grows clear that a profound and easy way to start is with simple relaxation. Ease eases. Especially it unwinds my inborn urge to clutch onto the innumerable *whats* that I desire, and therefore to clutch onto the me that desires them. Ease easily softens this constricting urgency. Ease is a friend of expansiveness.

In a more relaxed state, my obsessions also relax. Seeing the extent to which I freshly grow aware of the many gestures by which I consistently get in my own way is a bit embarrassing and also a great relief. These "supports" grow more transparent with ease and training. If seeing through these is possible, if spaciousness can open at all, then it must be possible actually to live in the spaciousness that emerges right there inside the problem itself.

The renowned Geshe Wangyal, with whom I spent as much time as I could during the last twelve years of his life, called bodhisattvas "true cosmopolitans." Cosmopolitans know that their way is not the only way, that today's self is just that, not an eternal fixation. Eschewing narrow-minded habits, their hearts and interests include everyone. Friendship with oneself and others can begin.

Refuge, like all Tibetan ritual enactments, includes cognitive, imaginal, somatic, sonic, devotional, and other affective states that open toward a kindly and inclusive horizon. Aspiring to mountain peaks with valley views, we gaze at the peak from below even as we already sense how this valley looks from on high. This is essentially what occurs in Jigme Lingpa's story-meditations when, as the intrepid traveler, we newly recognize a landscape that includes both death and awakening. Finally, we see that we are neither small nor alone. This changes everything, and the path is joined.

The pith practices invite an awareness that encompasses the entire universe in our experience. At such moments, this knowing indeed feels like the ground of everything we know, as if the true nature of everything we experience is wisdom "indescribable, inconceivable, and inexpressible," an "unconfused and authentic state of mind."[296] There is no looking, just then, at some object out there. Full awakening may not be at hand, but the fusion of our human state with a more expansive one feels more than possible.

Gazing at the clear night sky offers an immediate passage to expansiveness. Feeling part of this immensity, our challenges no longer consume us quite as before; they are ripples on our ocean. Jigme Lingpa, addressing Samantabhadra at the opening of his *Stairway to Liberation*, writes:

> The display of your manifest ground is like the moon's reflection in water . . .

Even while appearing in the water with stunning clarity, there is no moon in the water. This is how it is with everything! Sometimes the mind cracks open a bit and this is not just an idea, but a real seeing, in light of which we can, just possibly, simply relax and enjoy the dance. Knowing reality means being at ease.[297] Ease means an openness to others' pain. It is precisely to release these compassionate energies that Jigme Lingpa writes:

> Like moons in water, sights deceive us
> We ever roam bound in cyclic chains
> So all may rest in their clear-mind sphere,
> I awaken through four boundless states.[298]

There is only one moon, but many ways of living in moonlight. We're not asked to look away from it, only to rest in the actual water in which it appears, our own clear mind sphere, the dharmadhātu. Real rest lets go of the heavy armor of false confidence, the effort of pretending. Pretending is animated by a wish to connect, but we end up feeling more alone.

My failure to recognize how things are—as attention-grabbing as they are illusory—obscures the innate bodhicitta that is part of my original nature. To the extent that I can recognize habitual patterns and whizzing distractions as "cyclic chains," compassion can flow. I also freshly appreciate Śāntideva's famous dedication:

> For as long as space abides, as long as the world remains,
> just so long may I be here, resolving all beings' pain.[299]

The dharmadhātu is a space that endures and, says Longchenpa, is an essential realm, the source and arena of everything.[300] This same real and empty arena is also the source (though never the cause) of our ordinary, befuddled sensibilities. Following these back to their source takes us to nothing less than the sheer buddha form, the dharmakāya itself.[301] Longchenpa wants us to know right off that this is what bodhisattvas have to work with.

The things that grate when I am hungry or tired are often of no consequence when I'm rested and on track. My annoyance depends less on external causes than on my own state. And what exactly in me does that depend on? Habits and history have their influence, but the situation is not static or given. I am a sea of shifting currents. There is movement, there is stillness. Joy and sorrow come and go. Knowing is ongoing. And there is a brightness to knowing, like the clear light inside a mirror. The space of my mind is not preconfigured. It is open, empty in essence. Even my body softens—inside/outside is no longer the core structure of my experience, in that objects don't so much arrive from elsewhere as open right inside my senses. Generosity and human connection flow more naturally than before.

Reading and reflecting on Longchenpa's words helps me appreciate that my responses in practice are not random, but a function of the kind of organism I am and all human beings are. His words shed light on my experience, my experience sheds light on his words. Sometimes, uncomfortable in the not-knowing that practice requires, I naively demand certainty: "Is this experience correct? Did I do it right?

What's supposed to happen?" What's supposed to happen is that we look into what does happen. That's the practice.

For example, descriptions of the dharmadhātu, especially Long-chenpa's emphasis that it encompasses everything, match a nascent sense of barriers melting, of a horizon emerging that is at once vast and intimate. Just as seeing even a small piece of sky reveals a slice of infinity, even a swift taste of our deeper nature reveals how reliably we are held in ways impossible to describe and easy to sense, wholly insubstantial, utterly unassailable, and compelling enough to bring respite from my tiresome self-spiraling. It does feel like refuge.

This relaxation is an easing into clarity. Following your breath is an excellent path to such ease. Opening to loving kindness is another. Jigme Lingpa's first pith practice is explicitly an easing into a state of freedom, mind not hooked by anything.

It is no small thing to have a life with space in it for reflection. In my case, finding a life-long Dharma partner as well as secure and satisfying work were huge supports. But that alone would not have been enough. I also needed close connection with wisely compassionate teachers whose seeing didn't stop where mine did, and who generously shared, in words and gestures, their wisdom and skillful means.

Gradually, really slowly in fact, my mind began to relax. By the time I encountered buddha-nature teaching in Dzogchen, I was more open and, most especially, the teaching now came from living human beings who knew what these words meant in experience, and I could talk to them about this again and again. They saw my real nature just as clearly as they saw my inner warts. Being seen so wholistically is healing. Geshe Wangyal scolded me a lot, told me to leave, and never let me down. Years later, as I was leaving to continue graduate school, he mildly observed to another student, in my presence, "From the beginning, I always liked her."

Longchenpa's fourth training emphasizes the significance of a living teacher, or teachers. That is my experience and Buddhism's lineage legacy.

As the example of many accomplished practitioners shows, practice taps into something that, without eliding differences, connects us across racial, religious, and ethnic boundaries. We are all the same in being different.

Reminders of this deeper sameness powers the resolve to be kind and to be hopeful, bringing us strength for the work that serves our human lives—reaching for justice, disbanding habits that work against us, rejecting habits of manufacturing and governance that undermine our well-being and our environment. In the flux and fade of our own experience we realize that sometimes impermanence is on our side—our troubles too can change.

Within this larger perspective, as Longchenpa and Dzogchen traditions understand it, primordial wisdom is the way things are. This is a truth born of first-person experience, because everything we see is undeniably part of our knowing. The ultimate support of even ignorant knowing is wisdom, just like the ultimate support for shade is light. Our ultimate face is a freedom from twoness, a fundamental unity of experience unbroken into subject and object.[302] We know a state free of duality only when our knowing is freed of duality. This can only be understood by wisdom in the same way that English can only be understood by English speakers. Great sculptors are said to see their creation already there in the stone, only needing to remove what gets in the way of other people seeing it. This is how Longchenpa also looks at ordinary beings and their buddha nature. In each other all along.

In many ways, Buddhism teaches what life teaches. Life teaches that it pays to pay attention, that kindness heals, and that there is more to things than meets the eye. The practices we've described, and the inner practices of Dzogchen as well, are ways to open our eyes, to forget what we thought we knew, and to see anew what we didn't know is already part of our knowing.

Primordial wisdom is a gift that keeps on giving. It is not caused or causable. Does this make it seem like the wisdom and karmic narratives are finally on a collision course? They are not. We are only now finally understanding the horizon shift toward which we are headed:

How marvelous! How truly marvelous and superb!
The secret of all the perfect buddhas
is that all things are born within what is unborn,
yet in the very act of their birth, there is no birth . . .[303]

Contradictories exclude each other. But contradiction is not the last word. Logic teaches that hot and cold, black and white, are such that when you have one, you don't have the other. But life teaches that this is not entirely true. Seeing for yourself, for example, that motion and stillness are creative partners animating your own mind, may open a broader horizon that can feel like home.

All these strengthen attention. Attention is the start of love. Each training moves us toward bodhicitta, ultimate love. The first three trainings do this with smashing directness: to recognize our mortality, how we spend our short lives creating more suffering rather than less, all open the heart to want to address pain wherever we can. In this unstable world in which everything perishes, what can be more meaningful than this?

The middle trainings gather resources for this purpose, learning how to learn, to commit to our training, and finally, in the seventh training, to see directly for ourselves what the pith practices also reveal, that our own minds and bodies have the wherewithal for greater compassionate and wisdom. Bodhicitta is the throughline.

As we move more deeply in the wisdom narrative, we are inspired less by a wish to escape than by a sense of wonder, falling in love with the newfound ease and trust we are discovering. Why not continue?

CONTEMPLATIVE INTERLUDE:

FOURTH PITH PRACTICE

Examine the doer of movement and stillness.[304]

འགྲོ་གནས་ཀྱི་མཁན་པོ་ལ་བརྟག་གོ །

Mani stone at nuns' practice grounds,
Adzom Gar, Sichuan

7. Open Secret, Open Mandala

Dzogchen's secret is naked knowing. It's an open secret because nothing impedes it and knowing is always at hand. When I examine the originator or "doer" in Jigme Lingpa's fourth pith practice, I seem to find something unstoppable in the infinite, unbounded middle of my chest. When Rumi says, "You have a fresh spring inside your chest," perhaps this is what he is talking about. This fresh constancy is the truest and most beloved lover of all time. I toggle between a sense that I'm looking *at* this, and that what occurs is way too intimate for the preposition *at*. My usual "I" is on the verge of dissolving and won't be missed because something else is expanding.

These are just examples of the kinds of openings that can occur in practice. They are just scenery along the way; we are not really looking for this kind of thing, we are looking for ongoing realization. But we can appreciate when they occur that some movement is occurring.

This is not to say that anyone else should or will experience this way. These tastes are only to suggest how rich these practices can be, and as harbingers of what more might come. Practices impact practitioners differently; that's part of why we need a teacher who can respond to our own specific situation. The right words at the right time can be profoundly transformative.

Find a teacher or teachers; talk to them, let your experiences go, leave aside attachment to them while you also take inspiration that they are a beacon onward.

In this light, Jigme Lingpa's observation that mind watching your own mind is not sheer awareness of your deepest nature becomes a tremendous support for not taking ordinary, dualistic observation at face value.

The intimacy of being present to your own knowing can be

intoxicating, like finally falling in love after reading about love for years. But how does this happen? Here again, I draw delight and comfort from Rumi, whose Sufi wisdom often seems to mirror Dzogchen, as when says:

> The minute I heard my first love story,
> I started looking for you, not knowing
> how blind that was.
> Lovers don't finally meet somewhere.
> They are in each other all along.[305]

The mirroring intimacy with which wisdom knows itself, Longchenpa tells us, *is* the great completeness.[306] Sheer self-recognition (*rang rig*) is perfect buddhahood.[307]

Such perspectives might feel alien, as they certainly did to me. Today, Nāgārjuna's famous words from his *In Praise of Dharmadhātu* come to mind; Longchenpa cites them in connection with the bodhisattva approach:

> Not having heard how they are constituted, and
> owing to the flaw of belittling themselves,
> those who are faint-hearted
> might not give rise to awakened mind.[308]

When we don't know what we're made of or how much we've simply made up, these grand vistas do seem strange. Nāgārjuna gets that. And so a little encouragement is in order: Don't be fainthearted! Don't be proud! Just have a good look and get to know your knowing.

When we don't see any real alternative to the status quo, we are not motivated. This is why Buddhist traditions, and perhaps especially in Tibet, emphasize anchoring your practice in deep appreciation for the potential and opportunities you already have. This is also why we all must work for a world where such opportunities are increasingly available for everyone.

Our inborn nature is an inalienable aspect of the bodhisattva path, the powerful impetus behind the seven trainings and all Mahāyāna practice, and utterly central in Dzogchen. All teachers and students of the Great Way are bound by bodhicitta and its *samaya*, the commitments to create and maintain a safe holding for practice and practitioners.[309] Seeing your own purity means staying awake to the essence, nature, and responsive quality in every being, shorn of image and story. This means recognizing that even the most violent murderer has, but lacks access to, this nature.

The ability to see purity requires trust in inner knowing. It helps if we have built up trust in other areas of life as well. Do you trust your friends? Your family? Your coworkers? Anyone? There is wisdom in skepticism, but if it erodes our capacity to trust, it limits our capacity to grow whole.

> If your mind is pure, everyone is a buddha.
> If your mind is impure, everyone is ordinary.[310]

Longchenpa, with the weight of the entire Indian and Tibetan Buddhist traditions behind him, down to present-day teachers in those lineages, is giving full permission to feel that yes, I can do this. I have seen some rays from the sun of full awakening.

Ordinary mind is erroneous due to habit patterns that result from ignorance, habits that are literally a failure of awareness.[311] Until we recognize—any moment now—that the ultimate, the dharmadhātu, that wisdom-flooded sheer arena, is fulsomely inclusive. It is part of everything, the source of everything, and everything participates in it.[312] The ultimate dance floor.

Dualistic seeing cannot know the serene arena of experience, the dharmadhātu, or the wisdom that suffuses it. This is why, again, words cannot express the ultimate:

> Wisdom beyond talk, thought, or story
> Unborn, unceasing, essence of space[313]

The seven trainings prepare us to recognize that everything occurs in that space, which is open and inseparable from our being. Just as all images arise in the clarity of a mirror, just as all waves emerge through and dissolve back into the ocean, so everything you know is part of your knowing. May wisdom know wisdom!

Likewise, every scene in a film is simply colors and shapes on the screen. Everyone knows this. Yet almost no one makes this knowing part of the experience of watching a film. It would ruin the film! That's exactly the point. As practitioners, we are determined to ruin conviction in meaningless activities and to instead maintain awareness of their essence.

Actually, for skilled practitioners, awareness doesn't ruin the film. It enhances playful enjoyment of films and everything else. What it ruins is being helplessly lured into feeling that something is real when it isn't. Letting go that delusion, everything is a delightful play of sound and light in this wondrous world, even more enjoyable than what our ordinary minds experience.

> Mind-nature is the essence of awakened mind.[314]
> Sheer knowing is the expanse of awakened mind.[315]
> Sheer knowing is the space of primordial wisdom.[316]
> Sheer knowing itself is buddhahood.[317]

Primordial wisdom encompasses all the above, and like them, primordial wisdom is free of frills. It has no object. How could it? An object by definition is separate from a subject. Wisdom is the nature of ordinary mind and all it knows. If this is puzzling, enjoy feeling puzzled! Don't always be addicted to knowing, especially ordinary knowing. The seven trainings, the five pith practices, all practice and the whole of living, will be that much more delightful.

Each of Jigme Lingpa's guided story meditations is a chance to flow from karmic to wisdom perspective. Each of the piths offers another set of chances, as do the nonconceptual practices of the seventh training. Through all these, we approach the intimate space of mind-nature, the essence of awakened mind.[318] This nature connects seen and seer. As such, it midwifes increasing freedom from the gravitational pull of sense objects. Ordinary consciousness, by contrast, is not free and gets owned by what it sees, much as mirrors take on the aspect of their objects.[319]

This bears exploration. So, if you like, once again take a moment to gaze out your window and let your gaze fall on something and rest there. A tree, a garden, a building. It doesn't matter, so long as it is comfortably in the frame of your seeing. As you look at it, or perhaps you smell, touch, or taste it, can you separate your sensing from the thing you sense? Can you separate your seeing from the tree that you see? What do you do to try to separate them? What happens when you try? Does the sense of distance shift, remain the same, get stronger?

Maybe you cannot separate them, just as you cannot pull apart the empty sky and the sunlight suffusing it. Words like "different" and "same" fall apart.

When I feel totally puzzled about what "nondualism" or "wholeness" actually feels like, or how it is that wisdom can be called the actual nature of everything, I cannot shake the allure of this remarkable exploration that calls me back again and again to unstoppable curiosity.

All we most fervently seek is already our own. Yet we must look where we are capable of looking. Again, Rumi has words for this:

> If I had known the real way it was,
> I would have stopped all the looking around.
> But that knowing depends
> on the time spent looking![320]

Looking is a delicious state of not-knowing. We *don't know* what we will find. How exciting. We enjoy the freshness. Contemplative practice, like life, thrives as we make friends with all parts of ourselves, the parts we don't know yet.

Our two faces, like the karmic and wisdom narratives, suggest the different inner landscapes where life, study, and practice take place. Each of the seven trainings moves through these radically distinct landscapes, finally transcending the apparently irrevocable boundaries that enclose them. Personal as well as cultural variations on this theme abound.

The sixteenth-century essayist Michel de Montaigne wrote that too much fealty to rational judgment limits our freedom, especially our freedom of inquiry. The European Enlightenment exalted the new freedom from blind obedience to received religiosities and replaced this with obedience to the claims of reason. This became a different, but also limiting, cage. Obedience to norms of addiction and to the binding neatness of nouns can hide flux and an intrinsic spaciousness.

In the sixteenth and seventeenth centuries, the philosophical divide between heart and mind, or emotion and reason, reinforced a landscape of conflicting territories—Descartes' "I think, therefore I am" finds the landscape lit by reason; Pascal's "The heart has its reasons of which reason knows nothing" sees the limitations of that light. But heart and reason remained secret from each other.

In more modern times, internal landscapes of Western individuality were divided into the known and unknowable—the conscious and unconscious—by Sigmund Freud (1856–1939). Freud felt that painful or shameful memories and impulses were likely to be hidden from view. William James (1842–1910) offered a similar narrative when he concluded that we spend nearly one-third of our lives in fringe states and that despite our being unaware of it, this fringe greatly influences our overall feelings and judgments.[321]

Up to a point, Freud and James are saying what Longchenpa and Jigme Lingpa also say—that we do not know ourselves very well. Their concern and ours throughout these pages is our poignant ignorance of our genuine face. Which we cannot see without coming to grips with our other face.

In the radically consummate wholeness of Dzogchen, the awakened state includes everything. This awakened mind, bodhicitta, is the real nature of the practitioner's mind. In Longchenpa's metaphor, recognizing the sun of primordial wisdom lights up the intimate and infinite space of the dharmadhātu, inseparable from wisdom's light.

This convergence of bodhicitta and reality is crucial to Dzogchen and completes the arc of Longchenpa's gnostic turn. This bodhicitta—invincible, irrevocable, requiring no tinkering whatever—is always present. Tinkering obscures it. And the more we look, the more we see how pervasive is our tinkering. The pervasiveness of pretending.

With awakening, as at sunrise, everything in our experience changes color. All Longchenpa's pivots are for this. The five pith practices are all for this. And they don't point only in one direction. Reality is everywhere. It just keeps showing up.

CONTEMPLATIVE INTERLUDE:

FIFTH PITH PRACTICE

Cut the threads that weave thought.
Let your mindfulness and awareness
ease into unbridled openness.[322]

རྟོག་པའི་སྤྲུན་ཐག་བཅད་ནས་དྲན་ཤེས་ཁ་ཡན་དུ་གློད་པར་བྱའོ།

Acknowledgments

B UDDHISM'S GUIDING PRINCIPLES of dependent arising, whole-ness, and great-heartedness mean that the threads of my thanks extend far and wide. First, bows to the tradition itself, and to all the great beings who over the past fifty years and counting have helped me appreciate it.

I had the fortune to meet, hang out with, and, above all, study deeply with some of the premier Tibetan scholars and practitioners of their generation, especially Geluk Geshes, starting with Gyume Khensur Ngawang Lekden (1900–1972), who taught at the University of Wisconsin, Madison, when I was just beginning to study Buddhism in 1970; Geshe Rabten and Geshe Ngawang Dargye, whom I soon thereafter met in Dharamsala; at the University of Virginia, Lati Rinpoche and Denma Locho Rinpoche; and in both India and Virginia, first and last, the great Loseling Khensur Yeshe Thupten. Jeffrey Hopkins, the founding director of the still-thriving Buddhist Studies Program at the University of Virginia, invited several of these teachers to work with us individually, and himself read Tibetan texts closely with us for years, making everything else possible. He read with all the graduate students individually on a weekly basis on our individual topics, reading widely around each topic to better inform our meetings. Geshe Wangyal, my touchstone throughout, illuminated all these matters in his own unique ways.

During these same years, I also encountered Dzogchen masters who introduced me to Longchen Nyingthig practices, especially Khetsun Sangpo Rinpoche, who completed his training in Tibet before taking exile in India and Nepal, and with whom I met whenever possible between 1974 until his passing in 2009; Lama Gonpo Tseten of Amdo, who spent several years teaching in California in the 1980s; and Chogyal Namkhai Norbu Rinpoche, whom I also met in the mid-1980s and took as many retreats with as I could for many years. All these great beings have now passed.

Since 1996 the Dzogchen master Adzom Paylo Rinpoche, who gave me my Dharma name at our first meeting and in 2010 honored me with the title Dorje Lopon, has been central to my learning in Dzogchen, as has been Khetsun Rinpoche's outstanding Dzogchen student and scholar, Lama Tenzin Samphel, whose teachings I have regularly orally translated, as I and the Dawn Mountain community have for a dozen years been regularly studying Dzogchen literature with him, especially the works of Longchenpa. Conversations with colleagues in David Germano's Dzogchen initiative, a collegial cohort of Dzogchen scholars and practitioners, provided much background support, and especially Gyurme Lodro Gyatso (Khenpo Yeshi), whom I first met in that context and whose reflections on the pith practices discussed here were vibrantly illuminating.

I also benefited greatly from the opportunity to be a fellow at Rice University's Humanities Research Center, where I developed the manuscript, discussed portions of it with my co-fellows from across the humanities, and presented segments of this work at two Gnosticism, Esotericism, and Mysticism (GEM) seminars to my outstanding colleagues and the graduate student community at Rice's Department of Religion. And deep thanks to Dr. Phyllis McBride, Director of Rice's Office of Proposal Development, for her skillful perspectives and encouragement.

Thanks as well to David Kittelstrom at Wisdom, who gave encouragement and helpful guidelines from the very start, and Mary Petrusewicz, who took over in the completion phase of pulling it all together.

More recently still, Learned Foote, an outstanding PhD candidate at Rice University, read an early version and gave helpful comments. Teaching the seven trainings and pith instructions to practitioners at Vækstcenteret in Denmark, thanks to the invitation of Jes Bertelsen and the help of Martijn van Beek; at Ganden Chokhor Switzerland, thanks to the gracious welcome of Ven. Geshe Lodro Tulku Rinpoche, with the further support of Natascha Keller-Gasserman and

Mary O'Beirne, and at Dawn Mountain, where it initiated our ongoing Dzogchen Cycles Program, gave me the opportunity to think through many practical as well as philosophical matters with many participants, as did preparing for the Wisdom Academy class based on this book. Likewise thanks to numerous Rice undergraduates, especially Tiffany Padilla, for their curiosity and questions when we read Cortland Dahl's *Steps the Great Completeness* in class, itself obviously an important basis for this book. Cort was a most gracious conversation partner for me as well, as was Martijn van Beek. In the last months of finalizing the manuscript I was lucky to have impactful conversations with Gyurme Lodro Gyatso (Khenpo Yeshi). In the rush of final edits, Jann Ronis, the head of BDRC, stepped in with vital bibliographical help, as did Karma Gongde. Thanks to Dzogchen Nyingthig friends who shared their notes from Adzom Rinpoche's oral teachings on the Seven Trainings on Whidbey and in Germany, and also to students who attended my Barre Seven Trainings course at Barre, Massachusetts, for their notes and conversation, especially Moses Mohan, Jungeon You, Cara Snajczuk, Melanie Jane, Isabelle Freda, Nancy Thompson, Joseph Hennessey, and Patricia Crain.

And a nod to other friends with whom I didn't discuss this book but whose brilliant conviviality definitely contributed to the energy of inspiration and finishing it, including scholar friends at Rice and elsewhere—Marcia Brennan, David Germano, Bill Parsons, Niki Clements, Sarah Jacoby, Ann Gleig, Renée Ford, Walter Goodwin, Nathanial Rich, and Steven Tainer—as well as Sharon Jackson and the amazing past and current board members of Dawn Mountain and Dawn Mountain Tibetan Buddhist Temple, and Dr. Mark Yurewicz, who for many years has carefully designed and typeset Dawn Mountain Research Institute's publications of Adzom Rinpoche's treasure-text sādhanas, adroitly assisted by Elizabeth Wallett.

And finally, joy and infinite gratitude for sharing my whole life's Dharma adventure and everything else important to me to Harvey B. Aronson, Lama Namgyal Dorje, who has supported me in every possible way since we met in 1970, and who in the waxing days of this

Sagadawa moon, as I was finalizing this manuscript on deadline, offered unending time and mind to closely read and give crucial suggestions on every last page until it was done. Today.
Sagadawa Full Moon, June 14, 2022.

NOTES

1. *All-Creating Majesty* (*Kun byed rgyal po*), cited by Longchenpa in his *Precious Treasury*, 200.4–6. This translation can be sung to any seven-syllable Tibetan melody. For Barron's excellent translation, see his *Precious Treasury of the Basic Space of Phenomena*, 209.
2. Klein and Wangyal, *Unbounded Wholeness*, 38.
3. Thich Nhat Hanh, "Real Peace," https://justdharma.org/category/thich-nhat-hanh/.
4. https://www.brainyquote.com/quotes/martin_luther_king_jr_115064.
5. Borges, "The God's Script," 172.
6. Genesis 1:1–5.
7. Basham, *The Wonder That Was India*, 247. For the Sanskrit, see https://sanskrit-documents.org/sanskrit/major_works/.
8. Pagels, *Beyond Belief*, 140–41.
9. Adapted from Tulku Thondup, *Masters of Meditation*, 77.
10. Longchen Rabjam, *Commentary on the "Precious Dharmadhātu Treasury,"* 43.8ff. (my translation); see also Barron, *Treasure Trove*, 5.
11. Petitmengin, "Anchoring," 1.
12. Suchness, or nonconceptual realization of reality (*chos nyid*), awareness, or open presence (*rig pa*), and vast expanse (*klong chen*) are key Dzogchen terms that will recur throughout our discussion.
13. These nine pathways are known as "vehicles" (Tib. *theg pa*, Skt. *yāna*) because they engender states of mind that yield a "platform or something that can hold you up." Levinson, "Metaphors of Liberation," 84.
14. Longchen Rabjam, *Sevenfold Mind Training: Practical Instructions on the Foundational Practices* (*Sngon 'gro sems sbyong bdun gyi don khrid*).
15. Here is a chantable English translation that can be sung to any traditional Tibetan melody for a nine-syllable line:

> Respectful homage through my three doors
> to lama, yidam, ḍākinī hosts.
> Seven mind training points make clear how
> to stepwise enter their core meaning.

The Tibetan word *sbyong* means "to train" and also "to purify." Afflictions require purification, your heart essence does not. Likewise, the mistaken mind (*sems*) requires training, but your innate buddha nature does not. Hence the term *sems sbyong* ("mind training") could also be translated as "mind purification."

16. "*Precious Copper Letters*" is a section of the *Fourfold Heart Essence* (*Snying thig ya*

bzhi) and its topics are more fully elaborated in the *Yangthig* teachings, Long-chenpa's commentarial syntheses of Vimalamitra's and Guru Rinpoche's Heart Essence teachings. For an overview of the Fourfold Heart Essence, including the place of "Precious Copper Letters" in it, see Dahl, *Entrance to the Great Perfection,* appendix 3, 218–29.

17. His mention of *rig pa* here, particularly in the context of mentioning "Precious Copper Letters," is a further indication that Longchenpa is discussing Dzogchen.

18. Adzom Rinpoche glosses this as the impermanence of our own bodies, and notes that the secret impermanence includes also your own thoughts, mind, or mood.

19. Commenting on the meaning of "fortitude" *(bsran tshugs)* in *Sevenfold Mind Training* (Tibetan text 329.3 and 329.6), Adzom Rinpoche notes: "For example, even though you are very sick, cultivate patience. Make effort. Never mind how much difficulty there is. You take medicine even though you don't like it because it brings benefit. This practice too will bring great benefit." Lama Tenzin Samphel, acclaimed student of Khetsun Sangpo Rinpoche, says that fortitude means continually doing your best, conjoining effort and courage both. Your concentration helps you avoid distractions. If, for example, you are instructed to stand on one leg for a long time, you would feel pain, you would be shaking, but still you persevere."

20. These reasons can be drawn from this or other texts and teachings. For example, at this point you could reflect that, as stated earlier, practical instructions are needed because without such intervention the sufferings of cyclic existence are endless. Or that because of your definitive decision to depart cyclic existence, or the medicinal quality of the teaching, or that this is a means by which you can benefit others. In other words, you have permission to be creative here.

21. Jigme Lingpa gives slightly different instructions here, advising that this holding begins while the nectar is descending—that is, earlier in the practice. Adzom Rinpoche, who mainly followed Jigme Lingpa's way of practice here, comments: "You do not inhale or exhale while you hold, but you let go when you need to breathe again" (March 2015 and 2017).

22. Khetsun Sangpo Rinpoche, *Strand of Jewels,* 19: "In terms of how these [winds and elements] function [10a4], in summer the fire-wind [is strongest], in fall the wind-wind, in winter the water-wind, and in spring the earth-wind. Therefore [to create balance] one meditates on the opposite, which acts as its antidote. [For example, fire is the antidote to the water-element."]

23. The term *ngöndro (sngon 'gro)* literally means that which goes *('gro)* before *(sngon).* The practices referred to by this rubric are often, and misleadingly, translated as "preliminary practices," making them sound like something one leaves behind; hence, Dzongsar Khyentse Rinpoche uses the phrase "so-called preliminary practices." "Foundational" is meant to indicate the ongoing importance of these practices. A house is as strong as its foundation. Whenever you enter your house, the foundation supports you, and you depend on it to do so.

24. For more details, see "Mark of Vermillion," in Kapstein, *Tibetan Assimilation,* 38.

25. From this encounter developed Adzom Paylo Rinpoche's *Mañjuśrī Dzogchen,* a revealed treasure *(gter)* from Mañjuśrī through the intermediary of Vimala-mitra. Rinpoche has thus far published only two prayers from this, whose

opening lines indicate the transmission on Wutai Shan from Mañjuśri to Vimalamitra to himself.

26. See Ying, "Being and Knowing," especially chaps. 3 and 4.

27. Of special note is the heady progress of 84000, formed in 2010 with the goal of translating all scriptural transmissions (sūtras) attributed to Buddha within one hundred years. They have already accomplished more than 10 percent of their goal. Their constantly updated reading room is accessed at https://read.84000.co/.

28. Jigme Lingpa correlates the traditional stages of the path with the Great Completeness in his *Padma Garbo*, a background text for *Yeshe Lama*, the famous practice text students traditionally engage after completing the foundational practices. Those foundational practices are very much in alignment with the seven trainings. The translations of these works are restricted to practitioners with the requisite background.

29. In Longchen Rabjam, *Commentary on the "Precious Dharmadhātu Treasury,"* 49!7 (my translation; the symbol ! indicates lines counted from the bottom of the page; so 49!7 is seven lines from the bottom of p. 49). See also Barron, *Treasure Trove*, 14.

30. Longchen Rabjam, *Commentary on the "Precious Dharmadhātu Treasury,"* 385.3; Barron, *Treasure Trove*, 437.

31. Nyoshul Khenpo Jamyang Dorje, *A Marvelous Garland of Rare Gems*, 144. *The Profound Heart Essence (Zab mo yang thig)* is contained in the *Fourfold Heart Essence*. See also Dahl, *Entrance to the Great Completeness*, appendix 3.

32. Barks, *Essential Rumi*, 274.

33. For example, wholeness as described in systems theory, or science's use of Francisco Varela's enactive approach, can heal or at least address distorted conviction in separateness. More simply put, asserting the superiority of one's own racial, religious, social, gendered, or geographical location expresses and creates alienation from those whose race, religion, and so forth differ from ours. For Buddhists, these mostly uninvestigated differentials derive from an unacknowledged conviction in an (unproveable, unfindable) objective, solid, monolithic, and inevitable ordering. See also King, *Gods of the Upper Air*.

34. Adapted from Barron, *Treasure Trove*, 100; Longchen Rabjam, *Commentary on the "Precious Dharmadhātu Treasury,"* 115.15.

35. In the tenth century, the great Buddhist master Gampopa, born in central Tibet and versed in Indian, Chinese, as well as Tibetan culture, commented that being a "person" (Tib. *gang zag*, Skt. *purusha* or *pudgala*), a term not limited to humans, is by definition to have capacity or ability. Gyaltsen, *Jewel Ornament of Liberation*, 63. For more on the varying definitions of personhood, see Klein, *Meeting the Great Bliss Queen*, 44–47.

36. Dahl, *Steps to the Great Perfection*, 17.

37. Jigme Lingpa, *Treasury of Precious Qualities: Book Two, Vajrayana and the Great Perfection*, 85.

38. Longchenpa makes this very clear in his discussion of the four boundless states: equanimity, love, compassion, and sympathetic joy. See also Longchen Rabjam, *Now That I Come to Die*, 41–66; and Jigme Lingpa, *Treasury of Precious Qualities*, chap. 8.

39. Barron, *Basic Space*, 32–33; Longchen Rabjam, *Commentary on the "Precious Dharmadhātu Treasury,"* 63!4ff.

40. Adzom Rinpoche taught the seven trainings only twice in the West. This chapter was compiled based on oral translations from Tibetan to English by Erik Drew and Anne Klein, and on Martin Kalff's oral translation from Tibetan and English into German. These translations have been reviewed and amplified through my further discussions with Rinpoche.

41. Gyurme Dorje, *Biography of Adzom Drukpa*, 186.

42. Growing up at Adzom Gar, Adzom Paylo Rinpoche and his sister, Jetsun Khacho Wangmo, herself regarded as an incarnation of Tārā, studied with the yogischolar Karmabenzra and with the immediate incarnation of Adzom Drukpa, Adzom Drukpa Thupten Pema Trinle (1926–2001), who was one of the most influential Dzogchen masters in China in the 1980s and 1990s and to whom other Nyingma masters sent their students for Dzogchen instruction and transmission. Likewise recognized as Adzom Drukpa's incarnation was Chogyal Namkhai Norbu Rinpoche (1938–2018), founder of the internationally known Dzogchen Community, prolific author and one of the great pioneers introducing Dzogchen to the West.

43. Adzom Rinpoche has also noted that in tandem with Longchenpa, Jigme Lingpa guides us through his discussion of the stage-by-stage path (*lam rim*) in *Stairway to Liberation* (*Thar pa'i them sgas*), his commentary on Longchenpa's *Instructions on the Meaning of the Sevenfold Mind Training*. The full title of Jigme Lingpa's commentary on the seven trainings, *Stairway to Liberation: Instructions on the Meaning of the Shared Mahāyāna Foundational Mind Training*, indicates that all the key points of mind training are found here, and that the wisdom to which mind training leads brings forth all good qualities.

44. So far we have not been able to locate this verse.

45. Rinpoche uses the word *yangthig* in speaking here, apparently referring both to the *Khandro Yangthig*, Longchenpa's commentary on Guru Rinpoche's *Heart Essence of the Dakinis*, and to the *Lama Yangthig*, Longchenpa's commentary on Vimalamitra's *Heart Essence*. Possibly however, he intends mainly to point to the latter. See Dahl, *Entrance to the Great Perfection*, appendix 3.

46. See Klein, *Knowing, Naming, and Negation*, 186–89.

47. Rinpoche first sang this song spontaneously at this point in the teaching on Whidbey Island, December 2007:

ཀློང་ཆེན་ཆོས་སྐུའི་དགོངས་དོན་བརྙེས༔ རབ་འབྱམས་ཤེས་བྱའི་མཁའ་ལ་བརྡལ༔

མ་དོར་ཐེག་རྩེ་སྐྱོན་མཛད་པའི༔ དྲི་མེད༔ དྲི་མེད་འོད་ཟེར་གྱས་ཕྱུག་འཚལ༔

ཀློང་ཆེན་འོད་གསལ་འཇའ་ལུས་སྐུ༔ འཕོ་བར་མེད་པའི་རོ་རོར་བཞུགས༔

རྟག་ཁྱབ་ལྷུན་གྲུབ་སར་རྟོགས་ནས་༔ འགྲོ་དོན་ནམ་མཁའ་མཉམ་པར་སྦོག༔

བདག་ནི་རྗེ་བཙུན་ལ་ཧཱུ་མི་དང་༔ ནས་ཡང་འབྲལ་བར་མེད་པ་ཡིས༔ ཆོས་ཀྱི་བདུད་ཉྱིད་རོ་སྲོང་ནས༔

ཆོས་རྣམ་དུ་གཞིན་དུ་སངས་རྒྱས་ཕོག་༔ ཅེས་འགྱུར་མེད་ཐུབ་བསྟན་རྒྱ་མཚོས་འཕལ་དུ་སྤྲས་པ་དགོ།

48. Longchenpa is known as Longchen Rabjam and also as Drime Ozer. The first part of this song is woven around these names. "Vase Expanse" in the first and fifth lines is Longchen (*klong* = expanse; *chen* = vast). In the next line "Great Array" translates Rabjam (*rab 'byams*), the second part of Longchenpa's best-

known name. On the fourth line "Stainless Light" renders Drime Ozal (Dri med 'od gsal), another important name for Longchen Rabjam.

49. In private undated conversation, Adzom Rinpoche added, "We need to identify the essence (*ngo bo*) of meditative stabilization, because its essence includes all other methods."

50. Rinpoche added, "See also the two side channels: the red *Roma* and white *Gyangma*, right and left for men, and (sometimes, but not in this case) reversed for women" (March 15, 2017, Chengdu). Jigme Lingpa's text does not mention the side channels.

51. Jigme Lingpa, *Stairway to Liberation*, just says "red *ah*." See Dahl, *Steps to the Great Perfection*, 95.

52. This rotation from front to back was described to me by a monastic of Adzom Gar as unique to the Adzom lineage of channel-wind practices.

53. Adzom Paylo Rinpoche, March 2015 and March 2017.

54. Jigme Lingpa's instructions are to pull in and up once your channels are full of nectar (perhaps even during descent, though Adzom Rinpoche did not fully support this), whereas Longchenpa suggests this pulling up and in only while focused on the white *ah*. In our conversation, Adzom Rinpoche went with Jigme Lingpa overall here.

55. This paragraph added by the translator.

56. Oral instructions on the channel-wind practices are from Adzom Rinpoche, March, 2015, as he generously responded to my questions to considerably amplify what Longchenpa and Jigme Lingpa say in their texts. Different lineages likely offer different nuances on these practices. Check with your own teacher to clarify instructions in your own context and, again, do not undertake these unless you are under the guidance of an experienced practitioner.

57. Adzom Rinpoche, continuing oral commentary of March 2015.

58. Jigme Lingpa, *Wisdom Chats*, nos. 65 and 66, 773.4ff. (Anne Klein, unpublished translation).

59. Tulku Thondup, *Masters of Meditation*, 118.

60. Goodman and Davidson, *Tibetan Buddhism*, 133.

61. Different lists of Longchenpa's incarnations are found in Goodman and Davidson, *Tibetan Buddhism*, 133.

62. Translated and discussed by Janet Gyatso in *Apparitions of Self*.

63. Dahl, *Steps to the Great Perfection*, 5.

64. Dahl, *Steps to the Great Perfection*, 16. Tibetan text of homage in Jigme Lingpa, *Stairway to Liberation*, 141.3.

65. Dahl, *Steps to the Great Perfection*, 29; Jigme Lingpa, *Stairway to Liberation*, 144.3.

66. For a comprehensive look at mind training in Tibet, don't miss Thupten Jinpa, *Essential Mind Training* and *Mind Training: The Great Collection*.

67. Dahl, *Steps to the Great Perfection*, 25.

68. Adapted from Dahl, *Steps to the Great Perfection*, 31.

69. Jigme Lingpa, *Stairway to Liberation*, 147.6–148.1 (my translation); see also Dahl, *Steps to the Great Perfection*, 31.

70. For more on the importance of pith-practice instructions, *man ngag*, often translated as "quintessential instructions" in the oral traditions of Tibet, see Klein, *Path to the Middle*, introduction.

71. Longchenpa uses *kha yan* ("unbridled openness") twice in his *Commentary on the "Precious Dharmadhātu Treasury,"* and he uses *glod* ("ease") a dozen times.
72. Longchen Rabjam, *Precious Treasury*, 71.12 ff. See also Barron, *Treasure Trove*, 42.
73. This is a central principle. In a mahāmudrā context, Ju Mipham extols the power of engaging the triad of stillness, movement, and awareness (*gnas, brgyud, rig gsum*) of mind. Oral teachings by Lama Tenzin Samphel at Dawn Mountain Center for Tibetan Buddhism, 2020–23, provide an excellent background for exploring this triad. Recordings available by contacting info@dawnmountain.org.
74. Barron, *Precious Treasury of Philosophical Systems*, 117 (*Grub mtha'*, 807.4).
75. These meditations are replete with what Antonio Damasio calls the "somatic markers" of religious experience. Damasio, "Somatic Marker Hypothesis," 51.
76. Becker, *Denial of Death*.
77. For the psychological benefits of reckoning with impermanence and death, see Yalom, *Existential Psychotherapy*, especially chapter 2.
78. Bateson, *Steps*, 309–37.
79. An observation derived from an inspiring moment in a story by Michael Lewis, "How I Got into College," aired September 6, 2013, https://www.thisamericanlife.org/504/how-i-got-into-college (accessed June 28, 2022).
80. Ghent, "Masochism," 109.
81. Ghent, "Masochism," 214.
82. Ghent, "Masochism," 221.
83. Stern, *Interpersonal World of the Infant*, 54. Daniel Stern discusses what he calls "vitality affects," which he describes as "an extension of holistic thinking." See also Stern, *Forms of Vitality*, 10.
84. These insights are also found in the writings of A. H. Almaas, the renowned innovator of the Diamond Approach and the oral teachings related to them, for example by senior teachers and Diamond Approach synod members Deborah Ussery and Morton Letofsky.
85. Adapted from Dahl, *Steps to the Great Perfection*, 31.
86. This does happen. See the mountain climber and videographer Jimmy Chin's astounding true story in the remarkable film *Meru*. He was swept away in an enormous class-3 avalanche in the Tetons, the kind that carries off buses and houses. He tumbled down an entire mountainside, 2,000 feet, thinking, "I've always wondered how I would die," until the fall finally slows and he is expelled from the toe of the avalanche to sit on the snow at the mountain base, completely unharmed. Numerous clips of the scene are available online, best seen, though, as part of the whole film, a galvanizing tale of holding on and letting go. See *Meru: Believe in the Impossible*, a film by Jimmy Chin and Elizabeth Chai Vasarhelyi, Music Box Films, 2015 (www.merufilm.com). Among the clips is this description of his experience: "Jimmy Chin: Trapped in an Avalanche," https://www.youtube.com/watch?v=OF696aPoSUI.
87. Here too Jigme Lingpa can be seen to be drawing from Longchenpa's *Precious Treasury of Philosophical Systems*. "The initial step of meditating on emptiness is the dharmakāya principle. Meditating on the form of deity in that context is the sambhogakāya principle. Ensuring benefit for beings by visualizing light rays shining forth and being reabsorbed is the nirmāṇakāya principle." See also Barron, *Precious Treasury of Philosophical Systems*, 253 (*Grub mtha'*, 1036).

88. The difference between these two types of knowing is akin to memorable moments of silence in the *Vimalakīrti Sūtra*. When Śāriputra is unable to answer a question, he is silent. When Vimalakīrti declines to speak, he leaves his thousands of guests in a profound silence that yields wisdom. Śāriputra's silence results from not knowing. Vimalakīrti's silence is a strategically chosen moment for leaving speech aside to communicate a state beyond ordinary talk, thought, or story. Mañjuśrī applauds Vimalakīrti's silence, calling it a superb teaching on nondual wisdom.

89. This also allows us to consider afresh how it is that the tantric practices of creation and completion have come to be seen as a Dzogchen practitioner's best friend (Khetsun Sangpo Rinpoche, private conversation, 2009).

90. Smith, *Great Commentary of Vimalamitra*, 165.

91. In a passage that resonates deeply with what can occur here, the Zen teacher Henry Shukman describes an experience he had as a student when, after days of nothing but torment in a strict Zen *sesshin*, "suddenly something happened. The knee pain was still there, the sound of the wind was still there, but there was no one experiencing them. It was the strangest thing. There was no me. The very center of my being, the core of my life, vanished. *I* vanished. Where had I gone? What had happened to me? *Where I used to be, there was just a broad openness* [italics mine]. All things were happening just as before, nothing had really changed, yet everything had changed, because there was no *me* to whom everything was happening.... The relief was indescribable. All the worrying, all the fretting—and all along there had been no one home." Shukman, *One Blade of Grass*, 151.

92. Dahl, *Steps to the Great Perfection*, 31, 36, 43, 45, 49.

93. The Kalmyks are Buddhist and most are Gelugpa. Historically, the clergy received their training either on the steppe in Kalmyk monasteries or in Tibet. The Kalmyks are of Mongolian descent, and in Russia most live in the Republic of Kalmykia, in the southeast European part of Russia, between the Volga and Don rivers, its eastern border the Astrakhan region and its southeast border the Caspian Sea.

94. Dahl, *Steps to the Great Perfection*, 36.

95. Dahl, *Steps to the Great Perfection*, 36.

96. Jigme Lingpa, *Stairway to Liberation*, 153.1; see also Dahl, *Steps to the Great Perfection*, 36.

97. Longchen Rabjam, *Commentary on the "Precious Dharmadhātu Treasury,"* 194!4ff; Barron, *Treasure Trove*, 202–3.

98. Jigme Lingpa's "Vajra Verses on the Natural State" on Lotsawa's website is a helpful text for practitioners seeking to understand the special features of the cutting-through practice itself. See https://www.lotsawahouse.org/tibetan-masters/jigme-lingpa/vajra-verses-on-the-natural-state. Thanks to Gyurme Lodro Gyatso (Khenpo Yeshi) for this suggestion, and for clarifying several points in this paragraph.

99. Jigme Lingpa, *Stairway to Liberation*, 1302–4; see also Dahl, *Steps to the Great Perfection*, 16;.

100. See the marvelous three-volume translation by Padmakara of Longchenpa's *Trilogy of Rest*.

101. Bertelsen, *Gateways of Empathy*, 1–2.

102. Longchen Rabjam, *Commentary on the "Precious Dharmadhātu Treasury,"* 266!3; Barron, *Treasure Trove,* 296.
103. Longchen Rabjam, *Commentary on the "Precious Dharmadhātu Treasury,"* 113.11–12 (my translation); see also Barron, *Treasure Trove,* 99. For more reflection on the significance of effortlessness and its relation to spontaneity in Dzogchen, see Klein and Wangyal, *Unbounded Wholeness,* especially chapter 3.
104. Longchenpa uses this analogy three times in his *Commentary on the "Precious Dharmadhātu Treasury,"* 61.7, 65.8, and 306, which you can find in Barron, *Treasure Trove,* 29, 34, and 345.
105. Longchen Rabjam, *Commentary on the "Precious Dharmadhātu Treasury,"* 278!6–5; Barron, *Treasure Trove,* 301.
106. Dahl, *Steps to the Great Perfection,* 5.
107. The *locus classicus* for Śāntideva's fourfold method is found in the *Guide to the Bodhisattva's Way of Life* (*Bodhisattvacaryāvatāra,* 8.90 through remainder of chapter) where he moves from his discussion of meditative stabilization to introduce the mind of awakening as the new focus of meditation (*byang chub sems ni bsgom par bya*), understanding this as the fruition of the previous bodhisattva trainings and, most especially, of the instructions about to be given on equalizing self and other, reflecting on the faults of self-cherishing and the benefits of cherishing others, and, finally, exchanging self-cherishing for full-hearted cherishing concern for others' happiness and freedom from suffering.
108. For Longchenpa and the wisdom narrative in general, this is not the fruition of training—though training is needed—but of one's very nature.
109. The *Perfection of Wisdom in Eighteen Thousand Lines* (*Aṣṭādaśasāhasrikāprajñāpāramitā*), trans. Gareth Sparham, https://read.84000.co/translation/UT22084-029-001.html (accessed July 1, 2022). For the verse cited above, see the Introduction, chap. 21, v. i.71. It's important to note that awakening is in their nature, even though bodhisattvas do a great deal of practice before earning that title.
110. Dahl, *Steps to the Great Perfection,* 40.
111. Dahl, *Steps to the Great Perfection,* 40–41.
112. For a contemporary and very useful take on this traditional material, see the discussions of the hell realms in McLeod, *Wake Up,* 139–42.
113. Barron, *Treasure Trove,* 312; Longchen Rabjam, *Commentary on the "Precious Dharmadhātu Treasury,"* 280.1–1.
114. Jigme Lingpa, *Stairway to Liberation,* 162.6; see also Dahl, *Steps to the Great Perfection,* 43.
115. Dahl, *Steps to the Great Perfection,* 42; Jigme Lingpa, *Stairway to Liberation,* 162.2–3.
116. Jigme Lingpa, *Stairway to Liberation,* 162.6; see also Dahl, *Steps to the Great Perfection,* 31.
117. Longchen Rabjam, *Commentary on the "Precious Dharmadhātu Treasury,"* 279!1–280.2; Barron, *Treasure Trove,* 312.
118. Jigme Lingpa, *Stairway to Liberation,* 165.5; see also Dahl, *Steps to the Great Perfection,* 45. Gyurme Lodro Gyatso (Khenpo Yeshi) glossed *mkhan po* here as "source" or "originator." Taking account of this, we could read this line as "the doer that initiates movement and stillness" (*mkhan po* is commonly agentive, and Lama Tenzin read it simply as "doer"). Cortland Dahl renders it as "Examine what it is that moves and what it is that is still." All these interpretations are useful in

practice, and all agree that the attentional focus is not on movement and still-ness, as was the case in the first pith.

119. Thanks to Gyurme Lodro Gyatso (Khenpo Yeshi) for his pivotal discussion of key points in this paragraph, June 2022. He received the Dharma name Gyurme Lodro Gyatso from Adzom Paylo Rinpoche (who himself holds the name Gyurme Thupten Gyatso).

120. Lopez, *In the Forest*, 29.

121. This untitled verse by Jigme Lingpa is cited in Tulku Thondup, *Masters of Meditation*, 125; it appears in Jigme Lingpa's *rnam thar* (spiritual biography), in the *Collected Works*, vol. 9, 87.6ff, https://library.bdrc.io/search?q=%22%27jigs%20 med%20gling%20pa%20rnam%20thar%22~1&lg=bo-x-ewts&t=Etext. Thanks to Martijn van Beek for sharing reflections on this passage and downloading the Tibetan.

122. Dahl, *Steps to the Great Perfection*, 49; Jigme Lingpa. *Stairway to Liberation*, 171.5. Like Dahl, and based on discussion with two Tibetan-trained scholars, I take the text's *rtogs*, meaning "to realize," to be a misspelling of *rtog*, meaning "thought."

123. Longchen Rabjam, *Commentary on the "Precious Dharmadhātu Treasury,"* 1.3; Dahl, *Steps to the Great Perfection*, 49.

124. Dahl, *Steps to the Great Perfection*, 55.

125. Thought is contrasted with direct perception in Klein, *Knowledge and Liberation*, chaps. 1 and 2. Chapters 4 and 5 discuss the functioning of thought through a process of elimination of all that is not its focal object (*apoha, gzhan gsel*). Text available on the academia.edu site of Anne Carolyn Klein. For an overview of classic stages of the path, see Levinson, "Metaphors of Liberation."

126. For an excellent summary of basic principles of conceptual thought (*rtog pa, kalpanā*), see Napper, *Mind in Tibetan Buddhism*, especially the discussion of conceptual consciousness under the category of inferential cognizer in her introduction, 20ff., and passim.

127. This nature is also called primordial wisdom (*ye shes, jñāna*), the way things are (*gnas tshul*), the ultimate, basic space of phenomena (*chos dbyings, dharmadhātu*), open awareness (*rig pa, vidyā*), awakened mind (*byang chub kyi sems, bodhicitta*), and union of primordial purity and spontaneous presence *(ka dag lhun grub bzung 'jug)*.

128. Jigme Lingpa, *Stairway to Liberation*, 147.6–148.1; Dahl, *Steps to the Great Perfection*, 49.

129. Thānissaro Bhikkhu, trans., *Bāhiya Sutta*, https://www.dhammatalks.org/suttas/ KN/Ud/ud1_10.html (accessed July 5, 2022).

130. Imagination is also discouraged in popular modern iterations of Theravāda, such as S. N. Goenka's insight meditation; one focuses on bare experience in the present moment. Theravāda's final goal of *nibbāna* is the cessation of all cognitive and sensory overlays. However, more recent scholarship questions this description of Theravāda and maintains that it includes visual and other sensory engagement. See Crosby, *Theravada Buddhism*.

131. *All-Creating Majesty*, in Longchen Rabjam, *Commentary on the "Precious Dharma-dhātu Treasury,"* 75!6 (my translation); see also Barron, *Treasure Trove*, 47. This venerated text is a key source for the Dzogchen mind collection teachings (*sems sde*). See also Neumaier-Dargyay, *Sovereign All-Creating Mind*.

132. We see this writ large in his Heart Essence of the Vast Expanse cycle (*Klong chen*

snying thig rtsa pod), and commented on by Patrul Rinpoche, *Words of My Perfect Teacher*, and Adzom Drukpa, *Lamp Lighting the Path* (trans. Anne C. Klein and Elizabeth Napper, forthcoming Wisdom Publications, 2024, House of Adzom series).

133. Neurological research on the effect of visual meditation practices is relatively scarce. See Kozhevnikov et al., "Enhancement of Visuospatial Processing."

134. Neuroscientists such as David Eagleman are now suggesting that reality is not something passively observed by the brain, rather the brain actively consructs the reality it perceives.

135. Klein, *Heart Essence,* 65.

136. Klein, "Imagining the Real," 500–513.

137. Stern, *Interpersonal World,* 40, notes that before two months of age infants show interest in the human voice, preferring it to other sounds of similar pitch and loudness, and that they prefer looking at faces rather than at other visual patterns. He discusses the research on imitation in this context.

138. This has been widely mentioned. See, for example, "Secret Life of Babies," https://www.youtube.com/watch?v=ersyQKAIMPI (accessed June 28, 2021).

139. This process is a little-discussed yet central part of tantric practice and most especially delicate in the Dzogchen-oriented revealed treasures of Adzom Paylo Rinpoche. I will discuss this in a commentary he requested I write on his Yeshe Tsogyal-centered treasures from his *Luminous Heart Essence* cycle, to be published by Wisdom in the House of Adzom series.

140. Neuroscience finds that mental imaging leads to brain activation in the areas related with visual and spatial proficiency. Evidence collected to date does not support the brain's capacity to sustain a complex image for anything more than a few seconds, although this ability is credibly attributed to many exemplary practitioners across the Buddhist traditions. In any case, sustained imaging is not the point of Jigme Lingpa's meditation here. See Kozhevnikov, "Enhancement of Visuospatial Processing," 645–53.

141. Stern, *Interpersonal World,* 154; on vitalities see especially 53–54, and on intensities 51 and 56.

142. See, for example, his discussion of the mind class's seven perspectives in Barron, *Treasure Trove,* 311–15. I am not saying that Longchenpa and Stern are describing identical experiences, but that there is a family resemblance that is meaningful.

143. Gendlin, *Focusing.* On the importance of "lived experience" as a category, see for example Petitmengin, "Anchoring in Lived Experience" and "Intuitive Experience"; Bitbol and Petitmengin, "Science of Mind as It Could Have Been"; Bitbol, "Is Consciousness Primary?"; and Klein, "Feelings Bound and Freed."

144. See Klein, *Knowledge and Liberation,* chaps. 2 and 3.

145. See, for example, the discussion of "mental image" (sometimes translated as "generic image," *don spyi*) in Klein, *Knowledge and Liberation*; and Dendar Hlarampa's juxtaposition of phenomena (like mental images) that have only general characteristics with sensory objects that have specific characteristics, in Klein, *Knowing, Naming, and Negation,* 42–87.

146. For a classic Tibetan Geluk discussion of this, see for example Klein, *Knowledge and Liberation,* chaps. 2 and 3; also, Dendar Hlarampa's discussion of general

and specifically characterized objects of thought and direct perception in Klein, *Knowing, Naming, and Negation.*

147. Stern, *Present Moment,* xiii.

148. However, Middle Way Buddhist philosophers, specifically the Prāsaṅgika school, maintain that what we see with direct perception is not fully representational either, because things erroneously appear to be more substantial than they are.

149. This inseparability is especially richly described in the Mind Only and Middle Way schools of Buddhist philosophy. It comes to be deeply felt through many practices.

150. Toni Morrison, "The Reader as Artist," Oprah.com, https://www.oprah.com/omagazine/toni-morrison-on-reading/all (accessed June 28, 2021).

151. These are all associated with the equally crucial feeling of trust, a kind of sublime trust related with what Longchenpa calls "the three confidences." Barron, *Precious Treasury of Philosophical Systems,* 362 (*Grub mtha',* 1218.1).

152. Part of this paragraph is edited from my article "Feelings Bound and Freed."

153. *Blang dor bya rtsol med pa'i chos chen ni/ rang jung ye shes byang chub sems nyid kyi/ . . . ngo bo thad drang ngang las ma g.yos par/ mngnon du byed pas gzhan du rtsol mi dgos/ rang la bzhag nas gzhan du 'tsho mi byed.* Longchen Rabjam, *Commentary on the "Precious Dharmadhātu Treasury,"* 117.4–5; Barron, *Treasure Trove,* 104–5.

154. These are anonymous distilled remarks from conversations among a circle of seven-trainings practitioners in different retreat settings.

155. Barron, *Precious Treasury of the Basic Space of Phenomena,* 12–13 (Tibetan script, 12).

156. For interesting perspectives on this, see Dachille, "Body Mandala Debate," especially chap. 8.

157. Gill, *Native American Religions,* 134ff. Of interest also is Prof. Gill's *Dancing Culture Religion.*

158. Kapstein, *Presence of Light,* esp. the preface and chap. 10.

159. Barron, *Precious Treasury of Philosophical Systems,* "Vajra Heart-Essence" chapter, 344 (*Grub mtha',* 1188.4).

160. Barron, *Precious Treasury of Philosophical Systems,* 345 (*Grub mtha',* 1189.4–5).

161. See Barron, *Precious Treasury of Philosophical Systems,* 341 (*Grub mtha',* 1183.1). Longchenpa continues: "In the heart center—'the palace of the true nature of phenomena'—the essence of timeless awareness, naturally occurring and utterly lucid, is steadfastly present" (345; *Grub mtha',* 1189.4). Here Longchenpa seems to bridge the paradigm of the channel-wind practices, which understands wisdom to abide in the central channel, and the unique physiology of Dzogchen, on the basis of which Longchenpa describes wisdom as everywhere in the body. Adzom Rinpoche refers to bodily suffusion poetically in his *Becoming Guru Rinpoche,* from his *Luminous Heart Essence* cycle, where the practitioner, on becoming Guru Rinpoche, is referred to as a "city that is a heap of vajras"—meaning that the body is simply filled with vajra-like buddhas. These perspectives do not so much contradict each other as they express valid views from different parts of the tradition. When you discuss the channel-wind *(rtsa rlung)* practices, there are very specific parameters, just as when you discuss Abhidharma or Madhyamaka, which never mention, for example, infinite pure array *(dag pa rab 'byams),*

which is taught in Mahayoga tantras. Thanks to Gyurme Lodro Gyatso (Khenpo Yeshi) for these last examples.

162. Barron, *Treasure Trove*, 39; Longchen Rabjam, *Commentary on the "Precious Dharmadhātu Treasury,"* 68!4.

163. Dzogchen discussions of this ground (*gzhi*) is relevant but beyond the scope of what is covered here.

164. Thanks to Dharmachakra Translation Committee for its translation, under the patronage of 84,000: Translating the Words of the Buddha, of *The Teaching on the Indivisible Nature of the Realm of Phenomena*, https://read.84000.co/translation/toh52.html (accessed July 5, 2022).

165. Slightly adapted from Dharmachakra Translation Committee, *The Teaching on the Indivisible Nature of the Realm of Phenomena*, 1.5.

166. Mañjuśrī's observation aligns with Dzogchen's frequent observation that the primordial general ground that is prior to either buddhahood or ordinary mind has neither ignorance or affliction, and that the ordinary mind has both. This is one of many moments in the sūtra that seems to sync well with Dzogchen views.

167. This crucial statement is meaningfully analogous to Longchenpa's noting that the way of being of all mind-states is wisdom (see note 123).

168. Adzom Paylo Rinpoche glossed this mantra as referring to the five sūtra paths, the fifth being complete awakening, with nowhere further to go (oral commentary on the *Heart Sūtra*, Upaya Zen Center, Santa Fe, New Mexico, 1999/2000).

169. In Sanskrit, all verbs of going are verbs of knowing. To go for refuge is to know refuge. Hence one could translate this mantra as "Known, known, thoroughly known, thoroughly and completely known. Awake!" To my knowledge, no one translates it this way, nor have I heard an ethnic Tibetan scholar gloss it this way (though I have not yet asked anyone if they would accept such a gloss).

170. Dharmachakra Translation Committee, 84000, *Teaching on the Indivisible Nature of the Realm of Phenomena*, Toh 52, https://read.84000.co/translation/UT22084-040-003.html, v.13.16 (2022).

171. Dharmachakra Translation Committee, 84000, *Teaching on the Indivisible Nature of the Realm of Phenomena*, Toh 52, https://read.84000.co/translation/UT22084-040-003.html, v.1.30. This passage too is remarkably consistent with classic Madhyamaka and with some of Dzogchen's own ways of exploring what it calls the hidden "defect" of the mind or the "rickety shack" of the mind. What is needed is confidence to continue the exploration.

172. Rumi, "In Baghdad, Dreaming of Cairo," 139.

173. Jigme Lingpa, *Stairway to Liberation*, 147.6–148.1 (my translation); see also Dahl, *Steps to the Great Perfection*, 31.

174. Dahl, *Steps to the Great Perfection*, 57; Jigme Lingpa, *Stairway to Liberation*, 180.5–6.

175. Dahl, *Steps to the Great Perfection*, 57.

176. Dahl, *Steps to the Great Perfection*, 47.

177. Dahl, *Steps to the Great Perfection*, 21.

178. Dahl, *Steps to the Great Perfection*, 20.

179. Dahl, *Steps to the Great Perfection*, 21.

180. Dr. Richard Davidson, founder of the Center for Healthy Minds (centerhealthyminds.org), University of Wisconsin, Madison, has called brain plasticity one of the most crucial discoveries about the brain in the last fifteen years.

181. David Brooks, "Students Learn from People They Love," January 17, 2019, https://www.nytimes.com/2019/01/17/opinion/learning-emotion-education.html. This paragraph is based on his reporting.

182. Dahl, *Steps to the Great Perfection, 50.*

183. For an important discussion of the difference between psychologically healthy attachment and the attachment Buddhist practice means to eliminate, see Aronson, *Buddhist Practice on Western Ground*, "Attachment East and West," 151–63.

184. Buddhist scholars and communities are working hard to better understand how and what has gone awry in Buddhist communities, and how the resulting harm can be addressed and not repeated. Among important current resources are: Bhante Sujato, "The Buddha Would Have Believed You," in *Lion's Roar*, https://www.lionsroar.com/the-buddha-would-have-believed-you/; Willa Blythe Baker, "How You Can Support a Victim of Clergy Sexual Misconduct" and "Advice for Wome in Secret Sexual Relationship with Their Buddhist Teacher," https://www.lionsroar.com/support-victim-sexual-misconduct/; and Ann Gleig and Amy Paris Langenberg, "Abuse, Sex, and the Sangha, Conversations for Healing," a series on YouTube, https://www.reddit.com/r/Buddhism/comments/vb2ps6/abuse_sex_and_the_sangha_conversations_for_healing/.

  Attempts to address racial traumas, especially in the United States, are also in process. This is a vast topic, beyond the scope of this present work. Among the helpful resources are Gleig, *American Dharma*; Owens, *Love and Rage*; Jan Willis, *Dreaming* Me; as well as talks by Ann Gleig, Rhonda Magee, Jan Willis, and other speakers at Rice University's Rockwell Lecture series *Black Lives Matter* in 2021 that can be found at https://reli.rice.edu/event-videos.

185. Dahl, *Steps to the Great Perfection,* 78; Jigme Lingpa, *Stairway to Liberation,* 205.3.

186. Dahl, *Steps to the Great Perfection,* 79; Jigme Lingpa, *Stairway to Liberation,* 205.304.

187. Translation lightly tweaked from Dahl, *Steps to the Great Perfection,* 90; Jigme Lingpa, *Stairway to Liberation,* 220.3.

188. Jigme Lingpa, *Wisdom Chats* (*Shes rab gtam tshogs*), nos. 66.774.6.–775.3.

189. Method path (*thabs lam*) is a reference to the completion stage (*rdzogs rim*) of tantra, as becomes clear in the following lines.

190. Jigme Lingpa, *Stairway to Liberation,* 153.2 (my translation); see also Dahl, *Steps to the Great Perfection,* 36.

191. Lama Tenzin Samphel points out that the three nonconceptual states, while necessary for training, are not themselves regarded as causes of the nonconceptual realization of reality (*chos nyid, dharmatā*). Commenting in response to my queries on the seventh training, May 31, 2021 and June 7, 2022.

192. In Tibet, everyone understood that such practices required personal guidance. Longchenpa discloses important relevant material in the final chapter of his *Precious Treasury of Philosophical Systems*, which is not restricted. Still, interested readers should seek out personal instruction. When in doubt, go gently. It took my asking questions every now and then over a ten-year period before Adzom Rinpoche kindly granted the pithy oral instructions mentioned here and permission to include them.

193. Adzom Gar, the seat of Adzom Drukpa, and now overseen by Adzom Paylo Rinpoche, is famous for its channel-wind expertise. The biography of Adzom Drukpa by his son, Gyurme Dorje, describes his utter mastery of these practices,

due to which "he could reach out and play with rocks as if they were dough, or leave handprints in rock . . ." (Adzom Gyalse Rinpoche, reading from the biography of Adzom Drukpa, oral translation by Erik Drew, June 5, 2022). I was able to study the early part of channel-wind practices briefly with Ani Tenzin Drolma, the main teacher of this practice to Adzom Rinpoche's nuns. She had begun her studies with another famous channel-and-wind (*rtsa-rlung*) practice master, Lama Gonpo Tseten of Amdo. The late Ani Tenzin Drolma told me that he was regarded as an incarnation of Vimalamitra. Also, that at the age of seventeen she was barely able to walk, and this disability completely disappeared through her channel-wind practices with Lama Gonpo. After his death, she became the main *Rtsa-rlung* teacher for the nuns of Adzom Paylo Rinpoche's monastery. I had the good fortune to study with her on several brief occasions between 1981 and 1983. Her kindness to me was tremendous; her utter humility notwithstanding, her expertise and depth of practice were obvious. She died of cancer in 2016 in a hospital in Chengdu. Her body was transported back to Rinpoche's home monastery in Rege, at least two days by steep and winding roads. When the vehicle carrying her arrived at Rege, it was officially acknowledged that she had not yet left her body; she was still in *thugs dam*. Several people described this to me afterward. At least one other nun who died that year at the monastery was also reported to have spent time in *thugs dam*, a state in which one remains in deep union with reality before leaving the body. Adzom Rinpoche trains his Rege students very profoundly.

194. Barron, *Precious Treasury of Philosophical Systems*, 350 (*Grub mtha'*, 1198.3): "In the approach of the vajra heart essence, the subtle energies settle into a natural state of quiescence and so need not be made to enter the central channel." In the next passage Longchenpa observes the different types of confusion, or ignorance, that Dzogchen discusses in connection with the basis, path, and fruit.

195. The crowning moments in the classic cultivation of calm abiding, a complete relaxation of distraction and unified ease of focus, arrive after experiencing the subtle movement of wind currents that bring pliancy and bliss to mind and body. See, for example, the discussion of the four pliancies that occur between the attainment of the ninth state and actual calm abiding, in Geshe Gedun Lodro, *Walking Through Walls*, 110–11.

196. Barron, *Precious Treasury of Philosophical Systems*, 240 (*Grub mtha'*, 1014.3–5).

197. Jigme Lingpa gives slightly different instructions here, advising that this holding begin while the nectar is descending—that is, earlier in the practice. Adzom Rinpoche, who mainly followed Jigme Lingpa's way of practice here, comments: "You do not inhale or exhale while you hold, but you let go when you need to breathe again (oral commentary, March 2015 and 2017).

198. Dahl, *Steps to the Great Perfection*, 92.

199. Adzom Paylo Rinpoche, oral comments, China, probably 2015.

200. Shenphen Dawa Rinpoche, "Bumchung," 11 (unpublished, undated, and privately distributed).

201. Adzom Paylo Rinpoche, oral comments, March 7, 2015. Because this information is hard to come by, with Rinpoche's permission I am sharing it here. However, by no means should anyone practice this without the required demonstration and instruction from an experienced teacher. There is always

the danger of holding too strongly, or too long, or in the wrong place, even when you think you are doing it right, and this can be harmful.

202. Jigme Lingpa, *Wisdom Chats*, no. 71, 799.5–6.

203. Jigme Lingpa, *Wisdom Chats*, no. 71, 799.6.

204. This summarizes Lama Tenzin Samphel's comment on the meaning of Jigme Lingpa's *Wisdom Chats*, no. 71, 799.6, on the inexpressibility of wisdom. In this way, Jigme Lingpa explains the gap or boundary between wisdom and ordinary mind. That is, ordinary experience does not recognize that all objects are included in its own open field of subjectivity. After writing this, I listened to a brief exchange between the Dalai Lama and Russian neuroscientists, who were talking about the relationship of mind to brain. The Dalai Lama said, "We see in ordinary mind the possibility of enlightenment. But we cannot say the same of the brain." One of the Russians replied, "So there is no such thing as an enlightened brain?" Good question. The wisdom cultivated in Dzogchen is understood to run through circuits throughout the subtle body, even if the brain might today be acknowledged as participating in some way.

205. Barron, *Precious Treasury of Philosophical Systems*, 341–42 (*Grub mtha'*, 1182.3).

206. Dahl, *Steps to the Great Perfection*, 11.

207. Barron, *Precious Treasury of Philosophical Systems*, 345 (*Grub mtha'*, 1188.4–1189.4).

208. Barron, *Precious Treasury of Philosophical Systems*, 342 (*Grub mtha'*, 1188.3).

209. Barron, *Precious Treasury of Philosophical Systems*, 345 (*Grub mtha'*, 1189.2–4).

210. Ackerman, Nocera, and Bargh, "Incidental Haptic Sensations," 1712–15, explores these specificities beyond what is possible here. Thanks to Prof. Larry Barsalou for bringing this to my attention. And to the Mind and Life Summer Research Institute (SRI) and other programs that brought me into contact with the larger scientific-contemplative conversation.

211. Adzom Paylo Rinpoche, conversation, March 2017.

212. In presenting tantra, however, the Geluk school, and all Tibetan systems, move away from emphasizing the "mere negative" aspect of reality.

213. Dodrupchen Jigme Trinle, *Commentary on Root Verses of Jigme Lingpa's "Treasury of Precious Qualities,"* 574!8ff.

214. That is, primordial purity or emptiness itself are not the whole picture of Dzogchen's understanding of the reality. Luminosity is also spontaneously present. See chapter 11.7 of Jigme Lingpa's *Precious Treasury of Good Qualities*, vol. 2, 44. See Dodrupchen Jigme Trinle, *Commentary on Root Verses of Jigme Lingpa's "Treasury of Precious Qualities,"* 573.8–574.5. This section then goes on to discuss specific qualities of teachers and trainees.

215. Pelzang, *Guide to "The Words of My Perfect Teacher,"* 276.

216. Based on discussion with Lama Tenzin Samphel, November 7, 2018.

217. Barron, *Precious Treasury of Philosophical Systems*, 306 (*Grub mtha'*, 1123–24).

218. Tulku Thondup, *Masters of Meditation*, 124–25; Tibetan text, Jigme Lingpa's *rnam thar* (spiritual biography), in the *Collected Works*, vol. 9, 42a.4.

219. Shenphen Dawa Rinpoche, *Bum Chung*, 19.

220. Bertelsen, *Gateways of Empathy*.

221. Bertelsen, *Gateways of Empathy*, 6–7.

222. The *how* of the mind is an important focus for uncovering fresh depths of

experience in or out of meditation. Claire Petitmengin often emphasizes the importance of moving from *what* to *how* in her studies on intuition and the micro-phenomenology of human experience and in her in-person trainings. *How* is grounded in lived experience rather than secondary observations about it. Accessing this lived state involves freedom from our inner narrator, including freedom from self-judgment, which for many of us is a virtually ceaseless commentary on personal inadequacy. *How* also moves away from the narrative of what we are anxious about, the endless review of items of concern, to what specific instances of anxiety *feel* like. This yields awareness of inner gestures we make to support or relieve it.

223. For further discussion see Ackerman, Nocera, and Bargh, "Incidental Haptic Sensations," whose finding we previously summarized on p. 151 and note 209.

224. They do so in dimension-specific and metaphor-specific ways. Exploring these specificities is beyond our scope here.

225. Theise, "Beyond Cell Doctrine," 263–69. Neil Theise is a senior student of Zen Buddhism at the Village Zendo, New York City, under the guidance of Roshi Enkyo O'Hara. See more of his work at https://www.closertotruth.com/contributor/neil-theise/profile.

226. See, among other resources, McEvilley, *Shape of Ancient Thought.*

227. Theise, "Beyond Cell Doctrine," 267.

228. Theise, "Beyond Cell Doctrine," 266.

229. Theise, "Beyond Cell Doctrine," 267 (italics mine).

230. For key differences in Buddhist and contemporary psychology's understanding of selfhood, see Aronson, *Buddhist Practice*, esp. 41–52.

231. Barsalou, Wilson, and Hasenkamp, "On the Vices of Nominalization," 335; see also 343.

232. Barsalou, Wilson, and Hasenkamp, "On the Vices of Nominalization," 334–60. Thanks to Prof. Barsalou for his compelling public and private discussion of this and related issues.

233. Barsalou, Wilson, and Hasenkamp, "On the Vices of Nominalization," 335–36.

234. Barsalou, Wilson, and Hasenkamp, "On the Vices of Nominalization," notes 199, 200.

235. One Christmas when I was about five, my father read me "A Visit from St. Nicholas" by Clement Clarke Moore, which I loved and which begins "'Twas the night before Christmas, when all through the house . . ." When he got to the line "The moon on the breast of the new-fallen snow/ Gave a lustre of midday to objects below," I stopped him. I wanted to know what "objects" were. He explained for several minutes. I don't recall what he said, but I clearly recall my puzzlement as he spoke. I couldn't get what it meant. "Objects" remained a mystery to me. Perhaps this was a starting point for my life-long interest in ontology and epistemology. Reading the line again now, it's interesting that "lustre" didn't stop me, but this generic noun "objects" did. Hence, in part, my interest in what Barsalou says here.

236. It seems not too farfetched to suggest that perceiving and putting words to the complex processes of body-sensing that include multivalent, holographic, and kinesthetically sensed dynamic elements reveals sensing to be a complex category of knowledge. The study of interoception, the manner of experiencing the

spaces and phenomena associated with one's own body, has been much studied of late. See for example Farb et al., "Interoception."

237. The subtle shift in sensations at one's throat, shoulders, gut, heart, or chest as emotions open or get shut down are more likely to be overlooked, both in life and in science, than neater, noun-able objects. Barsalou's main interest here is how this leads scientists to overlook messy contexts. He writes, "Science is well known for valuing elegance, parsimony, and power in theoretical and empirical research. When possible, scientists like to avoid messy complexity, imprecision, and weak effects." He further notes that "once a process is nominalized, the process is viewed as something that exists discretely, remains relatively constant across time and context, is easy to manipulate, and enters into simple causal relationships. Platonic blindness follows, viewing the process as a context-free mechanism, analogous to a simple manipulable object." Barsalou, Wilson, and Hasenkamp, "On the Vices of Nominalization," 341. See also Dunham and Banaji, "Platonic Blindness," 201–13.

238. Suzuki Roshi, *Zen Mind*, 41, 49, 71, and passim.

239. Suzuki Roshi, *Zen Mind*, 48.

240. Body awareness is now subject to scientific research across a wide range of health topics and is described as "awareness of internal body sensations." Such sensations are subtle kinesthetic sensations, and what is being felt is movement. Movement, in the logos of Buddhist traditions, is the activity of *prāṇa*, or energy. From this perspective, all measurements of heart rate, blood pulse, and even brain activity are the movement of *prāṇa*. Thus, despite the wholesale absence of such discourse in classic Western medicine, anatomy, or biology, the two narratives are not contradictory.

241. Compelling examples of this, in my experience, are the dialogical processes at the heart of micro-phenomenology. See for example the listed works by Claire Petitmengin and A. H. Almaas. Petitmengin's research has launched a broad spectrum of scientific work based on careful phenomenological inquiry. Methods of inquiry described by Almaas, especially in *Spacecruise*, are central to the inner work of the Diamond Approach. Such first-person emotionally-based approaches conjoin cognitive and somatic elements to create powerful ways of coming home to one's own actual experience.

242. This paragraph summarizes points from Stern, *Interpersonal World of the Infant*, 54–58, but can only hint at his fascinating detailing of this experience. His narrative of how self-sensing develops in relation to others is also relevant for Buddhist tantric practice, as I will discuss in a future volume in this series. Further development of his ideas is found in Stern, *Forms of Vitality*.

243. Those familiar with Tibetan practices related to the elements will recognize that this involves at the least a shift from an overly earth-bound state to the greater fluidity, and connectedness, of water. The *seeing to being* cycle I have developed through the inspiration of Adzom Rinpoche has practices based in the elements. Here too one works with body, mind, and energy, and for many it provides easy access to the kinds of shifts suggested throughout these trainings and has traditionally been an important part of tantric and Dzogchen training. Tenzin Wangyal Rinpoche in *Healing with Form, Energy, and Light*

has written eloquently of this using Bon sources, with the overall picture very similar.

244. Jigme Lingpa, *Wisdom Chats*, no. 66, 776. Jigme Lingpa actually uses the term "heretic brahmans," here but in our cosmopolitan world that designation only detracts from his real point: we become heretics in the sense of looking askance at the reality that the practice is meant to reveal.

245. Jigme Lingpa, *Stairway to Liberation*, 162.6 (my translation); see also Dahl, *Steps to the Great Perfection*, 43.

246. Other famous examples of karmic-narrative bodhicitta practice are Candrakīrti's seven cause-and-effect precepts (*rgyu 'bras man ngag bdun*). See Tsongkhapa, *Great Treatise*, 2: 35–50. Also Hopkins, *Compassion in Tibetan Buddhism*, 26ff.

247. We find this in Candirkīrti's famous homage to compassion at the beginning of his *Entering the Middle Way*, and in Śāntideva's praise of the bodhisattva's open heart in the opening chapters of his *Guide to the Bodhisattva Way of Life*. Similarly, Tsongkhapa's *Great Treatise*, drawing extensively from Candrakīrti, opens by describing the loving intention to awakening (bodhicitta) as the hallmark of the Great Way, the Mahāyāna. He supports this with a passage from Asaṅga's *Sublime Mindstream*; Tsongkhapa, *Great Treatise*, 18.

248. Aṅguttara Nikāya, 1.51–52, trans. Thānissaro Bhikkhu (https://suttacentral.net/an1.51-60/en/thanissaro?reference=none&highlight=false).

249. Brunnhölz, *In Praise of Dharmadhātu*, 73.

250. Barron, *Precious Treasury of Philosophical Systems*, 174 (*Grub mtha'*, 904.1).

251. Thus he emphasizes that Mahāyāna includes both the compassion (*thugs rjes*) refers both to the compassion that takes living beings as its object and the sublime knowing that suffuses the dharmadhātu. Barron, *Precious Treasury of the Basic Space of Phenomena*, 10–11, and *Treasure Trove*, 53; Longchen Rabjam, *Commentary on the "Precious Dharmadhātu Treasury,"* 79!4.

252. Barron, *Treasure Trove*, 87; Longchen Rabjam, *Commentary on the "Precious Dharmadhātu Treasury,"* 104.

253. Barron, *Precious Treasury of Philosophical Systems*, 149 (*Grub mtha'*, 860.1): *sems kyi rang bzhin 'od gsal gang yin pa / de ni nam mkha' bzhin du 'gyur med de/*.

254. See also Barron, *Precious Treasury of Philosophical Systems*, 84 (*Grub mtha'*, 744.5). Here Longchenpa is citing the *Complete Display of Primordial Awareness Tantra* (*Ye shes rnam par bgod pa'i rgyud*).

255. Barron, *Precious Treasury of Philosophical Systems*, 149 (*Grub mtha'*, 860.1).

256. Longchen Rabjam, *Commentary on the "Precious Dharmadhātu Treasury."* Indeed, eight of the thirteen chapters of this key Dzogchen text has "awakened mind" in the title.

257. Longchen Rabjam, *Precious Treasury of Philosophical Systems* (*Grub mtha'*, 860.4–5): *'di la bsal bya ci yang med, bzhag bar bya ba cung zad med*. See also Barron, *Precious Treasury of Philosophical Systems*, 149. Freedom from any effort that either erases or places—subtracts or adds—to what is currently unfolding is an important and fairly common trope in refuge verses in tantric practice texts (*sādhana*). In Adzom Rinpoche's own twenty-first-century Treasure Revelation (*Gter*) *Luminous Heart Essence* cycle, a key line in the practice of Yeshe Tsogyal echoes Asaṅga in succinctly showing the way to refuge and universal compassion:

Rest, neither erase nor place:
Face known. Refuge. Mind awakes.

Rang babs gsal bzhag bral ba la / Rang ngo shes pas skyabs sems bskyed. In Klein, *Foundational Dakini Practice*, 15.

258. Dorje Choying Tobden, *Complete Nyingma Tradition*, 332.

259. Longchen Rabjam, *Precious Treasury of Philosophical Systems* (*Grub mtha'*, 872.2–3, my translation); see also Barron, *Precious Treasury of Philosophical Systems*, 155.

260. Klein, tr., *Foundational Dakini Practice*, 9, third line of refuge.

261. Longchen Rabjam, *Precious Treasury of Philosophical Systems* (*Grub mtha'*, 874.4–5; my translation); see also Barron, *Precious Treasury of Philosophical Systems*, 157. Longchenpa cites this early in his discussion of the bodhisattva path. When he describes Atiyoga, Dzogchen, he shows that the cluster of terms introduced earlier all refer to one another. The stainless dharmadhātu is mind-nature, naturally pure. It is also uncontrived primordial wisdom that arises of its own accord.

262. Jigme Lingpa, *Wisdom Chats*, no. 66.

263. This and other of Rinpoche's Dzogchen-inflected cycles are taught at Dawn Mountain (www.dawnmountain.org). For information on joining live or via video recordings, see Dzogchen Cycles Program, https://www.dawnmountain.org/teachings/dzogchen-cycles/.

264. Barron, *Precious Treasury of Philosophical Systems*, 151 (*Grub mtha'*, 863.5). See also Barron, *Treasure Trove*, chap. 3. Jigme Lingpa too uses this metaphor in *Wisdom Chats*, no. 798.4.

265. Barron, *Treasure Trove*, 101; Longchen Rabjam, *Commentary on the "Precious Dharmadhātu Treasury*,*"* 115.

266. And it resonates with central perspectives of Dzogchen. For example, one of the core principles of the mind class of Dzogchen teachings is that everything and everyone is inseparable from primordial wisdom, for this is "the true nature of phenomena in which they are not in fact anything at all." Barron, *Precious Treasury of Philosophical Systems*, 314–15 (*Grub mtha'*, 1133.1).

267. Barron, *Treasure Trove*, 104; Longchen Rabjam, *Commentary on the "Precious Dharmadhātu Treasury*,*"* 117: *Rang la bzahg nas gzhan du 'tshol mi byey.*

268. The phrase "unborn, unceasing," a famous part of Rāhula's *Praise of Mother Perfection of Wisdom*, is found in numerous Dzogchen tantras; Longchenpa also embroiders on it extensively in his *Commentary on the "Precious Dharmadhātu Treasury."* In Adzom Rinpoche's increasingly influential *Ḍākinī Ngöndro* and *Becoming Yeshe Tsogyal*, he reveals their meaning in Dzogchen in ways that bring them to deep experience.

269. The Tibetan text reads *rtogs pa* (realization), but oral consultation as well as context makes it clear that *rtog pa* (thought) is what is meant. In giving the Tibetan on the fifth pith practice's interlude page, I have changed *rtogs pa* to *rtog* based on discussion with two Tibetan scholars.

270. Longchen Rabjam, *Commentary on the "Precious Dharmadhātu Treasury*,*"* 49.2: *Sku gsum klong nas 'khor 'das rang shar kyang / dbyings las ma g.yos chos nyid bde ba'i zhing.* See also Barron, *Treasure Trove*, 13.

271. Dahl, *Steps to the Great Perfection*, 43.

272. Barron, *Treasure Trove*, 345.

273. Tulku Thondup, *Masters of Meditation*, 124–25; Tibetan text, Jigme Lingpa's *rnam thar*, in the *Collected Works*, vol. 9, 442.6.

274. Barron, *Precious Treasury of the Basic Space of Phenomena*, 32–33.

275. Yampolsky, *Platform Sutra*, 125–83.

276. Yampolsky, *Platform Sutra*, 130.

277. Yampolsky, *Platform Sutra*, 132.

278. See Barron, *Precious Treasury of Philosophical Systems*, 226 (*Grub mtha'*, 993.1–2). This entire section is a forthright statement about the fundamental nature of wisdom. It ties into its preceding section, which details the interwoven nature of the three buddha dimensions, or *kāyas*. Adzom Paylo Rinpoche's revealed treasures include numerous Dzogchen-inflected practices (*sādhana*) that help bring these themes to experience, as will be discussed in a future volume in this series.

279. Conversation with Gyurme Lodro Gyatso (Khenpo Yeshi), fall 2022.

280. See Dorje Choying Tobden, *Complete Nyingma Tradition*, Books 1–10, "Foundations of the Buddhist Path," 332.

281. Germano, "Architecture."

282. Van Schaik, "Early Dzogchen IV."

283. Van Schaik, "Early Dzogchen IV."

284. For an excellent reflection on how the term *phyogs ris med*, translated in different contexts as "unbiased," "nonsectarian," or "omnidirectional," is both a principle of Dzogchen and a historical movement toward more ecumenism in Tibet, see Deroche, "On Being Impartial." In a modern context, we can say that this sense of non-leaning, of not turning one's back on anything, is a basis for what we think of as fairness, which is meant to be a hallmark of justice, which is not to be blind, but all-seeing, offering fair care to everyone.

285. Adapted from Dahl, *Steps to the Great Perfection*, 16; Jigme Lingpa, *Stairway to Liberation*, 130.1–3.

286. Barron, *Treasure Trove*, 335; Longchen Rabjam, *Commentary on the "Precious Dharmadhātu Treasury*," 158a. These three are frequently mentioned in key Dzogchen tantras and are also referenced in a slightly different way in Nāgārjuna's *In Praise of Dharmadhātu*.

287. Klein, *Heart Essence*, 69. These nine-syllable lines of chantable English can be sung to a number of traditional Tibetan melodies. A long-verse translation of the same, adapted from Klein, *Heart Essence*, 102:

> Until full enlightenment,
> I seek refuge in the Three Real Jewels, the Ones Gone to Bliss (*sugata*)
> In the three roots (Guru, Deva, Ḍākinī)
> In the nature of the channels, winds, and bright orbs, which are my
> awakened mind
> And in the maṇḍala of essence, nature, and flowing compassion.

288. The first line here is the refuge of the sūtra bodhisattva path; the second is the refuge of the outer tantras; the third is the refuge of the inner tantras; and the fourth is the Dzogchen way of taking refuge in the actual tripartite nature of mind itself—empty essence, luminous nature, and the all-suffusing flow of compassion throughout the world.

289. See Khetsun Sangpo Rinpoche, *Strand of Jewels*, 4–5.
290. These three are organizing principles in the Seventeen Dzogchen Tantras, which are part of the *Vima Nyingthig* (*Bi ma snying thig*, Seminal Heart of Vimalamitra) collection and said to have been revealed in the eleventh century by Zhangdon Tashi Dorje. Malcolm Smith's annotated translations of the Seventeen Tantras is in progress, with volumes 1–4 available as of this writing through Wisdom Publications (https://wisdomexperience.org/product/tantra-without-syllables-vol3-and-blazing-lamp-tantra-vol4/).
291. *All-Creating Majesty* (*Kun byed rgyal po*) is the main tantra for the mind class (*sems ste*) of Dzogchen.
292. In Barron, *Treasure Trove*, 21; Longchen Rabjam, *Commentary on the "Precious Dharmadhātu Treasury*, 54 (see also 14; 49!7). Note that the order of the first two, nature and essence, is reversed from Jigme Lingpa's order, as we often see when they appear in the Dzogchen tantras. An interesting development that could be charted through computer search technology now available.
293. Especially the *Ḍākinī Ngöndro* and *Troma Severance*, different editions privately printed by Dawn Mountain and Tārā Maṇḍala for use in practice.
294. These paragraphs are drawn from my article "Feelings Bound and Freed: Wandering and Wonder on Buddhist Pathways, https://www.tandfonline.com/doi/full/10.1080/14639947.2018.1443567. Hand-correct proofs available without paywall at: https://www.academia.edu/63821307/Feelings_Bound_and_Freed_Wandering_and_Wonder_on_Buddhist_Pathways.
295. Shukman, *One Blade of Grass*, 47.
296. Barron, *Precious Treasury of Philosophical Systems*, 112 (*Grub mtha'*, 799.2–3).
297. Longchenpa extensively unfolds the theme of ease in his famous *Trilogy of Rest* (*Ngal gso 'khor gsum*), first translated into English by Herbert Guenther as *Kindly Bent to Ease Us*. The root text and its commentary *The Great Chariot* (*Shing rta chen po*) have also been recently translated by the Padmakara Translation Group as *Trilogy of Rest*.
298. For the full English text in both chantable English (as here) and prose poem, see Klein, *Heart Essence*, 66. The verse translation, 95–96, reads: "The manifold [sensory] appearances are/ like the illusion that the moon is there in water./ We wandering beings continually roam/ the chain links of cyclic existence. So they may rest easily in the basic space/ of their own clear reflecting presence, I bring forth a mind intent on enlightenment/ as I dwell in fourfold boundlessness."
299. Śāntideva, *Bodhisattvacaryāvatāra*, verse X.55, 143.
300. Barron, *Precious Treasury of Philosophical Systems*, 158 (*Grub mtha'*, 875.4).
301. See also Barron, *Precious Treasury of Philosophical Systems*, 157 (*Grub mtha'*, 874.3).
302. Barron, *Precious Treasury of Philosophical Systems*, 115 (*Grub mtha'*, 803.2).
303. Longchen Rabjam, *Commentary on the "Precious Dharmadhātu Treasury,"* 73 (my translation); see also Barron, *Treasure Trove*, 71. Longchenpa is here citing from *Discourse Unifying the Enlightened Intent of All Buddhas* (*Sang rgyas thams cad kyi dgongs pa 'dus pa'i mdo; sarva tathāgathacitta jñāna guhyārtha*).
304. Jigme Lingpa, *Stairway to Liberation*, 165.5 (my translation); see also Dahl, *Steps to the Great Perfection*, 45.

305. Rumi, "In Baghdad, Dreaming of Cairo," 106.

306. *Pearl Garland*, cited in Barron, *Treasure Trove*, 104; Longchen Rabjam, *Commentary on the "Precious Dharmadhātu Treasury,"* 117.

307. This is getting ahead of our story and yet is a crucial element of it. In the fifth chapter of his *Precious Dharmadhātu Treasury*, Longchenpa cites the *Pearl Garland*: "Perfect buddhahood is just intimately self-mirroring awareness (*rang rig*)" (117!9), as translated in Barron, *Treasure Trove*, 104.

308. Longchen Rabjam, *Precious Treasury of Philosophical Systems*, 875.4 (my translation); see also Barron, *Precious Treasury of Philosophical Systems*, 158. The phrase "how they are constituted" here renders the Tibetan *khams*, which is mentioned again at 903.2 (Barron, 173).

309. I have often heard Tibetan lamas, in the course of teaching a retreat, summarize these as a commitment to maintain good relationships with teacher and fellow students.

310. Cited in Wolter, *Losing the Clouds*, 173.

311. Barron, *Precious Treasury of Philosophical Systems*, 113 (*Grub mtha'*, 800.2–3).

312. Barron, *Precious Treasury of Philosophical Systems*, 115 (*Grub mtha'* 803.2–3).

313. Rāhulabhadra's famous *Praise of Mother Wisdom*, https://www.wisdomlib.org/buddhism/book/bodhisattvacharyavatara/d/doc6290.html. Recited in Sanskrit, https://www.youtube.com/watch?v=QmWqyh-8YI4.

314. *Sems nyid byang chub sems kyi ngo bo*, in Longchen Rabjam, *Precious Dharmadhātu Treasury*, 107.4, as translated in Barron, *Precious Treasury of the Basic Space of Phenomena*, 34–35. Also Barron, *Treasure Trove*, 91.

315. *Rig pa byang chub klong*, in Longchen Rabjam, *Commentary on the "Precious Dharmadhātu Treasury,"* 17!6, as translated in Barron, *Treasure Trove*, 76.

316. Longchen Rabjam, *Commentary on the "Precious Dharmadhātu Treasury,"* 106; see also Barron, *Precious Treasury of the Basic Space of Phenomena*, 34; Barron, *Precious Treasury of the Basic Space of* Phenomena, 34, 35; and Barron, *Treasure Trove*, 89.

317. Barron, *Precious Treasury of the Basic Space of Phenomena*, 123. Barron, *Treasure Trove*, 352.

318. *Sems nyid byang chub sems kyi ngo bo la/ lta ba bsgom med spyod pa spyod du med/*, in Longchen Rabjam, *Commentary on the "Precious Dharmadhātu Treasury,"* 107.4; see also Barron, *Treasure Trove*, 91.

319. Longchen Rabjam, *Commentary on the "Precious Dharmadhātu Treasury,"* 72! 3; see also Barron, *Treasure Trove*, 43. For detailed sūtra discussion on how sense consciousnesses take on the aspect of their object, see Klein, *Knowledge and Liberation*, chap. 3.

320. Rumi, "In Baghdad, Dreaming of Cairo," 206.

321. Recent research suggests that fringe states are in fact very useful. Intuition, for example, itself typically a fringe state, brings new understandings into awareness. For James, the fringes of consciousness hold material not presently in awareness but potentially retrievable.

322. Jigme Lingpa, *Stairway to Liberation*, 171.5 (my translation); see also Dahl, *Steps to the Great Perfection*, 49.

TIBETAN AND SANSKRIT TERMS

	TIBETAN	SANSKRIT
all	*kun*	*samanta*
all-base	*kun gzhi*	*ālaya*
authentic knowing, or valid cognition	*tshad ma*	*pramāṇa*
authentic listening	*tshad dang ldan pa*	
awaken	*byang chub*	*bodhi*
awakened	*byang chub, sangs rgyas*	*bodhi, buddha*
awakened mind	*byang chub kyi sems*	*bodhicitta*
awareness holder	*rig 'dzin*	*Vidyādhara*
beyond	*'das pa*	*para*
bliss	*bde ba*	*sukha*
bright orb	*thig le*	
channel-wind practices	*rtsa rlung*	
complete certainty, definitive understanding	*nges shes*	*niścaya[-jñāna]*
compassion	*thugs rje*	*karuṇā*
complete, perfect, whole, all-inclusive	*rdzogs pa*	*niṣpanna*
completion stage	*rdzogs rim*	*niṣpannakrama*
conceptual thought	*rtog pa*	*kalpanā*

	TIBETAN	SANSKRIT
confluence of the three main channels	*rtsa gsum bsdud*	
constituent, realm	*khams*	*dhātu*
conviction in cause and effect	*rgyu 'bras yid ches gyi dad pa*	
cutting free, cutting through	*khregs chod*	
dawning of their own accord	*rang shar*	
dawning and freed	*shar 'grol*	
demolishing the rickety shack of the mind	*sems kyi khang bus debs*	
gradual process for developing understanding	*kho rim*	
dharma	*chos*	
dimension (of a buddha)	*sku*	*kāya*
east	*glod*	
emanation	*sprul sku*	*nirmāṇakāya*
emptiness	*stong pa nyid*	*śūnyatā*
essence	*ngo bo*	*svabhāva, vastu*
essential disposition	*khams*	*dhātu*
everything living and everything without life	*srog dang srog ma yin pa*	
expanse	*klong*	
felt, touched	*reg bya*	*spraṣṭavya*
fortitude	*bsran tshugs*	
foundational practices	*sngon 'gro*	

	TIBETAN	SANSKRIT
four applications	*sbyor ba bzhi*	*caturprayoga*
Fourfold Heart Essence	*snying tig ya bzhi*	
furthering, blossoming	*chub*	
general ground	*spyi'i gzhi*	
generic image	*don spyi*	*arthasāmānya*
giving	*gtong*	
go	*'gro*	*gate*
good	*bzang, bhadra*	*samanta*
grace-mind	*dgongs pa*	*saṃdhāya*
great, vast	*chen*	*mahā*
great array	*rab 'byams*	
Great Completeness	*rdzogs pa chen po*	
ground	*gzhi*	*ālaya*
habits of mind, predispositions	*bag chags*	*vāsanā*
heartfelt clarifying confidence	*dvang pa'i dad pa*	
heartfelt confidence wanting to awaken	*dod pa'i dad pa*	
heartfelt conviction in cause and effect	*rgyu 'bras yid ches gyi dad pa*	
helpful mind	*phan sems*	
honorable compassion	*btsun*	
imagine	*dmigs byed*	
indivisibility in essence, or wholeness, of body, speech, and mind	*lus ngag sems gsum ngo bo dbyer med*	

	TIBETAN	SANSKRIT
inexhaustible and complete wisdom	shes rab mthar phyin pa	prajñāparyanta
infinite pure array	dag pa rab 'byams	
irreversible heartfelt confidence	phyir mi ldog pa'i dad pa	
joined (combined) energies (or winds)	rlung kha sbyar	
kindliness	byams pa bzang	maitrī
knowledgeable	mkhas pa	
lineage, or human inheritance	rigs	gotra
manifestation wheel	sprul 'khor	nirmāṇacakra
meditative experience	nyams	
mind and awareness	blo rig	
mind	sems, blo, yid	citta, buddhi, manas
mind guidance	sems khrid	
mind training	blo sbyong, sems sbyong	
movement	'gyud	
naturally awakened dimension, full form	ngo bo nyid sku	svabhāvikakāya
nonconceptual primordial wisdom of reality	chos nyid rnam par mi rtog pa'i ye shes	
not knowing, unknowing ignorance	ma rig pa	avidyā
obscuration	gti mug	moha
observing	bya ra	
overreach	sgro 'dogs	āropa

	TIBETAN	**SANSKRIT**
open awareness, sheer awareness	*rigpa*	*vidyā*
person	*skyes bu*	*puruṣa*
power, feat	*'grub pa*	*siddhi*
practical instructions, pith practice instructions	*man ngag*	*upadeśa*
primordial wisdom	*ye shes*	*jñāna*
pure from the beginning	*gdod nas dag pa*	
real guru, authentic teacher	*don gyi bla ma*	*arthaguru*
reality	*chos nyid*	*dharmatā*
settling into reality	*rnal du dbab*	
realization	*rtogs pa*	
realm	*dbyings*	*dhātu*
resplendent dimension, enjoyment body	*longs spyod rdzogs pa'i sku*	*saṃbhogakāya*
resting at ease	*ngal gso*	
revealed treasure	*gter*	
reverse cyclic existence	*khor ba'i blo ldog*	
sanctum	*sbubs*	
sealed to silence	*kha tham*	
searching out the mind's defect	*sems kyi mtshang brtsal ba*	
self-mirroring awareness	*rang rig*	*svasavedana*
seven cause-and-effect precepts	*rgyu 'bras man ngag bdun*	

	TIBETAN	SANSKRIT
sheer form	chos sku	dharmakāya
spacious source, stainless matrix	chos dbyings	dharmadhātu
special deity	yi dam	iṣṭadevatā
stage-by-stage path	lam rim	mārgakrama
stainless light	dri med 'od gsal	vimalaprabhā
state of union with reality before leaving the body at death	thugs dam	
stillness	gnas pa	sthāna
sublime, marvelous	phun sum tshogs pa	saṃpanna
suchness, nature of reality	chos nyid	dharmatā
superb knowing	shes rab	prañjā
support	rten	adhiṣṭhāna
taking	len	
teach, teaching	bstan pa	upadeśa
teaching points	don khrid	
tenets	grub mtha'	siddhānta
mind of awakening as the new focus of meditation	byang chub sems ni bsgom par bya	
purify	byang	
train, purify	sbyong	śuddhi
unbiased in any direction	phyogs ris med pa	apradeśa
unbounded wholeness	thig le nyag cig	

	TIBETAN	SANSKRIT
underestimation	*skur 'debs*	*apavāda*
vast expanse	*klong chen*	
vehicle	*theg pa*	*yāna*
the way things are	*gnas tshul*	
wheel of ornamentation	*rgyan gyi 'khor lo*	
wholly open, unbridled openness	*kha yan*	
wind energies that circulate in the channels	*rlung*	*prāṇa*

BIBLIOGRAPHY

TIBETAN PRIMARY SOURCES

Adzom Drukpa, Drodrul Pawo Dorje (A'dzom 'gro 'dul dpa'o rdo rje). *Autobiography: Liberation and Treasure Revelations. Grub dbang rje btsun bla ma'i rnam thar zhal gsung ma byin rlabs gter 'byin.* In *The Collected Songs of Jetsun Drupwang Rikzin Drodul Pawo Dorje. Rje btsun grub pa'i dbang phyug rig 'dzin 'gro 'dul dpa' bo rdo rje'i mgur 'bum.* Rekhe, Tibet Autonomous Region: Re khe Dgon chen nang bstan shes rig spe tshogs (Publishing House of the Great Monastic Center), n.d. BDRC MW1AC333.

Adzom Paylo Rinpoche (A'dzom pad blo rin po che). *Becoming Guru Rinpoche. 'Od gsal snying thig las gu ru sgrubs thabs gsang ba'i thig le.* English translation, Klein, *Practice for Becoming the Guru.*

———. *Becoming Yeshe Tsogyal, from the "Luminous Heart Essence." 'Od gsal snying thig las mtsho rgyal dkar mo'i sgrub thab msbde chen dpal ster.* English translation, Klein, *Becoming Yeshe Tsogyal.* German translation, Claudia Webinger, privately printed for Ganden Chokhor, Chur, Switzerland, 2018.

———. *Ḍākinī Ngöndro, from the "Luminous Heart Essence." 'Od gsal snying thig las ḍāk'i sngon 'gro bde chen lam bzang.* English translation, Klein, *Foundational Dakini Practice.*

———. *From the Lotus Heart Essence: Great Compassionate One. Padma snying thig las thugs rje chen po yang snying 'gro ba kun sgrol.* English translation, Klein, *Great Compassionate One.*

———. *Troma Severance. 'Od gsal snying thig las khro ma'i sgrub thabs gzang ba'i ye shes.* English translation, Klein, *Troma Severance.*

Dodrupchen Jigme Trinle. *Commentary on Root Verses of Jigme Lingpa's "Treasury of Precious Qualities": A Rain of Joy. Yon tan mdod rtsa 'grel / Yon tan rin po che'i mdzod dga' ba'i char.* Chengdu: Si khron mi rig skrun khang, 1998.

Gyurme Dorje. *Biography of Adzom Drukpa. A 'dzoms rgyal sras 'gyur med rdo rje'i gsung 'bum,* vol. 1 of 5. Khrom: 'Jam dbyangs shes rig dar spel khang nas bsgrigs, 2011. https://www.tbrc.org/#!rid=W1PD159426.

Jigme Lingpa ('Jigs med gling pa). *The Application of Mindfulness: Instructions of the Unique Great Perfection Preliminaries of the Heart Essence of the Vast Expanse. Thun mong ma yin pa'i sngon 'gro 'i khrid yig dran pa nyer gzhag.* In the *Collected Works,* vol. 8, 905–43. Reprinted in the *Nyingthig rtsa pod,*

Dilgo Khyentse edition, vol. *hum*, 271–304. English translation, Dahl, *Entrance to the Great Perfection*, 61–80.

———. *The Collected Works of 'Jigs-med-gliṅ-pa Raṅ-byuṅ-rdo-rje Mkhyen-brtse'i-'od-zer*. Compiled by the First Dodrupchen. 9 vols. Gangtok: Derge Parkhang, 1985. BDRC W27300.

———. *Fruits of Excellent Deeds: A Biography of Rangjung Dorje Khyentse Ozer [Jigme Lingpa] from the South. Yul lho rgyud du byung ba'i rdzogs chen pa rang byung rdo rje mkhyen brtse'i 'od zer gyi rnam thar pa legs byas yongs 'du'i snye ma)*. In the *Collected Works*, vol. 9, 3–502.

———. *Heart Essence of the Vast Expanse. Klong chen snying thig rts pod*. Bodnath, Kathmandu, and Bodhgaya, Bhihar: Shechen Publications, 1994. BDRC MW1KG13585.

———. *Stairway to Liberation: Instructions on the Meaning of the Shared Mahā-yāna Foundational Mind Training. Thar ba'i them skas /Thun mong gi sngon 'gro sems sbyong bdun gyi don khrid thar pa'i them skas*. Bhutan: Lama Ngod-rub and Sherab Demy, 1985. English translation, Dahl, *Steps to the Great Perfection*.

———. *Treasury of Precious Qualities, Book One. Yon tan rin po che'i mdzod*. English translation, Padmakara Translation Group, *Treasury of Precious Qualities, Book One*.

———. *Treasury of Precious Qualities, Book Two. Yon tan rin po che'i mdzod*. English translation, Padmakara Translation Group, *Treasury of Precious Qualities, Book Two*.

———. *Wisdom Chats. Shes rab gtam tshogs*. In *Chats and Counsel, An Ocean of Spiritual Paths. Gtams gyi tshogs theg pa'i rgyal mtsho*. n.d., n.p.

Longchen Rabjam (Klong chen rab 'byams pa dri med 'od zer). *Commentary on the "Precious Dharmadhātu Treasury." Chos dbyings mdzod 'grel ba*. In *The Seven Treasuries*, vol. 3. Garze, Tibet: Adzom Chogar. English translation, Barron, *Treasure Trove*.

———. *Precious Treasury of Philosophical Systems. Grub mtha' mdzod / Theg pa mtha' dag gi don gsal bar byed pa grub pa'i mtha' rin po che'i mdzod*. BDRC WA3CN4960.

———. *Practical Instructions: A Sevenfold Mind Training on the Foundational Practices. Sngon 'gro sems sbyong bdun gyi don khrid*. In *Snying thig ya bzhi*, vol. 1, 323–32. Darjeeling: Talung Tsetrul Pema Wangyal, 1976. Reprint of the A'dzom 'brug pa chos sgar edition. Bod ljongs bod yig dpe rnying dpe skrun khang lha sa, 2011. BDRC WAS1KG18486,

———. *The Trilogy of Rest. Ngal gso skor gsum*. English translation, Padmakara Translation Group, *Trilogy of Rest*, 3 vols.

Translations and Secondary Sources

Ackerman, J. M., Christopher C. Nocera, and John A. Bargh. 2010. "Incidental Haptic Sensations Influence Social Judgments and Decisions." *Science* 328, no. 5986: 1712–15. doi 10.1126/science.1189993.

Almaas, A. H. [A-Hameed Ali]. *Spacecruiser Inquiry: True Guidance for the Inner Journey.* Diamond Body Series 1. Boston: Shambala Publications, 2002.

Apte, Varnan S. *The Practical Sanskrit-English Dictionary.* Poona: Shiralkar & Co., 1890.

Aronson, Harvey B. *Buddhist Practice on Western Ground: Reconciling Eastern Ideals and Western Psychology.* Boston: Shambhala Publications, 2012.

Barks, Coleman. *The Essential Rumi.* San Francisco: HarperSanFrancisco, 1996.

Barron, Richard (Lama Chokyi Nyima), trans. *The Precious Treasury of the Basic Space of Phenomena,* by Longchen Rabjam. Junction City, CA: Padma Publishing, 2007.

———. *The Precious Treasury of Philosophical Systems: A Treatise Elucidating the Meaning of the Entire Range of Spiritual Approaches,* by Longchen Rabjam. Junction City, CA: Padma Publishing, 2007.

———. *A Treasure Trove of Scriptural Transmission: Commentary on the "Precious Treasury of the Basic Space of Phenomena,"* by Longchen Rabjam. Junction City, CA: Padma Publishing, 2001.

Barsalou, Lawrence W., Christine D. Wilson, and Wendy Hasenkamp. "Conclusion: On the Vices of Nominalization and the Virtues of Contextualizing." In Mesquita, Barrett, and Smith, *Mind in Context,* 234–360.

Basham, Arthur Llewellyn. *The Wonder That Was India.* New York: Grove Press, 1954.

Bateson, Gregory. *Steps to an Ecology of Mind.* Chicago: University of Chicago Press, 1972.

Becker, Ernest. *The Denial of Death.* New York: Free Press, 1997.

Bertelsen, Jes. *Gateways of Empathy: The Pentagon Model.* Copenhagen: Danish Society for the Promotion of Life Wisdom in Children, 2010. https://www.academia.edu/38648218/Gateways_of_Empathy_The_Pentagon_Model_by.

Bitbol, Michel. "Is Consciousness Primary?: Moving beyond the 'Hard Problem.'" *NeuroQuarterly* 6, no. 1 (2008): 53–72.

Bitbol, Michel, and C. Petitmengin. "The Science of Mind as It Could Have Been: About the Contingency of the (Quasi-) Disappearance of Introspection in Psychology." *Science as It Could Have Been: Discussing the Contingency/Inevitability Problem,* edited by L. Soler, E. Trizio, and A. Pickering, 285–316. Pittsburgh, PA: University of Pittsburgh Press, 2015.

Borges, Jorge Luis. "The God's Script." In *Labyrinths: Selected Stories & Other Writings*. Edited by Donald A. Yates and James E. Irby. New York: New Directions, 1964.

Borges, Jorge Luis, and L. A. Murillo. "The God's Script." *Chicago Review* 17, no. 1 (1964): 5–9. https://doi.org/10.2307/25293818. [Borges, *La escritura del dios*, in *El Aleph*, Buenos Aires, 1949.]

Brunnhölzl, Karl, trans. *In Praise of Dharmadhātu, by Nāgārjuna*. Commentary by the Third Karmapa, Rangjung Dorje. Ithaca, NY: Snow Lion Publications, 2008.

———. *Straight from the Heart: Buddhist Pith Instructions*. Ithaca, NY: Snow Lion Publications, 2007.

Choying Tobden Dorje. *The Complete Nyingma Tradition: From Sutra to Tantra*. Translated by Ngawang Zangpo. Boulder, CO: Shambhala Publications, 2017.

Crosby, Kate. *Theravada Buddhism: Continuity, Diversity, and Identity*. West Sussex: Wiley-Blackwell, 2014.

Dachille, Erin. "The Body Mandala Debate: Knowing the Body through a Network of Fifteenth-Century Tibetan Buddhist Texts." PhD diss., University of California, Berkeley, 2015.

Dahl, Cortland. *Entrance to the Great Perfection: A Guide to the Dzogchen Preliminary Practices*. Ithaca, NY: Snow Lion Publications, 2009.

———. *Steps to the Great Perfection: The Mind-Training Tradition of the Dzogchen Masters*. Boulder, CO: Snow Lion Publications, 2016.

Damasio, Antonio. "The Somatic Marker Hypothesis and the Possible Functions of the Prefrontal Cortex." *Philosophical Transactions of the Royal Society B* 351, no. 1346 (October 1996): 1413–20. https://doi.org/10.1098/rstb.1996.0125.

Deroche, Marc-Henri. "On Being Impartial: The *ris-med* in Tibet: From Non-Sectarianism to the Great Perfection." *Revue d'Etudes Tibétaines* 44 (March 2018): 129–58.

Dharmachakra Translation Committee, under the Patronage and Supervision of 84,000: Translating the Words of the Buddha. *The Teaching on the Indivisible Nature of the Realm of Phenomena. Dharmadhātuprakṛtyasambhedanirdeśa*. Toh 52, dkon brtsegs, *kha*, 140.b–164.a. 2018. https://read.84000.co/translation/UT22084-040-003.html.

Dondon, Yeshe. *Health through Balance: An Introduction to Tibetan Medicine*. Translated and edited by Jeffrey Hopkins. Boulder, CO: Snow Lion Publications, 1986.

Duckworth, Douglas. *Mipham on Buddha-Nature: The Ground of the Nying-ma Tradition*. Albany: State University of New York Press, 2008.

Dunham, Yarrow, and Mahzarin R. Banaji. "Platonic Blindness and the Challenge of Understanding Context." In Mesquita, Barrett, and Smith, *Mind in Context*, 201–13.

Edgerton, Franklin. *The Buddhist Hybrid Sanskrit Grammar and Dictionary.* New Haven, CT: Yale University Press, 1953.

Farb, Norman, et al. "Interoception, Contemplative Practice, and Health." *Frontiers in Psychology*, June 9, 2015. https://doi.org/10.3389/fpsyg.2015 .00763.

Fenner, Peter. *Ontology of the Middle Way.* Studies of Classical India 11. Dordrecht: Kluwer Academic Publishers, 1990.

Garfield, Jay. *Madhyamaka and Yogacara: Allies or Rivals?* New York: Oxford University Press, 2015.

Gendlin, Eugene. *Focusing.* New York: Bantam Books, 1982.

Germano, David. "Architecture and Absence in the Secret Tantric History of the Great Completeness (*rdzogs chen*)." *Journal of the International Association of Buddhist Studies* 17, no. 2 (1994): 203–335.

Geshe Gedun Lodro. *Walking through Walls: A Presentation of Tibetan Meditation.* Translated and edited by Jeffrey Hopkins. Coedited by Anne C. Klein and Leah Zahler. Ithaca, NY: Snow Lion Publications, 1990.

Ghent, Emmanuel. "Masochism, Submission, Surrender: Masochism as a Perversion of Surrender." *Contemporary Psychoanalysis* 26 (1990): 108–36.

Gill, Sam. *Dancing Culture Religion.* Studies in Body and Religion 1. Lanham, MD: Lexington Books, 2012.

———. *Native American Religions: An Introduction.* Belmont, CA: Wadsworth Press, 1982.

Gleig, Ann. *American Dharma: Buddhism beyond Modernity.* New Haven, CT: Yale University Press, 2019.

Goodman, Steven, and Ronald Davidson, eds. *Tibetan Buddhism: Reason and Revelation.* Albany: State University of New York Press, 1992.

Guenther, Herbert. *Kindly Bent to Ease Us.* Varanasi: Dharma Publishing, 1972. [The first English translation of Longchenpa's *Trilogy of Rest* (*Ngal gso 'khor gsum*).]

———, trans. *Now That I Come to Die: Longchenpa's Parting Injunctions.* Berkeley, CA: Dharma Publishing, 2007.

Gyaltsen, Khenpo Konchog Rinpoche. *The Jewel Ornament of Liberation.* Translated by Gampopa. Ithaca, NY: Snow Lion Publications, 1998.

Gyatso, Janet. *Apparitions of the Self: The Secret Autobiographies of a Tibetan Visionary.* Princeton, NJ: Princeton University Press, 1998.

Hopkins, Jeffrey, trans. and ed. *Compassion in Tibetan Buddhism: Meditations of a Tantric Abbot, by Khensur Lekden, and Way of Compassion, by Tsongkhapa.* Ithaca, NY: Snow Lion Publications, 1980.

———. *Fundamental Mind: The Nyingma View of the Great Completeness, by Mi-pam-gya-tso, with Practical Commentary by Khetsun Sangpo Rinbochay.* Boulder, CO: Snow Lion Publications, 2006.

Jinpa, Thupten. *Essential Mind Training*. Boston: Wisdom Publications, 2011.

———, trans. *Mind Training: The Great Collection*. Boston: Wisdom Publications, 2005.

Jousse, Marcel. "Le jeu manuel de l'enfant." Cours à l'École d'Anthropologie du 24 janvier 1938. CDRom, edited by l'Association Marcel Jousse. (Transcription of course dates and titles at: http://www.marceljousse.com/wp-content/uploads/2016/01/CatalogueCoursEcoleAnthropologie.pdf.)

Kapstein, Matthew. *The Presence of Light: Divine Radiance and Religious Experience*. Chicago: University of Chicago Press, 2004.

———. *The Tibetan Assimilation of Buddhism: Conversion, Contestation, and Memory*. Oxford: Oxford University Press, 2000.

King, Charles. *Gods of the Upper Air: How a Circle of Renegade Anthropologists Reinvented Race, Sex, and Gender in the Twentieth Century*. New York: Doubleday, 2019.

Khetsun Sangpo Rinpoche. *Strand of Jewels: My Teachers' Essential Guidance on Dzogchen*. Translated, introduced, and compiled by Anne Carolyn Klein. Boulder, CO: Shambhala Publications, 2015.

Khetsun Sangpo Rinbochay. *Tantric Practice in Nying-ma*. Translated and edited by Jeffrey Hopkins. Co-edited by Anne C. Klein. Ithaca, NY: Snow Lion Publications, 1982.

Klein, Anne (Rigzin Drolma), trans. *Becoming Yeshe Tsogyal*. Houston: Dawn Mountain Research Institute, 2020

———. "Feelings Bound and Freed: Wandering and Wonder on Buddhist Pathways." *Contemporary Buddhism* 19, no. 1 (2018): 83–101. https://www.tandfonline.com/doi/full/10.1080/14639947.2018.1443567.

———, trans. *The Foundational Dakini Practice: Excellent Path of Great Bliss, from the "Luminous Heart Essence."* Houston: Dawn Mountain Research Institute, 2019.

———, trans. *Great Compassionate One: Essential Texts Liberating All Beings*. Houston: Dawn Mountain Research Institute, 2021.

———, trans. *Heart Essence of the Vast Expanse: A Story of Transmission*. Ithaca, NY: Snow Lion Publications, 2009. Reprinted as *Heart Essence of the Vast Expanse: Foundational Practices and Transmission of the Longchen Nyingthig*. Boulder, CO: Shambhala Publications, 2020.

———. "Imagining the Real: Buddhist Paths to Wholeness in Tibet." In *Cambridge Handbook of the Imagination*, edited by Anna Abraham, 500–513. Cambridge: Cambridge University Press, 2020.

———. *Knowing, Naming, and Negation: A Sourcebook on Tibetan Sautrantika*. Ithaca, NY: Snow Lion Publications, 1997.

———. *Knowledge and Liberation: Tibetan Buddhist Epistemology in Support of Transformative Religious Experience*. Ithaca, NY: Snow Lion Publications, 1998.

———. *Meeting the Great Bliss Queen: Buddhists, Feminists, and the Art of the Self.* Boston: Beacon Press, 1994. Boulder, CO: Snow Lion Publications, 2008.

———. *Path to the Middle The Spoken Scholarship of Kensur Yeshey Tupden.* Albany: State University of New York Press, 1994.

———, trans. *Practice for Becoming the Guru: The Secret Essence.* Houston: Dawn Mountain Research Institute, 2021.

———, trans. *Troma Severance.* Houston: Dawn Mountain Research Institute, 2021.

Klein, Anne Carolyn, and Elizabeth S. Napper, trans. *Lamp Lighting the Path.* Somerville, MA: Wisdom Publications, forthcoming 2024.

Klein, Anne Carolyn, and Geshe Tenzin Wangyal Rinpoche. *Unbounded Wholeness.* Oxford: Oxford University Press, 2006.

Kozhevnikov, M., O. Louchakova, Z. Josipovic, and M. Motes. "The Enhancement of Visuospatial Processing Efficiency through Buddhist Deity Meditation." *Psychological Science* 20 (2009): 645–53.

Levinson, Jules. "The Metaphors of Liberation: A Study of Grounds and Paths according to the Middle Way." PhD diss., University of Virginia, 1994.

Lopez, Donald S., Jr. *In the Forest of Faded Wisdom: 104 Poems by Gendun Chopel.* Chicago: University of Chicago Press, 2005.

McEvilley, Thomas C. *The Shape of Ancient Thought: Comparative Studies in Greek and Indian Philosophy.* New York: Allworth Press, 2002.

McLeod, Ken. *Wake Up to Your Life: Discovering the Buddhist Path of Attention.* New York: HarperCollins, 2001.

McGee, Rhonda. *The Inner Work of Racial Justice: Healing Ourselves and Transforming Our Communities through Mindfulness.* New York: TarcherPerigee, 2019.

Mesquita, Batja, Lisa Feldman Barrett, and Eliot R. Smith, eds. *The Mind in Context.* New York: Guilford Press, 2010.

Morrison, Toni. "The Reader as Artist." Oprah.com. https://www.oprah.com/omagazine/toni-morrison-on-reading/all (accessed June 28, 2021).

Napper, Elizabeth S., trans. and ed. *Mind in Tibetan Buddhism*, by Lati Rinbochay. Ithaca, NY: Snow Lion Publications, 1980.

Neumaier-Dargyay, Eva K. *The Sovereign All-Creating Mind: A Translation of the Kun Byed Rgyal Po'i Mdo'.* Albany: State University of New York Press, 1992.

Nyoshul Khenpo Jamyang Dorje. *A Marvelous Garland of Rare Gems.* Junction City, CA: Padma Publishing, 2005.

Owens, Lama Rod. *Love and Rage: The Path of Liberation through Anger.* Berkeley, CA: North Atlantic Books, 2021.

Padmakara Translation Group. *Treasury of Precious Qualities: Book One, The Rain of Joy, by Jigme Lingpa, with The Quintessence of the Three Paths, a Commentary by Longchen Yeshe Dorje, Kangyur Rinpoche.* Boston: Shambhala Publications, 2010.

———. *Treasury of Precious Qualities: Book Two, Vajrayana and the Great Perfection, by Jigme Lingpa, Commentary by Longchen Yeshe Dorje, Kangyur Rinpoche.* Boston: Shambhala Publications, 2013.

———. *The Trilogy of Rest, by Longchen Rabjam.* Vol. 1, *Finding Rest in the Nature of the Mind,* vol. 2, *Finding Rest in Meditation,* vol. 3, *Finding Rest in Illusion.* Boulder, CO: Shambala, 2018–2020.

Pagels, Elaine. *Beyond Belief: The Secret Gospel of Thomas.* New York: Random House. 2005.

Patrul Rinpoche. *The Words of My Perfect Teacher.* Boston: Shambhala Publications, 1998.

Pelzang, Khenpo Ngawang. *A Guide to "The Words of My Perfect Teacher."* Translated by Dipamkara with the Padmakara Translation Group. Boston: Shambhala Publications, 2004.

Petitmengin, Claire. "Anchoring in Lived Experience as an Act of Resistance." *Constructivist Foundations* 16, no. 2 (2021): 172–81.

———. "The Intuitive Experience." *Journal of Consciousness Studies* 6, nos. 2–3 (February 1999): 43–77. Reprinted in *The View from Within: First-Person Approaches to the Study of Consciousness,* edited by Francisco Varela and Jonathan Shear, 43–78. Thorverton, UK: Imprint Academic, 1999.

———. "Towards the Source of Thoughts: The Gestural and Transmodal Dimensions of Lived Experience." *Journal of Consciousness Studies* 6 (2007): 43–77.

Rumi, Jalal al-Din. "In Baghdad, Dreaming of Cairo." In *The Essential Rumi.* Translated by Coleman Barks. San Francisco: HarperSanFrancisco, 1995.

Samphel, Lama Tenzin. "Oral Commentary on Longchenpa's *Chos dbyings mdzod.*" Houston: Dawn Mountain Center for Tibetan Buddhism, 2016.

Śāntideva. *The Bodhicaryāvatāra.* Translated by Kate Crosby and Andrew Skilton. Oxford: Oxford University Press, 2008.

Shenphen Dawa Rinpoche. *Bum Chung: The Yoga of the Small Vase.* n.p.: Yeshe Melong, n.d.

Shukman, Henry. *One Blade of Grass: Finding the Old Road of the Heart.* Berkeley, CA: Counterpoint, 2019.

Smith, Malcolm. *The Great Commentary by Vimalamitra.* Boston: Wisdom Publications, 2016.

Stern, Daniel N. *Forms of Vitality: Exploring Dynamic Experience in Psychology, the Arts, Psychotherapy and Development.* Oxford: Oxford University Press, 2010.

———. *The Interpersonal World of the Infant: A View from Psychoanalysis and Developmental Psychology.* New York: Basic Books, 2000.

———. *The Present Moment in Psychotherapy and Everyday Life.* New York: W. W. Norton, 2004.

Suzuki Roshi. *Zen Mind, Beginner's Mind: Informal Talks on Zen Tradition and Practice.* New York: Weatherhill, 1970.

Thānissaro Bhikkhu. "Bāhiya Sutta." https://www.dhammatalks.org/suttas/ KN/Ud/ud1_10.html (accessed July 5, 2022).

Theise, Neil D. "Beyond Cell Doctrine: Complexity Theory Informs Alternate Models of the Body for Cross-Cultural Dialogue." *Longevity, Regeneration, and Optimal Health: Integrating Eastern and Western Perspectives* 1172, no. 1 (August 2009): 1–361. https://doi.org/10.1111/j.1749-6632.2009.04410.x.

Tsongkhapa. *The Great Treatise on the Stages of the Path to Enlightenment*, vols. 1–3. Translated by the Lamrim Chenmo Translation Committee. Edited by Joshua Cutler and Guy Newland. Ithaca, NY: Snow Lion Publications, 2000–2002.

Tulku Thondup. *Masters of Meditation and Miracles: The Longchen Nyingthig Lineage of Tibetan Buddhism*. Edited by Harold Talbott. Boston: Shambhala, 1996.

Wangyal, Geshe Tenzin Rinpoche. *Healing with Form, Energy, and Light: The Five Elements in Tibetan Shamanism, Tantra, and Dzogchen*. Edited by Mark Dahlby. Ithaca, NY: Snow Lion Publications, 2002.

Willis, Jan. *Dreaming Me: Black, Baptist, and Buddhist, One Woman's Spiritual Journey*. Sommerville, MA: Wisdom Publications, 2008.

Van Schaik, Sam. "Early Dzogchen IV: The Role of Atiyoga." Early Tibet blog, August 3, 2011. https://earlytibet.com/2011/08/03/eawrly-dzogchen-iv/.

Wallace, Vesna. *The Kālacakra Tantra: The Chapter on Sādhana, Together with the Vimalaprabhā Commentary: A Study and Annotated Translation*. New York: Columbia University Press, 2010.

Wolter, Doris. ed. *Losing the Clouds, Gaining the Sky: Buddhism and the Natural Mind*. Boston: Wisdom Publications, 2007.

Yalom, Irvin D. *Existential Psychotherapy*. New York: Basic Books, 1980.

Yampolsky, Philip B., trans. *The Platform Sutra of the Sixth Patriarch: The Text of the Tun-Huang Manuscript*. New York: Columbia University Press, 2012.

Ying, Chinghui Jianying. "Being and Knowing in Wholeness Chinese Chan, Tibetan Dzogchen, and the Logic of Immediacy in Contemplation." PhD diss., Rice University, 2010.

INDEX

A

activities, pointlessness of, 21–22, 54–56, 119

Adzom Drukpa, ii, 37, 208n42, 217n193

Adzom Paylo Rinpoche, ii, 2, 11, 25, 33–34, 97, 116, 157, 206n21, 206n25, 217n193, 222n257, 224n278

  commentary on mind training, 46–61, 136, 137–38

  lineage of, 37, 65, 208n42

  poem of praise, ii

  spontaneous song of, 55–56, 129, 149, 208n47

  See also *Luminous Heart Essence* cycle

afflictions

  dharmadhātu and, 114

  habitual tendencies and, 45, 54

  looking into face of, 175

  overcoming, 50–51, 57

  suffering and, 39, 43, 52

  unwholesome actions and, 51

Alcoholics Anonymous, 73–74

All-Creating Majesty (*Kun byed rgyal po*), 27, 85–86, 179–80

Almaas, A. H., 210n84, 221n241

Ani Tenzin Drolma, 218n193

animal realm, 93–94

appearance

  as magical display, 100

  as mistaken, 47, 53–54, 172, 184

Asaṅga, 162, 163, 164, 165, 166, 168, 176, 222n247

Atiśa, 26

Avalokiteśvara, 28

awakened mind, 45, 46, 56–57, 213n127

  in Dzogchen, 222n256, 224n287

  as goal and ground, 32–33

  Longchenpa on, 108

as real nature of mind, 194, 196, 225nn287–88

as reality, 194, 196, 225nn287–88

as source of all, 100, 174

awakening

  happiness and, 20

  heartfelt desire for, 39–40, 53, 73–74

  humanness of, 180–88

  as intrinsic, 15, 161

  in this lifetime, 11

  two elements of, 86

  as ultimate feat (*siddhi*), 45

awareness

  experience and, 6, 89

  of movement and stillness, 70–71, 84, 173, 210n73

  openness and, 94–95

  sheer, naked, or knowing, 19, 20, 112, 101, 110, 116, 191

  See also *rig pa* (open awareness); sheer awareness

B

Bāhiya Sutta, 100

Barsalou, Larry, 149, 154

Bateson, Gregory, 73–74

Becker, Ernst, 72

Bertelsen, Jes, 147–48, 202, 237

birthless

  birth from, 110, 170–71, 188

  nature as, 9, 28, 66

  unborn, 9, 66, 110, 171, 188

  unceasing, 28, 70, 130, 170, 193,223n268

  wisdom as, 70, 193

blessings. *See* waves of grace

bliss and emptiness, training in, 23, 58–59, 135, 137–38, 140–41, 206n21

bodhicitta

  Dzogchen and, 87, 116, 161–62, 196–97

Lineage Masters

Adzom Paylo Rinpoche was born in the Kham region of traditional Tibet in 1971. He was recognized as an incarnation of Jigme Lingpa, and of King Trisong Detsen, Vimalamitra, and Ngari Panchen, among others, as well as the speech dimension of Manjushri. Requested by one of his teachers to discourse on Patrul Rinpoche's *Words of My Perfect Teacher* at age thirteen at the prestigious, sacred seat of Samye Chimphu, he noted that "many lamas came, not to learn but to criticize me." How could one so young teach a text so profound? As his discourse progressed, they bowed to him in reverence.

He grew up and was trained at Adzom Gar, founded by Adzom Drukpa (1824–1942), who was Adzom Rinpoche's father in his previous life as Pema Wangyal. Currently he teaches where he mainly resides, at Ogyen Samden Ling, the monastery he founded circa 2000, located in the Rege area of the Tibet Autonomous Region, at a place long sacred to Guru Rinpoche and Yeshe Tsogyal. Over the years he has accepted invitations to teach in monastic centers of all four orders of Tibetan Buddhism, and Bon as well. In this way he continues and extends the nonsectarian (*ris med*) orientation of his prior life as Jigme Lingpa.

At Ogyen Samden Ling he masterfully teaches and transmits full traditional monastic and Dzogchen curricula and shares with his students a rare lineage of mind-nature instructions (*sems khrid*). He is a prolific terton, a revealer of texts or treasure finder. The treasures he has made known in recent years include the Luminous Heart Essence

(Osel Nyingthig), after seeing the face of Yeshe Tsogyal; the Lotus Heart Essence (Pema Nyingthig or Avalokiteshvara Dzogchen) cycles, received on Potu Island, sacred to Kwan Yin; and Manjushri Dzogchen, received in the cave of Vimalamitra at Wu Tai Shan in 1999. He is also holds Jigme Lingpa's Heart Essence, Vast Expanse (Longchen Nyingthig) cycle and the collection of Adzom Drukpa treasures known as the *Secret Treasure of the Luminous Vajra* (*Osel Dorje Sang Mdzod*). He holds both Dzogchen and Mahāmudrā lineages. He is known for many unusual accomplishments, including leaving foot and handprints in rocks at various place in Tibet, and, perhaps most famously, as a skillful means for inspiring dharma practice and learning, a headprint at Tedrom, which in the eighth century was a retreat site for Yeshe Tsogyal and Guru Rinpoche.

JIGME LINGPA (1730–98), an incarnation of Trisong Detsen and Vimalamitra, is renowned for his revelation of the Heart Essence, Vast Expanse cycle, which arose for him when he was twenty-eight and in retreat, after he wept with longing for Guru Rinpoche upon seeing him in a dream. At age thirty-one he experienced three pure visions of the wisdom body of Longchen Rabjam in which he successively received transmission of Longchenpa's teachings, speech blessings empowering him to teach as Longchenpa's representative, and the blessing of Longchenpa's wisdom mind, which transferred Longchenpa's knowing to him. Subsequently he received transmission of the Seventeen Nyingthig Tantras, Vima Nyingthig, Lama Yangthig, and others through Mindrolig monastery. At age forty-three he organized the printing of the Nyingma tantras in twenty-five volumes. As already noted, Jigme Lingpa was renowned as an early proponent of nonsectariaism in Tibet; his devoted students came from all ranks of society, from the most humble to the king and queen of Derge. At age seventy he retired to Tsering Jong, where he had established a nunnery. One clear bright day he gave a teaching on White Tārā. A sweet fragrance filled the area, a gentle rain fell from the clear sky, and after asking for new offerings to be set on the altar, he joined with primordiality.

LONGCHEN RABJAM (1308–64) is considered the reincarnation of Trisong Detsen's daughter, Princess Pemasal, who died while visitng Samye Chimphu. Guru Rinpoche revived her briefly, long enough to bestow on her the Dakini Heart Essence (Khandro Thugthig) cycle, indicating she would reveal the cycle in her future life as Pema Ledreltsal and promulgate it in her subsequent life as Longchenpa. Deeply learned, profoundly practiced, Longchenpa is the foremost compiler and creative interpreter of Dzogchen in Tibet. In addition to his own voluminous writings, he coalesced and expanded extensively on the Vima Nyingthig of Vimalamitra and the Dakini Heart Essence of Padmasambhava. At age twenty-seven he received the full Vimal-amitra teachings from Kumaradza, who empowered Longchenpa as his lineage holder. Following this, Longchenpa spent seven years in retreat, mainly at Samye Chimphu. Later, Vima Heart Essence teach-ings were received directly from Vimalamitra himself in a vision, and thus he was inspired to write the Lama Essential Essence (Lama Yangthig). He spent much of his life in solitude. When he arrived again at Chimphu at the age of fifty-six, he said that dying in Chimphu was better than being born in other places. He did pass there, and his stupa (visible in the fifth pith practice image) remains an object of ven-eration high above the valley to this day.

Jigme Lingpa's and Longchenpa's biographies were partly distilled from Tulku Thondup, *Masters of Meditation and Miracles*.

About the Author

ANNE CAROLYN KLEIN is a professor and former chair of the Department of Religion at Rice University, where she developed a contemplative studies concentration for graduate students, teaches courses on Buddhism, and reads with students in Tibetan. She is also a lama in the Nyingma tradition and a founding teacher at Dawn Mountain, a center for Tibetan Buddhism, where she teaches a variety of practices and texts, especially recently revealed (*gter*) practices from Adzom Paylo Rinpoche, whom she meet adventitiously in Tibet in 1996 and who named her a *Dorje Lopön* in 2009.

She has studied and translated in three of Tibet's five traditions. Her scholarly work encompasses both Tibetan texts and the learned oral commentary on them. Her books include *Knowledge and Liberation*, on Buddhist distinctions between intellectual knowing and direct experience; *Path to the Middle: The Spoken Scholarship of Kensur Yeshey Tupden*, on preparing to meet the ultimate; *Meeting the Great Bliss Queen*, contrasting Buddhist and feminist understandings of self; Khetsun Sangpo Rinpoche's *Strand of Jewels*, on essential Dzogchen teachings; with Geshe Tenzin Wangyal Rinpoche, *Unbounded Wholeness*, a translation and presentation of a Bön Dzogchen text; and *Heart Essence of the Vast Expanse*, on the foundational practices and lineage of Jigme Lingpa, with chantable English translations.

In all these endeavors her central theme is the embodied interaction between head and heart on the paths to wholeness, and delight in finding these throughout Buddhist literary and contemplative traditions.

ABOUT THIS COURSE

Longchenpa's Sevenfold Mind Training provides comprehensive training in bodhicitta—the awakening mind, the aspiration that your practice will benefit all beings—which is for Dzogchen the fundamental field of reality.

Bodhicitta can

- encourage heartfelt confidence in the path;
- create easeful joy in your practice and living;
- heal the separateness you feel;
- strengthen your sense of wholeness; and
- connect you with the liberating potential of primordial reality.

Through Longchenpa's seven trainings and Jigme Lingpa's innovative story-meditations, you'll learn to lean into full bodhicitta, a boundless resource that is simply the reality of your own mind.

WHAT TO READ NEXT
FROM WISDOM PUBLICATIONS

Liberation from Samsara
Oral Instructions on the Preliminary Practices of Longchen Nyingthik
Kyabjé Dodrupchen Rinpoché
Translated by Tulku Thondup Rinpoche and Sonam Paljor Dejongpa

In *Liberation from Samsara*, the Fourth Kyabjé Dodrupchen Rinpoché presents the Longchen Nyingthik preliminary teachings, with a special focus on guru yoga. These teachings, from the innermost secret instruction of Dzogchen, constitute a complete path to enlightenment.

Buddhahood in this Life
The Great Commentary by Vimalamitra
Malcolm Smith

"I rejoice and praise Acarya Malcolm Smith's direct translation from Tibetan into English of the *Aural Lineage of Vimalamitra* from the cycle of the *Pellucid Transcendent State of the Great Perfection*. Since it is certainly of great benefit to those faithful practitioners of Dharma around the world, I sincerely wish that once they have realized the secret of the mind in dependence on all of the book's instruction, which appear through the intimate instructions of the guru, they will be able to accomplish liberation into the body of light in one lifetime."—Tulku Dagpa Rinpoche

About Wisdom Publications

Wisdom Publications is the leading publisher of classic and contemporary Buddhist books and practical works on mindfulness. To learn more about us or to explore our other books, please visit our website at wisdomexperience.org or contact us at the address below.

Wisdom Publications
132 Perry Street
New York, NY 10014 USA

We are a 501(c)(3) organization, and donations in support of our mission are tax deductible.

Wisdom Publications is affiliated with the Foundation for the Preservation of the Mahayana Tradition (FPMT).